THE ECONOMICS OF PREVAILING WAGE LAWS

T0303962

The Economics of Prevailing Wage Laws

Edited by
HAMID AZARI-RAD
State University of New York – New Paltz

PETER PHILIPS
University of Utah

MARK J. PRUS
State University of New York – Cortland

Routledge
Taylor & Francis Group

LONDON AND NEW YORK

First published 2005 by Ashgate Publishing

2 Park Square, Milton Park, Abingdon, Oxon OX14 4RN
711 Third Avenue, New York, NY 10017, USA

Routledge is an imprint of the Taylor & Francis Group, an informa business

First issued in paperback 2016

British Library Cataloguing in Publication Data
The economics of prevailing wage laws. - (Alternative
    voices in contemporary economics)
    1.Wages - United States 2.Wages - Government policy -
    United States 3.Wages - Law and legislation - United States
    I.Azari-Rad, Hamid II.Philips, Peter, 1947- III.Prus, Mark
    J.
    331.2'973

Library of Congress Cataloging-in-Publication Data
Azari-Rad, Hamid.
    The economics of prevailing wage laws / by Hamid Azari-Rad, Peter Philips, and Mark J. Prus.-- 1st ed.
        p. cm. -- (Alternative voices in contemporary economics)
    Includes index.
    ISBN 0-7546-3255-5
    1. Wages--Construction workers--Law and legislation--United States. 2. Wages--Construction workers--
Law and legislation. I. Philips, Peter, 1947- II. Prus, Mark J. III. Title. IV. Series.

    KF3505.C65A993 2004
    344.7301'2824--dc22

                                                                            2004023404

ISBN 13: 978-0-7546-3255-9 (hbk)
ISBN 13: 978-1-138-25849-5 (pbk)

Contents

PART III PUBLIC POLICY: COMPENSATIONS

List of Contributors

Hamid Azari-Rad, Ph.D., is Assistant Professor of Economics at the State University of New York—New Paltz

Dale Belman, Ph.D., is Associate Professor of Industrial Relations at the Michigan State University

Cihan Bilginsoy, Ph.D., is Associate Professor of Economics at the University of Utah

Kevin Duncan, Ph.D., is Professor of Economics at the Colorado State University—Pueblo

Gerald Finkel, Ph.D., is the Director of Educational and Cultural Trust Fund of the Joint Industry Board of the Electrical Industry

Erin M. Godtland, Ph.D., is an Economist at the United States General Accounting Office

Jeffrey S. Petersen, Ph.D., is an Economist at the Allman Economic Analysis

Peter Philips, Ph.D., is Professor of Economics at the University of Utah

Mark A. Price, Ph.D., is a Research Associate at the Keystone Research Center

Mark J. Prus, Ph.D., is Professor of Economics and Dean of Arts and Sciences at the State University of New York—Cortland

C. Jeffrey Waddoups, Ph.D., is Associate Professor of Economics at the University of Nevada—Las Vegas

PART I
HISTORICAL CONTEXT FOR PUBLIC POLICY

Chapter 1

Introduction:
Prevailing Wage Regulations and Public Policy in the Construction Industry

Hamid Azari-Rad, Peter Philips and Mark J. Prus

Introduction

Prevailing Wage Laws in the United States regulate the wages paid on government funded construction projects. At the federal level the Davis-Bacon Act is probably the most well known prevailing wage law, though to many citizens, its existence is not recognized. The Davis-Bacon Act has set minimum wages by occupation and locality for federally financed construction projects since 1931. Thirty-one states along with the District of Columbia have prevailing wage laws. These acts are part of a larger set of regulations that began in the last half of the 19th century and developed through the 20th century and into the 21st. These laws include child labor laws, workers' compensation, fair labor standards including the eight-hour day, unemployment insurance, the rights of workers to collectively bargain for wages and benefits, minimum wage laws, Social Security, and the right to a safe workplace including state and federal Occupational Safety and Health Administrations (OSHA).

All of these laws come from one spirit—that the American economy, in general, and the U.S. labor market, in particular, should develop along a high-skill, high-wage, capital-intensive and technologically dynamic growth path. This is a vision of an economy where jobs are systematically good and safe and constantly getting better as employers, workers and society all join together in investing in both better technology, better tools and equipment, and higher skills. This is a vision of society where children are in school preparing for a better future for themselves, their families and their communities—rather than in dead-end jobs where the future is the first victim of employment. This is a view of competition where the playing field is level, and the worst employer does not chase out all of the better, safer, fairer employers. This is a vision of the labor market where workers have rights—rights to organize together and bargain collectively and rights not to be the victims of discrimination or exploitation. But this is a vision of society that is not shared by all.

There is now and always has been another view of the matter. There are those who believe that unregulated markets should be left alone to work out, how children are treated, how workers are treated and how the economy should develop. Whether the issue is the privatization of social security, the elimination of minimum wages, the toleration of child labor, the elimination of the 40-hour work-week, the gutting of workers' compensation, the watering-down of civil rights protections or the elimination of prevailing wage laws, this alternative view of America harkens back to the time of the Robber Barons in the post-Civil War period. This was a time when workers had no protections, black listing of union organizers was legal and widely practiced, there was no restriction on the formation of monopolies, and safety at work was a roll-of-the-dice.

We are in a topsy-turvy world here. The true conservatives in this debate are those who would preserve the laws and regulations that have developed over the last 150 years to protect workers, foster education, preserve the environment and safeguard civil rights. The true radicals are those who wish to erase this 150 years of progressive legislation as quickly and as completely as possible. We will see that the debate today is not new. We will see that critics of prevailing wage laws (among other protections) are using arguments that are 150 years old. Thus, we begin at the beginning when the notion of protecting workers was new, the notion of regulating markets was new and the idea of never, under any circumstance, intervening in the contracts agreed upon by employer and worker was the conventional wisdom of the day.

The First Federal Prevailing Wage Law (1868)

The first federal eight-hour day law was enacted on 25 June 1868. It also was the first federal prevailing wage law. The country had just passed through a Civil War that among other things had kick-started massive industrialization across the north and west of the country. The next thirty years would see the emergence of a new class of wealth and power in the country. Men such as J. P. Morgan, John D. Rockefeller, and Andrew Carnegie were using the rapid growth stimulated by the Civil War as a foundation for accumulating economic power never before seen in the country.

At the same time, the lives of working people were in flux. Hours of labor had always been long but they had moved to the pace and the rhythms of the farm. Shoe factories in New England, meat packing plants in Chicago, woolen mills in California, and silver mines in Nevada changed all that. Work was being harnessed to the time clock, the production line and the will of the foreman. People were being ground down by the pace of machinery, the demands of the supervisor, and the strain of 12 hour days and six day weeks.

In 1868 Congress addressed this issue with the National Eight-Hour Day Act. The idea was to set labor standards, to guide the labor market, to nudge it away from the stretching out of the workday towards competitive behavior that emphasized increased productivity within a limited set of hours. It was felt that the market could not get there by itself. Short-run competitive pressures would continually push for the longer day. But by regulating the market, it could be forced to find its own best interest, competition over productivity rather than competition over sweating labor.

At the time, the current legal doctrine of the individual's right to freely contract with others over wages and work conditions prevented Congress from directly regulating the labor market. Nonetheless, Congress could regulate its own contracts. Thus, public works were targeted as a way of indirectly trying to regulate all labor markets by regulating the contracts of contractors (and through them workers) on public construction. Republican Senator John Conness of California captured most of these ideas in one line of argument:

> [The eight-hour law] is but a very small boon that the working men of America ask from the Congress of the United States, namely: that the example be set by the Government of reducing the number of hours of labor. I know that the passage of this bill cannot control in the labor of the country; but the example to be set by the Government, by the passage of this bill, is due to the laboring men of the country, in my opinion. I know that labor in the main, like every other commodity, must depend upon the demand and supply. But, sir, I for one will be glad, a thousand times glad, when the industry of the country shall become accommodated to a reduced number of hours in the performance of labor. After forty or fifty years of such advance in the production of the world's fabrics by the great improvements that have been made by inventions, and the application of steam as a power, by which the capital of the world has been aggregated and increase many fold, I think that it is time that the bones and muscles of the country were promised a small percentage of cessation and rest from labor, as a consequence of that great increase in the productive industries of the country (U.S. Congress, 1868).

The eight-hour law as proposed applied only to government workers and the workers of those receiving government contracts. So it applied to shipyards and armament factories and construction, but it did not apply to all workers. Yet Senator Conness saw the law as a boon to all working men in America. Why not apply the eight-hour day to everyone? The answer is the Supreme Court, at the time, would not permit the Federal government from interfering in the private contracts between individuals. This was the doctrine of freedom of contract, and indeed, the recently fought Civil War was seen, in part, as a war over the rights of individuals to freely contract out their services. Slavery was seen as wrong by many because it violated the freedom to contract for one's labor services. One of the complaints of opponents of the national eight-hour day law was precisely that it violated this freedom of contract. Republican Senator Morrill of Vermont argued:

> Sir, I believe [that this Act] is a degradation of the working men of this country to deprive them of making contracts to work for just whatever sum and for whatever time they please (U.S. Congress, 1868).

The conventional wisdom that the Constitution forbade government interference with the freedom of individual contracts accounts for the focus of the National Eight-Hour Day Act on government workers and government contractors. If the government could not interfere with the contracts of others, it nonetheless could set the terms and conditions of its own contracts. Thus, it could require its contractors to meet the conditions of an eight-hour day. Both proponents and opponents of this law in the Senate viewed this Act as having the potential to reach beyond public works by setting a standard and custom that eventually would hold in the private sector.

Opponents of the National Eight-Hour Day Act wanted to leave the market completely unregulated and they were satisfied with whatever outcome emerged. Maine Republican Senator Fessendon summarized the laissez faire position of the opposition and the fear that such a law would make workers feel entitled to shorter hours:

> I oppose [this Act] upon principle, and because I believe that no good can come of it, and much evil probably will. The moment we have passed this bill there becomes an excitement throughout the country upon the same subject between the employer and the employed, and the evil example will go forth from this place. Let men make their contracts as they please; let this matter be regulated by the great regulator, demand and supply; and

so long as it continues to be, those who are smart, capable, and intelligent, who make themselves skilled workmen, will receive the rewards of their labor, and those who have less capacity and less industry will not be on a level with them, but will receive an adequate reward for their labor (U.S. Congress, 1868).

Prevailing wage regulations were an integral part of the first national eight-hour law. For the Act said that when hours on public works were cut from 12 to 8, the daily wage should not be cut from (say) $1.20 to 80 cents. In those days, construction workers were paid by the day. Congress said that when hours were cut, the contractor on public works still had to pay the daily wage that was current in the locale in which the work was being done. Proponents were not unmindful that such a provision would raise the hourly wage rate of workers. A popular doggerel of the time captured this position in rhyme:

Whether you work by the piece or by the day—
Decreasing the hours increases the pay (Hunnicutt, 1988).

Proponents of the National Eight-Hour Day Act, such as Senator William Stewart of Nevada argued that the increase in hourly pay would come primarily from and be justified by increased hourly productivity.

I say a man will do more per hour who is only required to work eight hours a day than will a man who is required to work ten hours. The less the number of hours a man works the more he can do in the hours that he does work ... Certainly, if a man only works a single hour a day, he can do more in that hour, make greater exertions, than if he had to work every hour in the day. So to adjust the wages *pro rata* according to the number of hours would not be fair (U.S. Congress, 1868).

This argument comes down to us today over whether higher paid construction workers are better trained and more productive. Proponents of prevailing wage regulation argue that these laws encourage collective bargaining in construction. Collective bargaining, in turn, creates joint labor-management apprenticeship programs that invest in the training of construction workers leading to higher productivity in (primarily) the union sector of construction. Opponents assert that there is no difference in the productivity of union and nonunion workers. If prevailing wages are cut, there will not be any corresponding fall in labor productivity.

Consequently, this view asserts that eliminating prevailing wages will save on construction costs rather than reduce construction labor productivity.

Stewart went on to argue that there were additional societal benefits from an eight-hour day law (with its prevailing wage codicil) that went beyond the cost-productivity issue:

> The [eight-hour day law need not be rejected even] if there was not as much work done in the eight hours, because there might be other good results following from it. There might be greater comfort given to the workingman; there might be an improvement in the condition of society; and if there should be an approximate amount of labor, something near the same amount as now, the other good results might be sufficient to justify the adoption of the reform. I have no idea but that taking the term of years through which men labor, an individual, in the course of his life, accomplishes more with eight hours a day than he will with ten hours a day labor. I think he will live longer, so that in the course of his natural life he will do more work if he works eight hours a day regularly than he will if he works ten hours. If you will put the value of men on the amount of labor they can do in the course of their natural lives I think men will be more valuable who work eight hours a day than if they work ten hours a day. I think they will accomplish more in their natural lives; they will not wear out so soon, and if there is any object in prolonging human life and increasing the aggregate of human happiness the argument would be in favor of this bill (U.S. Congress, 1868).

Stewart's arguments anticipate what proponents of prevailing wage laws will argue for the next 150 years—that high-wage, skilled labor can be as cost effective as low wage, unskilled labor. Even if this is not quite the case, having workers who are paid health insurance, paid a pension, adequately and safely trained and capable of making a career out of a casual labor market generates dividends to the worker, the worker's family, the community, and society as a whole so as to prolong human life and increase the aggregate of human happiness.

Republican Senator John Sherman of Ohio had led the effort to weaken the national eight-hour day law. In particular, he wanted daily wages to fall in proportion to the diminution in hours. When the final bill passed 26 to 11 Senator Sherman carped:

> The title of the bill ought to be changed, it seems to me to read: A bill to give to Government employees twenty-five per cent more wages than employees in private establishments receive.

To which Republican Senator from California, John Conness replied:

> That is an eccentricity if the honorable Senator from Ohio. The bill has a very good title as it stands.

In this last snippet of debate, we find an argument that critics will raise for the next 133 years—prevailing wages cost too much; they pay workers on public projects 25 percent more, and eliminating prevailing wage regulations will save taxpayers this unwarranted 25 percent. Proponents respond just as Nevada Senator Stewart argued 133 years ago. Prevailing wages support and promote higher productivity that offsets some or all of the increased costs. And furthermore, there are other benefits of this regulation associated with broader social benefits, a higher quality of life and safer work that mitigate any associated increase in costs.

Enforcement of the prevailing wage provision proved difficult. Twice Republican President Grant had to issue proclamations directing contractors and government agents to respect the prevailing wage provision of the eight-hour day law.[1]

Thus, the principle of a prevailing wage law at the federal level predates the current federal prevailing wage law, the Davis-Bacon Act (1931), by fifty years. The purpose of the first federal law was to set labor standards regarding hours and wage rates in the public sector presumably with the hope that these standards might spread to the private sector. That the purpose was thwarted in enforcement is indicated by Grant's need to make the same proclamation twice. It was also thwarted by legal decisions emphasizing the rights of individuals to contract without government interference.

Frustrated by problems of implementation and court rulings, the American Federation of Labor (AFL), in its first convention in 1881 stated what it thought the purpose of the law was and complained that it was not being enforced:

> Resolved ... that the National Eight Hour law is one intended to benefit labor and to relieve it partly of its heavy burdens, that the evasion of its true spirit and intent is contrary to the best interest of the Nation; we therefore demand the enforcement of said law in the spirit of its designers (Federation of the Organized Trades and Labor Unions of the United States and Canada, 1881, p. 3).[2]

The next year the AFL convention went on to argue 'that the system of letting out Government work by contract tends to intensify the competition between workmen, and we demand the speedy abolishment of the same'. Further by focusing on enforcing the federal law, 'the enforcement of the national eight-hour law will secure adoption of similar provisions in nearly all the States of the Union' (Federation of the Organized Trades and Labor Unions of the United States and Canada, 1882, pp. 4 and 18). Soon the AFL would turn to states to develop and enforce hours and prevailing wage legislation, but in the United Kingdom and in Canada, legislatures were preparing to follow the U.S. example.

Fair Wage Policies in England and Canada (1890)

> The country has no interest in keeping down the price of labour; on the contrary, the country is interested in the advancement of the labour market ... It is better for the workingman, for high wages enable him to supply himself with more of the necessaries, more of the comforts, more of the luxuries of life. This is better for the country also, as it stimulates the consumption of manufactured goods of all kinds. Higher wages benefit not only him who receives but him who gives, and they benefit not only the parties directly concerned, but the whole community.
>
> Canadian Postmaster General
1900 Workmen's Wages on Government Contracts Debate.

In England in 1890, the House of Lords issued the *Report of the Sweating Commission.* Sweatshop labor conditions had become a scandal. Construction was seen as one of the sweatshop industries. The system of contracting and subcontracting and lowest bidder acceptance led to a form of competition that was deleterious. To obtain a contract in the short run, contractors would ignore long term costs of the industry, such as training. Having shaved on a bid to win a government contract, contractors were trying to offset their costs through shoddy workmanship. Contractors who won a job would shop it around to laborers, seeing who would take the biggest pay cut to get a job. In response to these practices, Parliament enacted a prevailing wage law as part of a larger set of reforms designed to reign in the prevalence of sweatshop competitive practices.

Canada followed the English example in 1900. The Canadian Parliament was persuaded that there was a high-wage, high-skilled growth path and a low-wage, low-skilled growth path opening up before Canada. The high-wage path was seen as preferable because it promoted solid skills and good workmanship on public works, it created middle class citizens and it stimulated demand for local manufactured goods.

The First State Prevailing Wage Law—Kansas (1891)

In February 1891, Samuel Gompers,[3] President of the American Federation of Labor, visited Topeka, Kansas, to speak on what the local newspaper called 'the great topic of labor'. Ten years earlier, the AFL—at its own creation—had laid out legislative aims that included the eight-hour work day, the elimination of child labor, free public schooling, compulsory schooling laws, the elimination of convict labor, and prevailing wages on public works. These proposals were based on a belief that the American labor market should consist of highly skilled workers earning decent wages, with time for family, and with children free to earn an education.

On the morning of Gompers's arrival, the Alliance Party, known to history as the Populist Party, withdrew an earlier invitation for him to speak in the hall of the state House of Representatives, which that party controlled. Gompers, who represented 900,000 workers, had fallen out of favor with the Populists, reportedly because of his belief that the trade unions should not form a political party with the Alliance (*Topeka State Journal*, 1891a). Gompers and the AFL took the position that unions should be nonpartisan. Rather than form a labor party, Gompers advocated that unions support those of any party who would support the needs of working men and women. In Kansas in 1891, this made Samuel Gompers an ally of the Republican Party. The Republicans, who controlled the Kansas Senate, invited Gompers to speak there, and he did. In his Topeka speech, Gompers declared:

> Our banner floats high to the breeze and on that banner float is inscribed, 'Eight hours work, eight hours rest and eight hours for mental and moral improvement' (*Topeka Daily Capital*, 1891).

At that time, when there were no income supplement programs for the poor, low-income parents worked *and* had to send their children to work to make ends meet. This practice was later referred to by some as 'eating the seed corn'. Each generation of poor condemned its offspring to poverty because the children grew up as illiterate as their parents. The prevalence of cheap child labor, which accounted for 5 percent of the manufacturing labor force in 1890 and a larger proportion of service sector and agricultural workers, kept wages down and forced adult workers to put in the long hours to make ends meet. Gompers wanted regulation to force employers and the poor to adopt a strategy, however painful in the short run, of a high-wage, high-skilled growth path where children were in school and workers had the skills to justify wages that would allow for a family life. Gompers said,

> The Federation endorses the total abolition of child labor under 14 years of age; an eight hour law for all laborers and mechanics employed by the government directly through contractors engaged on public work, and its rigid enforcement; protection of life and limb of workmen employed in factories, shops and mines; ... the extension of suffrage as well as equal work for equal pay to women ... The Federation favors measures, not parties (*Topeka State Journal*, 1891b).

Gompers also pleaded for workers to be paid the 'current' daily wage so they could afford the reduced work time. Government was being asked to set a good example for the private sector, to show that a refreshed labor force could produce in eight hours what a fatigued and bedraggled labor force turned out in ten or twelve hours. With similar logic, the AFL called for an end to convict labor. Many states employed convicts to pay for their keep. Convicts built roads on chain gangs, operated farms, made textiles, and sewed garments. Convict-made goods were sold, forcing down prices and the wages of working free citizens.

In February 1891, the Second Annual Convention of the Kansas State Federation of Labor, in Topeka, approved a bill concerning state-paid wages. That month, the bill, which included the prevailing wage section, called 'for an eight hour law' and was brought forth by Mr. Avery of the Typographical Union No.121, Topeka. The bill stated:

> That in no case shall any officer, board, or commission, doing or performing any service or furnishing any supplies to the State of Kansas under the provisions of the act be allowed to reduce the daily wages paid to employees engaged with him (or them) in performing such service or furnishing such supplies, on account of the reduction of hours provided for in the act. That in all cases such daily wages shall remain at the minimum rate which was in such cases paid and received prior to the passage of the act (Oklahoma Department of Labor, 1913, p. 215).

The eight-hour bill, Senate Bill 151, failed in the Kansas Senate 6 March 1891, with the prevailing wage section removed. But by March 10 when the prevailing wage section was put back in, the bill became law. This first prevailing wage law stated:

> That not less than the current rate of per diem wages in the locality where the work is performed shall be paid to laborers, workmen, mechanics and

other persons so employed by or on behalf of the state of Kansas ...
(Laws of Kansas, 1891).

We do not know the immediate impact of the Kansas prevailing wage
law. But a report from the Oklahoma labor commissioner in 1910 may well
have applied to Kansas. The Oklahoma law was patterned after the Kansas
act. It was passed in 1908. It was reported to have had the intended effect of
setting wage and hour standards not only on public works but in related labor
markets. The Oklahoma Commissioner of Labor stated in 1910:

> The eight hour law has been of inestimable value to the laboring men of
> this state ... The common laborer, who was heretofore employed ten and
> twelve hours per day, is now, under the provisions of this bill, allowed to
> work but eight hours ... The law has not only affected the laborers and
> those who are dependent upon this class of work for a living, but it has
> gone further, and in many localities has gradually forced railroad
> companies, private contractors [i.e. private construction] and people of
> that class to pay a high rate of wages for unskilled labor (Oklahoma
> Department of Labor, 1910, p. 327).[4]

Prior to the Great Depression, eight states—Kansas (1891), New
York (1894), Oklahoma (1908), Idaho (1911), Arizona (1912), New Jersey
(1913), Massachusetts (1914), Nebraska (1923)—passed state prevailing
wage laws governing the hours of work and wages on state and municipal
public construction.

The Federal Davis-Bacon Act (1931)

For four years before the 1931 passage of the Davis-Bacon Act, several
bills were introduced in Congress to establish prevailing wages in
construction. Republican Representative Robert L. Bacon (NY) in 1927
introduced the first bill proposing a prevailing wage for construction, H.R.
17069. This member of Congress justified his measure as follows:

> The Government is engaged in building in my district a Veteran's Bureau
> hospital. Bids were asked for. Several New York contractors bid, and in
> their bids, of course, they had to take into consideration the high labor
> standards prevailing in the State of New York ... The bid, however, was
> let to a firm from Alabama who had brought some thousand non-union
> laborers from Alabama into Long Island, N.Y.; into my district. They
> were herded onto this job, they were housed in shacks, they were paid a

very low wage, and the work proceeded ... It seemed to me that the federal Government should not engage in construction work in any state and undermine the labor conditions and the labor wages paid in that State ... The least the federal Government can do is comply with the local standards of wages and labor prevailing in the locality where the building construction is to take place (U.S. Congress, 1927, p. 2).

Hearings for a federal prevailing wage law began in 1927 and continued in 1928 and 1930, but no bill was passed. On 3 March 1931, Bacon's original proposal, which he had reintroduced as H.R. 16619, was signed into law by Republican President Herbert Hoover (U.S. Congress, 1931).[5]

Since 1931, 33 states have passed prevailing wage laws, the last being Minnesota in 1973. Since 1979, however, 9 states repealed their prevailing wage laws starting with Florida in 1979 and ending with Louisiana in 1988. These states were concentrated in the South and the High Plains-Mountain states and they include Florida, Louisiana, Alabama, Colorado, Kansas, Utah, Idaho, Arizona and New Hampshire. In addition, Oklahoma's law was suspended by that state's Supreme Court in 1995 and it has yet to be reinstated. Today, 31 states and the District of Columbia have prevailing wage laws while 19 do not. The 19 no-law states are concentrated in the South and High Plains-Mountain area plus Vermont and New Hampshire.[6]

Determination of the Prevailing Wage

The Davis-Bacon Act required payment of prevailing wages on federally financed construction projects. However, the original language of the law was vague, and prevailing wages generally were not determined before the acceptance of bids. In 1935, Democratic President Roosevelt signed clarifying amendments to the act, which became the basis of the current Davis-Bacon Act.

In 1935, Roosevelt's Secretary of Labor, Francis Perkins, established the original rules for determining the federal Davis-Bacon prevailing rates. The prevailing wage was said to be the wage paid to the majority, if a majority existed; if not, the 30 percent rule was used. The 30 percent rule means if 30 percent of the workers in a specific construction occupation (such as carpenters) in an area are paid the same rate, that rate becomes the prevailing rate there. The 30 percent rule often resulted in the local union wage being declared the prevailing wage. If the 30 percent rule did not apply, because at least 30 percent of the workers in a given occupation in the local labor market did not receive the same wage rate, then the average wage rate was paid to workers doing the same job. The prevailing wage was determined this way for 50 years.

In 1985, Republican President Reagan changed administration of Davis-Bacon, creating the 50 percent rule. This rule holds that if 50 percent plus one of the wage rates for an occupation in a local labor market are the same to the penny, then that wage rate is said to prevail. If no one wage rate accounts for more than 50 percent of all wage rates for an occupation in a local labor market, then the average wage rate for that occupation prevails. Under the old rules, if union wage rates accounted for more than 30 percent of all wage rates for an occupation, then the union wage rate prevailed. Under the new rules, union wage rates must represent more than 50 percent of all wage rates in an occupation before union wage scales prevail under Davis-Bacon.

The choice of the average (mean) or the majority (mode) wage would not make a difference is wages in the construction labor market were normally distributed. In a normal or bell shaped distribution, the average of that distribution corresponds to the top of the 'bell'—namely the most commonly found observation or 'mode'. But many wage distributions are not normal in the statistical sense. In professional sports, for instance, the average wage can be quite high, but the vast majority of players make less than the average. That is because the average is being pulled up by superstars making unusually high salaries. In other words, there is a long tail in the wage distribution at the high end created by a handful of highly paid superstars while the majority of players are bunched together at the other end of the distribution. Construction is like this only in reverse. The construction labor market wage distribution has a long tail at the lower end of wages. Take plumbers as an example. Unionized plumbers, having gone through a five year apprenticeship program, having become trained in a variety of skills associated with industrial and commercial plumbing are lumped together with other plumbers whose skills consist of on the job experience at fixing sinks. Combining low-paid handy-men with high-paid skilled plumbers creates a wage distribution where the most commonly found wage (the mode) is a good deal higher than the average wage which is being pulled down by the wages of residential plumbers. This is particularly true in states where plumbers do not have to be individually licensed. Thus the divergence between two statistically accepted measures of the central tendency of a distribution—the mean and the mode—ends up mattering in prevailing wage determinations in construction.

When the federal prevailing wage switches between the mode and the mean, the law switches between encouraging and discouraging collective bargaining in construction. Much of the debate around prevailing wage regulation will reduce to the question of whether or not collective bargaining is good for the construction industry, and whether the government should encourage or discourage the practice of collective bargaining in this industry.

The Current Debate

The current debate over prevailing wage regulations circulates around six issues. Critics argue that prevailing wage laws raise public construction costs and are racially discriminatory in their intent and/or effect. Defenders of prevailing wage regulations deny that costs are raised substantially and claim that the race argument is false and misleading. They go on to assert that prevailing wage regulation encourage training of construction workers, better quality construction and a safer workplace. While academics have joined this debate at several points, the debate has played itself out primarily in legislatures and in newspaper editorials. Recently in Las Vegas Nevada, the two daily papers took opposite sides in this debate. In so doing, they fairly captured the viewpoints of the two sides. As critics of prevailing wage regulations, the editorialists of the *Las Vegas Review Journal* in an editorial from 21 January 2000 captured many of the basic position of the critics.

> The distortions caused by the state's version of the federal Davis-Bacon 'prevailing wage law' are not a matter of nickels and dimes. Cash Minor, chief financial officer of Elko County, testified before the 1999 Legislature that the state law required a contractor in Jackpot to pay $27.20 per hour to workers on a public golf course there, while the real market rate in northern Nevada at the time would have been only $15.

> All parties agree the ongoing Las Vegas construction boom—and the accompanying shortage of skilled tradesmen—would be keeping such wages high in Southern Nevada even without the state law. But in rural counties with lower costs of living, where men would gladly work for less, why should taxpayers have to shell out extra?

> If such a trend continues unabated, it's bound to drive up the price of some rural projects to the point where they simply won't be done at all. How would that benefit the local tradesmen?

Meantime, if the Las Vegas building boom were ever to slow, a state law which forbids wages from falling to reflect changing conditions of supply and demand would only throw more men out of work, as happened when Herbert Hoover famously twisted the arms of employers to keep wages artificially jacked up at 1929 levels, even as the Great Depression deepened.

'Prevailing wage laws' had their birth in racism, and their impact continues to be discriminatory. They are nothing but a ridiculous attempt to substitute busy bureaucrats and their calculators for the proper functioning of the free market, which is infinitely more flexible and accurate in determining the proper 'bid rate' for a given service.

How on earth can a 'market wage' be higher than the market will bear? If, as Bob Nard of the Southern Nevada Building and Construction Trades Council asserts, 'everybody benefits' when prevailing wage laws prevent out-of-state firms from lowering costs to taxpayers by paying lower wages which workers are happy to accept, why is state coercion required? For that matter, why not just set the 'prevailing wage' at $100 an hour, and 'benefit everyone' even more?

Because it's not true that 'everyone benefits' under such central planning schemes, of course. Not by a long shot.

The prevailing wage laws should be repealed (*Las Vegas Review Journal,* 2000).[7]

Not all cities have the benefit of more than one daily newspaper. Consequently, not all cities have the benefit of hearing more than one side of an issue. Las Vegas is fortunate in having two newspapers and in the case of prevailing wage regulations, Las Vegas readers benefit from the 'Paul Harvey' effect—they hear the rest of the story. In a 9 July editorial in the *Las Vegas Sun*, the argument in favor of prevailing wage regulations was presented in a signed editorial by Mike O'Callaghan, the executive editor and former Nevada governor:

Every few years there is an attack on the prevailing wage law in Nevada. The Silver State's law is often referred to as the 'Little Davis-Bacon Act'. Before taking a close look at how state prevailing wage laws work, let's discuss the federal Davis-Bacon Act.

The prevailing wage law, better known at the federal level as the Davis-Bacon Act, was passed in 1931 and signed into law by President Herbert Hoover. Both Davis and Bacon were Republicans who sponsored the law to guarantee fair bidding practices for contractors. Too many contractors were underbidding jobs, paid for with federal dollars, by paying laborers substandard wages. The low salaries of workers had become the cutting edge for the cutthroat bidders. It was hurting the communities, workers, taxpayers and the projects.

So it's not a Democrat or union gimmick to up the salaries of union workers. All workers benefit from the law and so does our economy. The 'little Davis-Bacon Act' requires that state and public works construction contractors pay workers the wage rates prevailing in local areas. Without this requirement, contractors can bring cheap labor into Nevada, gobble up our tax dollars set aside for public projects, and then return home, leaving behind nothing but an inferior product. Nevada's taxpaying workers, who must live in an area with a high cost of living, are left unprotected. Our taxpayers, contractors and workers are all victims without a prevailing wage law.

In 1985 and again in 1997 some of our legislators had the bright idea of doing away with, or at least weakening, the state's prevailing wage law. Again, as we look toward the 2001 legislative session we can see, smell and hear reasons being cooked up to attack the Nevada law. Before going too far, the enemies of the prevailing wage law should look east toward neighboring Utah.

A study, reported in 1995 by Peter Philips, Garth Mangum, Norm Waitzman and Anne Yeagle at the University of Utah, shows what happened after the Beehive State repealed its prevailing wage law in 1981. In Utah, whose experience was examined most closely, the state budget has not benefited from repeal of the prevailing wage law. The repeal helped drive down construction earnings and, as a result, the state has lost substantial income tax and sales tax revenues. In the decade before the 1981 repeal in Utah, construction worker earnings averaged about 125 percent of average nonagricultural earnings. By 1993, construction worker earnings had fallen to 103 percent of the average earnings for Utah workers. This decline in earnings is a result of both lower wages and a subsequent shift to a less-skilled construction labor force.

Also in Utah, the size of total cost overruns on state road construction has tripled in the decade since repeal in comparison to the previous decade. The shift to a less-skilled labor force—lowering labor productivity along with wages—and the greater frequency of cost overruns have lessened any possible savings in public works construction costs associated with the repeal.

Between 1979 and 1988, a total of nine states, including Utah, repealed their prevailing wage laws. The Utah economists, when viewing all of the nine states, concluded: Looking at all the states, and controlling for a general downward trend in real construction earnings, variations in state unemployment rates and regional differences in wages, repeals have cost construction workers in the nine states at least $1,477 per year in earnings, on average (in 1994 dollars). The costs may eventually be higher as the effects of the more recent repeals mature, driving wages and training down further.

Controlling for a general downward trend in the amount of construction training, variations in state unemployment rates and regional differences in training availability, the nine state repeals have reduced construction training in those states by 40 percent.

Minority representation in construction training programs has fallen even faster than have the training programs in repeal states. Until the various state repeals, minority apprenticeship participation mirrored the minority percentage of each state's population. After repeal, minorities became significantly under-represented in construction apprenticeship programs.

Occupational injuries in construction rose by 15 percent where state prevailing wage laws were repealed.

May I suggest that changes to the prevailing wage law of Nevada proceed slowly and not just be the first sneaky step in another attempt to destroy it (O'Callagham, 2000).[8]

In general, the outlines of the debate are clear. Do prevailing wage regulations raise public construction costs? Do they promote training, experience, quality construction and safety? Do prevailing wage regulations encourage the payment of health insurance and pension benefits and are these lost when prevailing wage regulations are repealed? Were prevailing wage regulations originally intended to keep blacks out of construction and/or is this the current effect of these laws? In short, should these regulations be retained or repealed.

Organization of the Book

The essays in this volume contribute to the prevailing wage law debate along its many dimensions. It begins with a section on the historical context and issues. Gerald Finkel provides an overview of the construction industry, and describes the major factors pertaining to the development of the construction industry alongside the rest of the industrial economy. He provides a historical background and explores: technological advancement in the construction industry, productivity and its connection to project costs, labor market segmentation and the wage structure, and the highly volatile nature of construction investment. Finkel looks at the determinants and the nature of both private and public construction expenditures. The latter issue established the context for considering construction labor market regulations and the related issues.

In 'Thoughtless Think Tanks: Sound Bite Thinking about the History and Intent of Prevailing Wage Laws', Azari-Rad and Philips conduct a detailed examination of congressional records, and historical data on racial composition of construction workers and their movements, to investigate the recent allegations that the Davis-Bacon Act was originally motivated by racial prejudice. Through careful examination of the congressional records and historical data from the U.S. Census, Azari-Rad and Philips demonstrate that the allegations about racist intentions behind the Davis-Bacon Act are baseless. They also describe the process by which 'Think Tanks' manufacture and disseminate factoids to advance ideologically charged policy agendas.

Regardless of the original intentions behind the passage of the Davis-Bacon Act, do prevailing wage laws act to exclude minority workers from the construction industry? In 'Prevailing Wage Laws, Unions and Minority Employment in Construction', Belman provides new empirical analysis estimating the effect of state prevailing wage laws on minority employment. Consistent with conservative claims he finds a simple negative correlation between state prevailing wage legislation and minority employment. However, this correlation disappears once he controls for the racial composition of states' non-construction labor force. More complete models of the racial composition of the construction work force also do not support the exclusion hypothesis. Belman concludes that the evidence typically cited in support of current prevailing wage laws negatively affecting minority employment is derived from simple models which do not adequately account for factors beyond prevailing wage laws which may impact the racial composition of the construction labor force.

The next two sections focus on contemporary policy issues related to the prevailing wage laws. These issues are central to current debates taking place at the federal level as well as in state, county and municipal governments across the nation. The first three issues address, specifically, the impact of prevailing wage law on public construction costs, training and the maintenance of a skilled workforce, and workplace safety.

'Prevailing Wage Laws and Construction Costs: Evidence from British Columbia's Skills Development and Fair Wage Policy', examines the issue at the center of much of the contemporary debate surrounding the continuation of prevailing wage laws. Policy makers across the nation have based arguments both for and against prevailing wage laws on their effect on public construction project costs. In this chapter Duncan and Prus review major research on the impact of prevailing wage laws on total project costs. Unlike earlier works that extrapolate a cost effect from wage differentials, this study looks at total costs and employs the appropriate controls for differences between public and private construction. In this case, empirical evidence from public construction in British Columbia, under the Skill Development and Fair Wage Policy, shows no inflationary impact from prevailing wage laws.

The prevailing wage laws may affect the recruitment and retention of apprentices mainly through its effect on trade unions whose participation in apprenticeship training is extensive. If the elimination or weakening of the prevailing wage laws adversely affect union strength, it could reduce the volume of training, unless the open-shop sector can overcome the skill free rider problem, and make up for the emerging gap by expanding its own training programs. In 'Wage Regulation and Training: The Impact of State Prevailing Wage Laws on Apprenticeship', Bilginsoy conducts an empirical study of the relationship between prevailing wage laws and the construction apprenticeship training. It focused on the impact of the prevailing wage laws on the recruitment of apprentices, completion and cancellation rates, and the minority share in apprenticeship programs, and finds that, controlling for the size of the trade, the supply of apprenticeship is higher in states that have prevailing wage laws. It also rises with the strength of the prevailing wage laws. Therefore, regulation clearly raises the recruitment rate. Bilginsoy also finds that apprentices complete graduation requirements at a slower rate in states without prevailing wage laws, indicating a lower efficiency in producing certified skilled workers.

Absence of prevailing wage laws may also negatively affect workers' safety. Adverse effects of eliminating prevailing wage regulations on union strength—collective bargaining—and training, as discussed by Bilginsoy, may result in more lax enforcement of safety rules, and increase the number of less skilled and experienced, and more accident prone workers. In 'Prevailing Wage Laws and Injury Rates in Construction', Azari-Rad investigates the relationship between the presence of the prevailing wage laws regulatory environment and workers' safety in terms of non-fatal injury rates in the construction industry reported by the Bureau of Labor Statistics. Utilizing four fixed effects models, Azari-Rad examines the effects of prevailing wage laws on total injury rates, and three more refined measures of injury rates, classified by the severity of injury. Controlling for employment, year and state, he finds that in absence of prevailing wage laws on the job injuries by all measures increase. The escalation becomes progressively greater as we move from less serious injuries with no lost workday to the more serious injuries with lost workday, and finally to the most serious injuries with days away from work.

The last section of this book addresses public policy issues regarding compensation and benefits. In 'Benefits vs. Wages: How Prevailing Wage Laws Affect the Mix and Magnitude of Compensation to Construction Workers', Petersen and Godtland use data from the 1980s and 1990s to compare compensation levels of construction workers in states that never had prevailing wage laws, states that repealed their prevailing wage laws, and states that have retained their prevailing wage laws. They examine the impact that prevailing wage laws, and their repeals, have on compensation to construction workers, in terms of both wages and benefits. They also examine the relationship between prevailing wage laws and the mix of compensation packages between wages and benefits. They find that compensation levels to construction workers are significantly higher under prevailing wage laws. When states repeal the prevailing wage laws, compensation levels decline to the levels of states that never had prevailing wage laws. Furthermore, prevailing wage laws are positively related to the share of benefits in compensation packages. Given the economic incentives in the construction sector that discourage the provision of benefits, the latter result is of particular importance.

In 'Health Care Subsidies in Construction: Does the Public Sector Subsidize Low Wage Contractors?', Waddoups finds that workers in the U.S. construction industry don't have access to employer based health insurance at exceptionally higher rates than their counterparts in other industries. He maintains that this is a negative externality resulting from market failures that shift the health care costs. To clarify the relationship between employer based health insurance and uncompensated health care, in connection to workers in the construction industry, Waddoups explores market failures that result in a low incidence of employer based health insurance among construction workers, the role of collective bargaining in resolving such market failures, and the relationship between employer based health insurance and uncompensated care costs at safety-net hospitals and clinics.

Finally, in 'Pension and Health Insurance Coverage in Construction Labor Markets', Price also finds that construction workers are less likely to have important fringe benefits like a pension plan and health insurance coverage compared to their counterparts in other industries. He asserts that the barrier to benefits coverage in construction are due to firm size, high turnover, and the absence of citizenship, and explores the role of collective bargaining in dealing with these barriers. Price finds that the repeal of prevailing wage laws leads to declining rates of pension and health insurance coverage for construction workers.

Unlike Petersen and Godtland's study which analyzes wages and benefits at the firm level, Price analyzes trends in pension and health insurance coverage rates using individual data from the Current Population Survey. This allows examination of the trends in coverage by individual characteristics such as turnover, race, ethnicity and citizenship. This chapter's focus on health insurance coverage rates also puts into perspective Waddoups's study which explores the consequences of the absence of health insurance coverage for taxpayers and other consumers of medical services. These themes are linked together through a focus on the influence of prevailing wage laws and collective bargaining on the trends in pension and health insurance coverage within the construction labor markets.

Conclusions

Prevailing wage laws emerged from a concern that cutthroat competition over wages in construction would lead the industry down a low-wage, low-skill development path. This was said to put the quality of construction at risk and lead to an itinerant, footloose low-wage construction labor force. Poor construction workers would make poor neighbors and potential burdens on the community. Reasonably paid construction workers, on the other hand, held out the possibility of being solid neighbors, good citizens and productive members of the community. Government, by the operation of prevailing wage laws, was supposed to get out of the business of cutting government costs by cutting the wages of its citizens. Whatever labor standards had been established, whatever wages prevailed in a local community, that is what the law said government should pay on public works.

The debate surrounding prevailing wage regulations is a microcosm for a larger debate current in the United States. This debate regards the benefits and the costs of deregulation in general. In recent years investment banking has been deregulated, the regulation of corporate accounting has been lax and the ability of the Security and Exchange

Commission to regulate stock trading has been starved for funds. De facto, the Attorney General of New York has become the primary regulator of the stock market. Debate rages over recent financial deregulations and whether or not they contributed to or exacerbated the recent bursting of the stock market bubble. The savings-and-loan, trucking, airlines and food processing industries have all experienced deregulation in the past twenty years with mixed and debatable results. Prevailing wage law regulatory debate should be held in the context of this larger recent trend towards deregulation. Each industry has industry specific questions. The heart of the question in construction is this—is the practice of collective bargaining good for the construction industry and should it be promoted through government regulation and should that regulation be prevailing wage laws? The heart of the larger question for the American economy and society is this—does an economy that is least regulated the best way to organize our material life or should the economy be constrained and channeled through regulations designed to short circuit the failures of the market? This volume is meant to contribute specifically to the first debate and contribute implicitly to the second. The general conclusion of this volume is that prevailing wage laws are, in the main, good and effective regulations of the American construction labor market because they allow market to create contracts that embed the true and long term costs of the industry—costs associated with training, safety, health insurance and pensions—into the short term bids on construction projects. The thrust of this volume also suggests that when embedded in a specific understanding of the details and practices of particular industries, well-thought-out regulations can contribute to industry performance and an effective delivery of goods and services at an economically efficient and socially responsible price.

Notes

[1] On 19 May 1869, President Grant issued the following proclamation:

> ... that, from and after this date no reduction shall be made in the wages paid by the Government by the day to such laborers, workmen and mechanics on account of any such reduction of hours of labor (*The Statutes at Large and Proclamations of the United States of America, from December 1869 to March 1871*, 1871, p. 1127).

On 11 May 1872 Grant reiterated with greater detail and emphasis in a second proclamation that per diem wages should not be cut with the required shorter hours:

... I, Ulysses S. Grant, President of the United States, do hereby again call attention to the act of Congress aforesaid, and direct all officers of the executive department of the government having charge of the employment and payment of laborers, workmen and mechanics employed by or on behalf of the government of the United States to make no reduction in the labor wages paid by the day to such laborers, workmen and mechanics on account of the reduction of the hours of labor (*The Statutes at Large and Proclamations of the United States of America from March 1871 to March 1873*, 1873, pp. 955-956).

[2] This organization changed its name to the American Federation of Labor in 1886.

[3] For a biography of Gompers, see Philips and Sinclair (2003).

[4] The primary concern in both Kansas and Oklahoma was to use public works hours and wage policies to set and improve local labor standards. A typical enforcement case in Oklahoma as reported by the Labor Commissioner follows:

[Anadarko. 10 May 1908] We were advised that the O'Neill Construction Company had cut the wages on public works at Anadarko from twenty-five cents to seventeen and one-half cents per hour ... [C]ontract was taken with the understanding that twenty-five cents per hour should be paid. The work was not progressing as rapidly as necessary to the cost within the estimate, hence the contractors tried to take advantage of the situation by reducing pay. After thoroughly discussing the matter before the [city] council and contractor, the wages were restored to twenty-five cents (Oklahoma Department of Labor, 1910, p. 327).

[5] Bacons proposal was re-introduced in 1930 as H.R. 9232 by Congressman Elliot W. Sproul from Illinois, while Bacon proposed a complementary bill.

[6] The no-law states include eight Southern states—Virginia, North Carolina, South Carolina, Georgia, Florida, Alabama, Mississippi and Louisiana—nine Plains-Mountain states—Oklahoma, Kansas, Iowa, South Dakota, North Dakota, Colorado, Utah, Idaho and Arizona—plus the upper New England states of Vermont and New Hampshire.

[7] We would like to thank the *Las Vegas Review Journal* for permission to reprint this article.

[8] We would like to thank the *Las Vegas Sun* for permission to reprint this article. Readers should notice that O'Callaghan relied upon work written by one of the editors of this volume along with colleagues at the University of Utah. The study cited by Callaghan, 'Losing Ground—Lessons from the Repeal of Nine Little Davis-Bacon Acts', has been criticized by A. J. Thieblot, a consulting economist in Baltimore Maryland on the basis of two arguments. First, Thieblot asserts that prevailing wage laws increase the risk of injuries in construction. Second, he asserts that any tax revenues lost from lower construction wages due to the repeal of prevailing wage laws would be offset by lower public construction costs. In another paper in the same journal, Thieblot goes on to argue that prevailing wage regulations also restrict blacks from construction work. Two of the editors of this volume published a rejoinder to Thieblot's paper that he then

responded to. See: Thieblot, A. J. (1996); Thieblot, A. J. (1999); Azari-Rad, Hamid and Philips, Peter (2003); and Thieblot, A. J. (2003).

References

Azari-Rad, Hamid, and Philips, Peter (2003), 'Race and Prevailing Wage Laws in the Construction Industry: Comment on Thieblot', *Journal of Labor Research*, vol. 24(1), pp. 161-168.

Federation of the Organized Trades and Labor Unions of the United States and Canada (1881), 'Declaration of Principles', in *Proceedings of the American Federation of Labor, 1881 to 1888*, Reprinted in 1905, Pantograph Printing, Bloomington, IL.

Hunnicutt, Benjamin K. (1988), *Work Without End*, Temple University Press, Philadelphia, PA.

Las Vegas Review Journal (2000), 'An Absurd Calculation: State Can Never Determine a "Proper" Wage', 21 January, p. B10.

Laws of Kansas (1891), Chapter 114, pp. 192-193.

O'Callagham, Mike (2000), 'Where I Stand—Mike O'Callaghan: A Law that Makes Sense', *Las Vegas Sun*, 9 July.

Oklahoma Department of Labor (1909), *Second Annual Report*, Oklahoma City, OK.

Oklahoma Department of Labor (1910), *Third Annual Report*, Oklahoma City, OK.

Oklahoma Department of Labor (1913), *Sixth Annual Report*, Oklahoma City, OK.

Philips, Peter, Mangum, Garth, Waitzman, Norman, and Yeagel, Anne (1995), *Losing Ground: Lessons from the Little Davis-Bacon Acts*, mimeo, Department of Economics, University of Utah, Salt Lake City, UT.

Philips, Peter, and Sinclair, Cory (2003), 'Samuel Gompers', in Joel Mokyr, *The Oxford Encyclopedia of Economic History*, Oxford University Press, UK.

The Statutes at Large and Proclamations of the United States of America from March 1871 to March 1873 (1873), vol. XVII, Boston, MA.

The Statutes at Large and Proclamations of the United States of America, from December 1869 to March 1871 (1871), vol. XVI, Boston, MA.

Thieblot, A. J. (1996), 'A New Evaluation of Impacts of Prevailing Wage Law Repeal', *Journal of Labor Research*, vol. 17(2), pp. 297-332.

Thieblot, A. J. (1999), 'Prevailing Wage Laws and Black Employment in the Construction Industry', *Journal of Labor Research*, vol. 20(1), pp. 155-159.

Thieblot, A. J. (2003), 'Race and Prevailing Wage Laws in the Construction Industry: Reply to Azari-Rad and Philips', *Journal of Labor Research*, vol. 24(1), pp. 169-177.

Topeka State Journal (1891a), 24 February, p. 4.

Topeka State Journal (1891b), 25 February, p. 1.

Topeka Daily Capital (1891), 25 February, p. 1.

U.S. 40th Congress, 2nd Session (1868), *Congressional Globe*, 24 June, Government Printing Office, Washington, D.C.

U.S. 69th Congress, 2nd Session (1927), *Hearings before the Committee on Labor, House of Representatives*, 18 February, Government Printing Office, Washington, D.C.

U.S. 71st Congress, 1st Session (1931), *Hearings before the Committee on Labor, House of Representatives*, 31 January, Government Printing Office, Washington, D.C.

Chapter 2

The American Construction Industry: An Overview

Gerald Finkel

Introduction

Construction has been a significant aspect of the human struggle against nature's elements, long before market economic relations came to dominate it and virtually every other form of human enterprise. From the earliest shelters to 21st century structures, the issues inherent in construction create a link across the millennia. Today, construction is a vibrant industry in the United States, accounting for $480 billion of output, or 4.8 percent of the gross domestic product; and employing 6.5 million workers, or 5 percent of the labor force. Yet the modern construction industry is inherently plagued by market instability, employment gyrations, and investment fluctuations, giving rise to pronounced periods of boom and bust.

The construction product market is diverse, consisting of residential, commercial, and public sector projects. Its labor market is no less diverse. The peculiar nature of construction products requires a relatively labor intensive production process and highly skilled workers. Construction trades are, therefore, divided along various crafts, and mom-and-pop shops operate alongside multi-billion dollar construction conglomerates in a highly competitive environment. The complex web of construction craft unions has a considerable presence on the medium to large-sized residential, commercial, and government projects, while the nonunion sector performs the bulk of work on small-scale jobs, and single-family residential developments.

Construction performance and labor productivity are major issues in the debate on union-nonunion wage differentials. Among other factors, the nature of the construction product and the turbulence of the market are fundamental determinants of private investments in this sector. At the same time government, as the purchaser of one-quarter of all construction services, has a significant impact upon both the product and labor markets.

These peculiarities of the construction industry provide the necessary context for examining its present economic issues. This chapter will provide a historical and institutional overview of the American construction industry, which will, in part, help to explain the evolution of wage protections and the various forms of companion legislations. It will begin with a description of the historical development of the American construction industry and then provide highlights of the product markets, structural divisions in those markets, and construction investment. The next section will review construction labor markets, their segmentation by union and nonunion status, variations in training, wages, and labor relations. The chapter then addresses the important issues of productivity, changing technologies and construction costs while the last segment considers the effects of prevailing wage laws.

Historical Development

Burgeoning 19th century capitalism thrust the construction industry into the mainstream of the American economy. Economic, technical, and social developments served to reshape the rudimentary system of contracting that was mired in the use of low level technologies and age old building materials (e.g., stone, wood, and iron). Nineteenth century technological inventions provided the basis for future commercial development. These scientific breakthroughs would rapidly expand wealth and value in the building industry. Economic expansion increased firm size and attracted new entrants at all levels of the industry. By the turn of the next century the labor-capital struggle over the division of this wealth would exacerbate the existing disorder of workplace relations. The result was the formation of a new set of building trades unions divided by skill but connected through their sites of employment.

The key elements from which market based construction was created were also the basic aspects of other nascent industries. The quest for viable markets, the drive for profits, mechanization, and efficiency were always important concerns for all builders and developers. It is the nature of the construction industry with its permanence of product, site specificity, and skill requirements that served to differentiate it from other developing parts of industrial America.

The real beginnings for the modern construction industry are found in the strengthening American economy of the post-Civil War era. The new markets for construction generated by economic expansion overwhelmed the artisan and master-apprentice system that had been the mainstay of the industry. The records of modern construction corporations begin in the antebellum period but are not prevalent until after the war. For example, many of the largest public and private pre-Civil War undertakings focused on transportation improvements by small firms and individual entrepreneurs who were engaged by companies with very specific charters.

In 1816, the State of New York appropriated money for a survey and construction of a 'grand canal'. In eight years (1817-1825), state surveyors and engineers oversaw the completion of a project that linked Buffalo with New York City. The Erie Canal was no more than a 4-foot deep ditch, 40-feet across, and 363 miles in length, but it became one of the nation's most important public works projects.

The work was done by small entrepreneurial farmers, who had property near the canal route, and their workers. As the project progressed, 'professional canal contractors' employing low paid immigrant labor added to the production process (Haven, 2004). However, contracts for the dig were let out for as little as a quarter of a mile—as was the first agreement with John Richardson, an individual contractor, to 'grub, clear, ... and construct a canal section' (New York State Archives, 2004). Work was performed almost completely by hand shoveling, which was augmented by tree and stump pulling equipment. A large supply of semiskilled laborers kept wages low and working conditions difficult.

Private transportation products centered on the building of 'for profit' turnpikes. Companies were regularly chartered as restricted corporations for the purpose of undertaking highway construction projects and sold stock to both private investors and public entities (Klein and Fielding, 1992). As such these were not public works projects, but, when connected to canals and ports, they significantly improved the country's transportation network.

As the century progressed the laws that regulated these corporations were enhanced with respect to liability, capitalization, and control. In particular, railroad companies used their corporate status to fulfill capital requirements and expand their spheres of influence. The Pacific Railroad Act (1862) provided incentives and loans for the construction of a transcontinental railroad from Omaha, Nebraska to Sacramento, California. The U.S. Congress chartered the Union Pacific to build westward and the Central Pacific, a California corporation to build to the east (Boorstin, 1965; Hoffstadter *et al.*, 1964). In turn, the construction was primarily subcontracted out to construction firms 'largely owned by the directors of the railroads they served' (Hoffstadter *et al.*, 1964). In local railway construction projects, a similar system was in place. An early forerunner of the New York City Transit system was the Brooklyn Steam Transit Company, incorporated in 1871 and chartered 'to construct any description of railroad in any part of the county of Kings' (*New York Times*, 1872).

As corporations came to dominate the American business enterprise in general, it also made headway into the construction industry. Infrastructure projects such as bridges and railways were of significant size and could only be carried out by the newly incorporated firms such as Turner Construction or Parson Engineering. The George A. Fuller Company was one of the premier construction firms at the end of the 19th century and even constructed its own Manhattan headquarters in 1902. Finally, to herald the coming era, J.P. Morgan spearheaded a consolidation of steel producers and erectors to create the American Bridge Company in 1900 (American Bridge Company, 2003). It included the Keystone Bridge Works, an early Carnegie steel company that had constructed the first steel bridge from 1867 to 1874. American Bridge subsequently became a subsidiary of the United States Steel Company in 1902, during a major period of corporate consolidation, and has built some of the largest public and private structures in the world.

The Product Markets

The demand for construction products varies from the most minor of installations to the creation of monumental public structures. The building industry has historically responded to the needs of other industries. Chandler noted the shift in steel usage when railroad construction declined in the 1890s and urban development increased. In 1887, Carnegie changed the focus of the Homestead Works from 'rails to structures' in order to capture the market for steel construction (Chandler, 1959, p. 77).

Excavation, erection, and structural work continued to be parceled out based on firm size and capital requirements. However, independent sole proprietors continue to exist in large numbers in large part because the building industry has relatively low barriers to entry and exit. Limited licensing restrictions and a general lack of regulation has created open markets with high turnover and no shortage of new entrants. In fact, historical development has produced distinct levels of market segmentation. Whereas the arguments for dual divisions between primary and secondary markets can be applied to manufacturing much more definitively, construction has both primary and secondary sectors composed of many internal markets. The competition among firms within these defined markets presents construction as a less structured industrial sector than that of the manufacturing or service sectors.

The product markets are widely varied but have some identifiable patterns regardless of their size. Primarily, 'construction' refers to contract construction. The implication is that there are a series of contracts for all parties involved in a project. The owner contracts with an architect and an engineer, the engineer with the general contractor, and the general contractor with the sub or specialty contractors. These contractors then enter the labor market and purchase 'contract labor', either formally or informally, for the duration of the project.

To the largest extent, this is the outline of market operations, whether it is for single-family residential work, commercial property development or in the public sector. Large and small contractors and developers coexist through a division of labor that often has the appearance of having ill-defined boundaries and chaotic forms of competition.

In an effort to provide order and self-protection for the purchasers of these services, private builders rely on managerial controls such as construction managers, design-build projects, and value engineering. The challenge is to rein in production costs while effectively coordinating a multitude of tasks. For the public sector, these controls have been in some instances augmented by wage regulation (prevailing wage laws) and job specific arrangements (project labor agreements).

Structurally, building industry markets are marked by a large amount of balkanization. Firms can range from the typical 'mom-and-pop' shops to corporations with over 1,000 employees. The U.S. Department of Commerce's *County Business Patterns* (1964-2001) lists categories from less than five to over 1000 employees in their nationwide county surveys. Firm sizes are routinely spread across these listings and within the major trade categories. The Census of Construction listed a total number of establishments with payroll engaged in construction (NAICS 23) as 656,448 (U.S. Department of Commerce, 1997). Of these, nearly two-thirds employed 1-4 people and only 75 firms employed 1,000 or more workers. When firms without payroll are included, the 1997 U.S. Census showed over 2 million construction firms (SIC 1987) with 1.73 million setup as individual proprietorships (U.S. Department of Commerce, 1997). With respect to race and gender, minority owned firms represented 11.5 percent of the total, and female owned businesses amounted to 6.7 percent (The Center to Protect Workers' Rights, 1997).

The actual divisions by product are based on skills or market type. Niche markets for motors or general contracting for high-rise construction can help to create insulated pockets of business activity. The largest sub-category of employers was residential builders, with over 95 percent involved in single-family housing. Not surprisingly, the residential value of construction put-in-place was 49 percent of the total value of construction installed in 2002 (U.S. Department of Commerce, 2002). This segmentation can be further divided by union and nonunion distinctions.

Ultimately, market structure's effect on productivity can appear to be contradictory. The positive side is reflected in market knowledge, skill enhancement, and specialization. Small, nimble firms in highly competitive markets such as alteration and low-end new construction are spurred on by low profit margins to become innovative and cost efficient. In addition, short-term relationships develop with repetitive mixes of these different contractors that further improve productivity through familiarity. Such positive externalities can flow to participants while they remain in these niche markets.

However, the low capitalization of the small shop does not bode well for capital-labor substitutions and has a negative impact on productivity growth. These types of contractors rely heavily on multi-function management, where the employer serves as foreman, estimator, and installer, and productive edges rely, to a great extent, on individual expertise. At the other end of the market spectrum is the large corporate entity. There are international firms (e.g., Kajima Construction, Bechtel or Bovis Lend Lease) employing thousands of construction personnel while mid-sized local companies dominate particular geographic areas with a few hundred workers. Yet the modern industry has followed its historical past by failing to develop large-scale economies of scale due to the ease of firm entry and exit, and a general lack of vertical integration (Cassamatis, 1969, p. 26).

As with any segmented market structure, firms are insulated from large and small competitors. Capital requirements, licensing, bidding track records, and labor agreements help to reinforce the divisions between primary and secondary firms. Yet intra-sector competitive pressure can be extensive, particularly during economic contractions. Large firms tend to move back down the bidding ladder—taking market share from smaller firms—while the process is reversed during an expansion.

Toward the end of the 20th century, the Jamaica Water and Power Company (JWP) experiment in New York was instrumental in shifting the notion of a single specialized firm to a much more inclusive business plan. JWP, a Long Island, New York based utility company began to purchase medium to large sized specialty contractors and 'supply houses' across the different mechanical trades. This represented, for the first time, a significant effort at both vertical and horizontal forms of economic integration. The objective was to become a 'full service' construction corporation that could offer complete installations and maintenance for the electro-mechanical portions of any project. Other companies, such as Integrated Electrical Service, have raised capital to purchase several electrical firms, and many large national general contracting firms have stakes and ownership of sub-contractors. BE&K, Keiwit and Fluor Daniel are examples of these types of companies.

The late 20th century concentration of capital was a direct effort to improve the economies of scale. Redundancy in management functions, barriers to capitalization, and weak purchasing power in the supply markets hindered construction firm development. The intricacies of local building codes, geographic construction practices and a broad range of collective bargaining agreements in the unionized segments compounded the difficulties in growth.

Construction investment, as in any business enterprise, must conform to a number of economic conditions. Internal rates of return, costs of production, opportunity cost, and return on investment are common considerations that are applied with varying levels of sophistication. Yet all firms, regardless of their market position, are guided by the cyclical nature of the industry. Investment opportunities are framed by the end of one downturn and the sudden onslaught of the next. In construction, the cyclical movements are intensified by the somewhat anarchic behavior of the industry's participants, the weak barriers to market entry, and the rush to profit during the expansion phase. Overbuilding is the most common manifestation of the missed market signals that would normally bring other industries to a gradual slowdown, but which has an abrupt impact on construction. Structures, unlike many other products, are built to last. Durability is an important consideration in every project, as opposed to the planned obsolescence that is the hallmark of the consumer products industry.

Clearly not every building is constructed like the Cathedral of St. Verbiana in Los Angeles, which was built with earthquake resistant design and a life expectancy of 300 years. However, replacement factors that would create inventory investment or waves of construction upgrading need an outside impetus. Long-term durability constrains the self-generating properties that can be found in other industries such as automobiles or clothing.

Commercial building feeds the needs of developers and workers alike for an anchor to any long run boom. Offices that are built by the actual user are one example of expansion that has its roots in the well being of other segments of the economy. Company headquarters, manufacturing centers, and warehouses are built with internal financing as the need arises. Commercial space that is built by a developer for a particular lessee adds an additional amount of risk to the market place. The Boston Properties tower was constructed in New York City for the Arthur Anderson Co. and was left without a tenant when Anderson folded in scandal. Finally, there is speculation building where builders and developers often partner with the hope of attracting a tenant during or after the construction phase. 'Will Build to Suit' may be a familiar sign found on newly erected small structures but it is implicit even on the largest of speculative construction projects.

These types of construction can be contrasted with residential construction. Home building ranges from single family to multi-family to high-rise. Repetition is the key to efficiency in the construction of most residential projects. Thirty story urban apartment houses and attached suburban condominium complexes can be designed for all income levels and tastes, but need to have units that are easily replicated during construction. This provides the speed in construction that makes housing for the mass market affordable.

Regardless of the type of private sector project being undertaken, investors, builders, and workers are cognizant of the impending time factors. The boom-bust cycle threatens to damage the economic outcome just as easily as interest rate fluctuations or price inflation dampens investor enthusiasm. As in a complicated game of musical chairs, nobody wants to be the last builder. As a boom picks up steam, contractors hoard workers, new entrants plow into the markets, and developers pump out blueprints. The upswing eventually ends with a bang. Widespread layoffs rapidly fill the benches at union hiring halls while excess space goes begging on the open market. In virtually every construction cycle the scenarios remain the same, with the product market being glutted and then gutted until conditions are ripe for revival.

There is every incentive then to keep the job on schedule during peak times. Profits and incomes are directly affected by interruptions at the workplace. Nonunion companies fear the encroachment of unions on the pace and control of the production process. Union employers are concerned about labor issues that have the potential to stop a job, while unions are sensitive to the negative impact of work stoppages on employment opportunities and member incomes. To that end, unions have established machinery for dealing with localized disputes, although all parties are guided by the National Labor Relations Act (NLRA).

Fast track construction, construction managers, at-risk managers, and design-build contracts are relatively new innovative employer tools to sustain job flow. The ultimate importance of project management, logistics, and scheduling cannot be understated. At the same time, commercial developers are concerned about the overall economic conditions that direct the demand for office and commercial space. Geographic reliance on particular industries serves to shape the crests and troughs of local cycles. Oil in the middle south, commodity markets in Chicago, and banks and brokerage houses in New York are examples of specific spheres of influence on the demand for construction services in these regions.

It is not necessarily the same situation in government-funded construction. This is because public building is a function of the distribution of a public good. Private sector entities are utilized for the actual construction, therefore, these projects still draw their building materials and services from the free markets. However, the appropriation decision remains an outgrowth of the political debate in which cost analysis remains a necessary but insufficient basis for the ultimate approval. Unlike the distribution of private sector goods, public sector construction is as much a function of the political process as it is of price and taste.

Public projects clearly account for a large portion of the annual total value of construction put-in-place. In 2002, $16.3 billion, or slightly more than 8 percent of the total public sector construction value put-in-place, was funded by the federal government. The remainder was included under the state and local sub-heading (U.S. Department of Commerce, 2002). While residential work is the largest component of private construction, the largest portions of public works are in highways and streets and the educational line. Educational construction has been growing steadily, reflecting recent political and social concerns, while roadwork has been a perennial leading category.

It is interesting to note that the Commerce Department's list of categories for public construction products is quite similar to those of the private sector. Construction workers are able to move between public and private workplaces—provided they possess the appropriate skills. It is the sources and operations of these labor pools that need to be examined next.

The Labor Markets

Construction labor markets satisfy a diverse set of demands for construction skills. In August of 2002, the Bureau of Labor Statistics reported that roughly 6,525,000 workers were employed in the construction industry. Their skills range from basic categories, such as general laborers, to highly trained operating engineers.[1]

The scope of skills and degrees of installation difficulty require a commensurate population of trained personnel. However, easy access to the secondary portions of the construction labor markets makes it nearly impossible to differentiate between unskilled and skilled employees listed under a job title for a particular firm. Contractors may list an employee as a journeyperson, but there is no verification of the individual's status or experience by the agency collecting the data. Remuneration is linked to skill, experience, training, and union status.

Union membership in the building trades has fallen over the past decade in the United States. It has decreased from 20 percent of those employed in the industry in 1993 to 16 percent in 2003 (U.S. Department of Labor, 2003). Allen (1985) presents a number of possible explanations for the fall in membership numbers. A long-term shift in building from urban (strong union) to suburban/rural (weak union) is one potential cause. Another is in the types of construction. Warehouse chain stores and residential projects require less skilled workers than industrial/commercial sites due to the repetitive nature of their design. Finally, there are continuing legal challenges that require unions to commit greater resources to organizing and membership drives.

Skill homogeneity has played an important role in shaping the industry's labor markets. The American building trades of the late 19th century developed in response to the construction booms of the developing economy of the United States. The structure of the trades flowed from earlier times when the master-journeyman-apprentice system existed. The remnants of the pre-Civil War unions, which were economically unsustainable, developed into manageable institutions as the economy and employment stabilized. Bricklayers, carpenters, and masons unions all began during this period.

Other trades grew directly out of the technological advances that helped create the 20th century construction market. Electrical workers gravitated from the telegraph and plumbing industries, iron and steel workers from the carpenters, and elevator constructors from hoist builders. It was also in the latter part of the 19th century that skilled building trades developed strong trade union movements. Electrical workers (1891), ironworkers (1896), and elevator constructors (1901) all have their union roots in locals established in the years following the Great Upheaval of the 1870s.

Specialization defines the labor divisions. Skilled trades generally recognize two categories of workers: apprentice or journeyperson.

Apprenticeships can last from three to five years. Such programs are usually certified by a State Apprentice Commission (SAC) or the federal Bureau of Apprenticeship Training (BAT) and may also exist within the nonunion sector.

Whereas the secondary markets with low-end construction have few barriers to entry in the helper category, apprenticeships have historically been a means for skilled workers to control the labor supply. Unions have made the size of the apprenticeship class a negotiable item and many trades add contract provisions defining apprentice to journeyperson ratios. Craft knowledge has been selectively passed to families and friends over the generations in an informal process dating back to the 18th century, while less clear cut barriers to entry—related to information, race and gender—existed throughout the 20th century.

The concept of 'father and son' created a pseudo-inheritance system for favoring the relatives of existing members. It has essentially given way to state supervised application processes. Public advertisements for programs help to close the information gap, while sponsored programs are required to take local demographics into account in their selection process. In 1997, 10 percent of the construction workforce was listed as minority, as opposed to 17 percent for all industries (The Center to Protect Workers' Rights, 2002). The U.S. Census Bureau reported in 2000 that approximately 3 percent of the actual trades workers were women (U.S. Department of Commerce, 2000).

Construction pay rates have always outpaced even the skilled industrial trades that perform similar tasks (Hirsch and Addison, 1986; Lewis, 1986). The apprentice to journeyperson path fits well with traditional economic arguments concerning wages and marginal productivity theory. The investment value of training is recovered by employers through increasing marginal revenue product, while the worker's return is captured in a higher wage. The quality of training has a relevant influence on the return on investment for both employer and employee.

However, on average, union workers receive more technical training than unorganized workers simply because of the costs and administration of such programs. Stand-alone training courses are cost prohibitive. Since unions are institutions with sizable memberships and employers are often part of an association, the costs of an apprentice operation can be pooled, sharply reducing the individual firm's expense. Vocational training through public schools or private training institutions remains an important source of manpower development. This type of education shifts the cost of generalized instruction away from the construction firm and over to the state or the individual.

For the nation as a whole, Lynch and Black (1998) found that only 17 percent of all workers reported that they received formal employer sponsored training and that construction was one of the industries 'least likely to provide formal training programs'. Considering that smaller firms were found to be much less likely to provide training than larger firms, the plethora of small nonunion construction shops would exclude large segments of the open market from training.

There are also several disincentives for nonunion firms to make significant investments in employee development. The first is the inability of the firm to capture the returns on these investments. Marginal revenue product that flows to firms, returns both the cost of training and additions to revenue over time. This is contingent on the worker staying with the firm—at least for a period long enough for the investment to pay for itself. The problem for open market contracting firms, in this regard, is that there is relatively weak firm specific labor attachment. The union sector offers a bureaucratic structure of benefits and advancement that is seldom replicated in the nonunion sector. The unorganized labor market is a patchwork of benefits and individual wage contracts that lack portability or permanence. Workers are economically free to move from firm to firm or from area to area without penalty. This increases the risk for a nonunion employer, even one offering high pay and relatively good benefits. If a worker leaves because he or she is hired away, or the work slows, the employer takes the chance of losing the entire training investment. There is no guarantee that the next worker hired from the market will have had prior training or familiarity with the company's method of operations.

A separate but equally important concern for the nonunion employer is that of training one's competition. Without any formal wage contract, workers are able to move as the free market dictates. An option for these employees is to move on to become contractors themselves. The capital requirements vary, as do the licensing rules, but entry into the employer side of the market remains relatively easy. In the small and medium markets, employers with no economic hold over their employees are virtually training their future competitors. The union employers run into the same quandary, but union employees have a greater incentive not to become employers due to their security, pay, and benefits. Not only can a nonunion employer lose their training investment but they may also be reducing their own future market share.

On the contrary, unionized firms sign contracts that are multi-employer or industry wide-agreements. Signatories are either independents or contractors who are affiliated with an employer's trade association (e.g., National Electrical Contractors' Association or the Association of General Contractors). One of the key aspects of these agreements is that the agreeing firms gain access to the unionized labor force. Thus, training costs incurred by these employers are returned through any productivity benefits that schooling produces for participating union members. Such benefits are captured from workers across the specific labor market (electricians, masons, plumbers, etc.) because there are major barriers to entry by untrained workers and economic penalties for worker exit from these labor markets.

Union membership in the building trades is attained, for the most part, through apprenticeship and, to a far lesser extent, through union organizing drives. Apprenticeships have entry criteria—such as residency, high school diplomas, or skill tests—and the size is limited by the terms of the collective bargaining agreement. These entry-level positions put the new employee into a series of job ladders with programmed advancement and proportionate pay increases. Workers develop a lifetime benefits stream, receive extensive training, and generally exhibit high labor market attachment. Therefore, training investments do not flow away from the market but are shared, even as workers move from shop to shop. Training also reflects the requisite skill levels needed for particular types of construction.

Regardless of the sources of the training (on the job, apprenticeship, or vocational) the labor markets need a mechanism for matching the suppliers of labor with the demanders for their skills and abilities. This selling of one's labor effort has both formal and informal aspects. In general, there is a distinction between union and nonunion labor markets. Hiring halls, referral halls, and shape-up rooms are associated with the union marketplace. Pay scales and skills are identified through collective bargaining and the contracts stipulate the time and purpose for which the labor is employed.

There are clear economies to employers and employees in the use of a hiring hall. Search and signaling costs are drastically reduced for all parties. Employers need only to contact the union hall or joint referral office to secure additional labor. Employees need not spend time and money seeking work, and their union affiliation serves as an ersatz resume. The process is not free because employers may be required to fund the administration of the hall while employees pay union dues that subsequently give them access to the referral system. It is also commonplace for many unions to establish hybrid hiring plans where members may either seek work by contacting union employers or opt to use the hiring list.

In the nonunion market, supply and demand are matched through an open process. Employers rely on personal referrals, employment agencies, and local advertisements to fill their demand. From the supply side, workers need to signal prospective employers accurately about their skill levels and wage expectations. The connections of the two sides can be fairly haphazard and expensive. Time spent searching and signaling, advertising costs, and agency fees need to be accounted for in the revenue added by the new employee. The wage bargain itself can vary from job to job. It can be as formal as a temporary contract for a particular job or as informal as a handshake.

The labor markets need to be able to match skills with the requirements of the installation. Private 40-story office towers are more sophisticated in design than a residential project of similar size. The residential project is, in turn, more complex than a Home Depot store while the Home Depot warehouse is, in turn, more difficult than townhouse type condominium developments.

Public projects can have the same distinction. The erection, for example, of a court house and office building structure requires a greater degree of expertise than a postal garage facility, while the garage is more complicated than a small renovation such as the replacement of a guardrail or a new front building door. While the government sector's needs mirror those of the private sector, the state has a more rigid process for awarding contracts. Criteria for awarding bids are legislated at the local, state, and federal levels while various public institutions are allowed alterations in the structure of their contracts (e.g., the New York State Dormitory Authority received permission to obtain bids through general contractors rather than direct bidding for sub-contracts).

Public sector labor markets reflect the size and technical requirements of the particular projects. Since public works projects are generally of significant size (roadwork, bridges etc.), the successful bidders need access to ample sources of skilled labor. In Vincent's (1990) study of Indiana's prevailing wage laws, the author determined that much of the state's construction work was completed by repetitive companies. The majority of these firms were unionized but, more importantly, he found that the scale of work was prohibitive for nonunion contractors.

In terms of the impact of public spending, it is important to note that governments draw from the same labor pools as private enterprise. Public works projects are bid out to private construction employers who then reach into the labor markets for their workers. There were roughly

1,306,000 workers on publicly funded construction sites in 1997. Government supported works comprised nearly a quarter of all construction, therefore, they have significant influence on the state of the labor markets and wages of workers.

Construction wages are explained through a number of industry variables. A short list of variables that influence wage levels and their changes include unionization, risk of injury, supply, demand, and training. However, the main force propelling wage change is productivity (Allen, 1994, and 1995; Gordon, 1981; Finkel, 1990). This is explored in detail in the next section.

Wage determination in construction clearly has a strong market outcome basis. The Smithian notion of a free market can be found, to a large extent, in the small nonunion construction shops. Wage bargains are made individually and for varying durations. These agreements may include health benefits, traveling time, 'off the books' bonuses—essentially, any perks or conditions of employment that can be negotiated (Foster, 1973). These informal arrangements stand in sharp contrast to collective bargaining agreements, which are legally binding contracts. In the open market, agreements are enforced by direct supervision by the individual employer. In the union sector, bureaucratic controls reinforce job site discipline, thus, increasing the costs to a worker for being terminated (e.g., the loss of health and welfare or pension benefits).

The imperfections of misinformation, identification, and assessment lead to a bumpy road in the free market hiring system. Yet the underlying theme of the hiring process is the value of the output produced by the prospective employee. In construction, this relies largely on the individual's physical skills and trade knowledge, but also the ability of the employer to monitor labor effort as if it was housed under the factory roof.

From an institutional perspective, the wage agreement is determined within guidelines that are a result of political-economic activity. For example, collective bargaining procedures are framed by the National Labor Relations Act (NLRA). In the construction industry, this includes specific laws that refer to organizing, strikes, picketing, and split shops. Common Situs provisions ban job site picketing under Taft-Hartley secondary boycott rules. Pre-hire agreements create efficiencies for all parties during organizing campaigns. Finally, it establishes legal tests for determining the existence of double-breasting and alter ego companies.

Individual effort and its collective expression also impact construction wages. Productivity frontiers, from which employers and employees draw their share of the wealth created in the industry, are expanded by technology and training. Heterodox theorists highlight this struggle over the division. Imbued with a focus on social relations, this alternative position argues that free enterprise sets the conditions for a capital-labor dispute over wealth (Gordon, 1981). In construction, the argument can be made that this conflict is a basis for the collective bargaining system. Workers organize based on skill homogeneity so that percentage organized gains in market share support wage demands during contract talks (Gordon, 1980).

The union's strength in dealing with employers stems from the size and activism of the membership (Finkel, 1997). Thus, the increase in the percentage organized affects wage change. Over time, the percentage organized is a function of organizing ability, which, in turn, is related to levels of involvement by the membership, market conditions and the level of commitment of union leaders. Since job sites are scattered, temporary, and difficult to identify, the union itself is highly dependent on the voluntarism and participation of the rank-and-file. In this view, unions become a rallying point in order to protect wages, benefits, and conditions from the incursions of employers. The collective will of the membership is pitted against individual employers or associations with respect to the size of the wage package and terms of employment. Still, the wage bargain remains a contest for the value of the daily or hourly level of output. Unions consider themselves protectors of the fair day's pay, while opponents claim unfair monopoly power over that segment of the labor market.

In 1999, median weekly wages for full-time employees with union membership were approximately 30 percent higher than those without membership. In construction, the differential was above 50 percent (Monthly Labor Review, 2000). Numerous industries are affected by the percentage of the workforce that is unionized. Research has established union to nonunion wage premiums for manufacturing, service, and construction (Lewis, 1963; Sobotka, 1953). The debate about such a differential centers on the notion of union monopoly power, as opposed to collective voice and worker solidarity theories. Construction organizing is limited in states that maintain right-to-work laws. These essentially ban the union shop, in which employees must become union members after a specific period of employment. In effect, this prevents workers from agitating for union-only work sites. The reduction in union market strength and bargaining power has a negative impact on the union-nonunion pay differential.

In addition to the unionization rate, safety is a factor that helps to capture levels and changes in wages. Safety concerns are often seen as being a wage determinant—particularly in an industry that annually competes with mining as the nation's most dangerous. Traditionally, injury rates are higher for inexperienced workers, and training programs play an important role in reducing those rates. Although there is often a general view that more dangerous work environments produce a wage premium, this is not necessarily the case in construction. Nonunion employees are perceived as working under less safe conditions than union workers because of union protections. Yet there is little evidence that nonunion employees receive additional compensation. Even in the union workplace apprentices who are at risk due to inexperience receive only a percentage of the journeyperson's wages and do not appear to be paid for their risk.

Recent research indicates that wage premiums attached to risk may exist to a far lesser extent than had been considered. Factors influencing market mobility and segmentation may supersede any union-nonunion hazardous pay differentials (Dorman and Hagstrom, 1998). It is also possible to argue that safer workplaces are more productive than those with high injury rates. Thus, there is a marginal productivity benefit to less hazardous conditions that can translate into a 'safety premium', particularly for unionized workers and their employers.

In addition to safety, wage studies typically include proxies for the supply and demand for construction labor. Data on the numbers of workers at the national level are available from the Bureau of Labor Statistics and to a lesser extent the County Business Patterns surveys. The real or perceived demand for workers causes a reaction in supply numbers. Thus, attachment can be relatively permanent—as found in the union sector—or as ephemeral as the day laborers who seek work at small-scale nonunion projects. In fact, the word journeyperson is derived from the French, *journey*, which is related to those who traveled around while plying their trade.

Productivity

At the core of the productivity debate is the issue of cost containment. This centers on the price of labor, the price of materials and the labor hours needed for a complete installation. Productivity analysis measures output per labor hour with various valuations for both numerator and denominator. The construction industry provides a unique statistical challenge in the form of its unique structure, specialty skills, and ever-changing types of building materials. Productivity studies typically employ real output, total worker hours, and non-supervisory data only, and attempt to account for union and nonunion differentials, public works regulations, and special

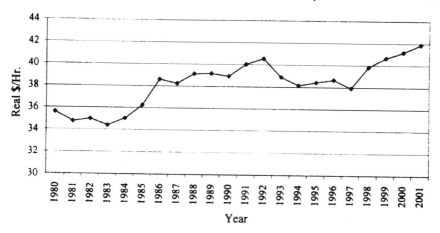

Figure 2.1 Real Construction GDP per production worker hours

Source: U.S. Department of Labor, Bureau of Labor Statistics.

agreements. Some attempt to integrate hourly output analysis with macroeconomic productivity explanations. Regardless of one's view, such analysis cannot be separated from the issues of measurement. This refers to both real price deflators and the changing product mix.

Deflation has always been problematic since productivity measures must capture a wide range of connected products and activities. Thus, the deflators themselves are related to total and unique indices, which are, in turn, based on specialty skills and a changing product mix.[2] Robert Gordon (1968) examined the difficulties arising from this range of deflator choices. The crux of the problem lies in the representative basket of goods used as a proxy for construction output. The United States Department of Labor provides detailed information on a stable basket of goods for either the consumer or producer price indices. Such groupings are designed to reflect typical family or business consumption. Construction cost indices include elements from roadwork, housing, concrete, or specific commodities such as lumber or steel. Weighting by the prices of concrete, steel, or wood tends to skew such deflators and reduce their accuracy.

As shown in Figure 2.1 the overall construction productivity has been rising over the past two decades. The ratio of the construction component of the annual real gross domestic product (GDP) to production worker hours has increased from \$35.61 in 1980 to \$41.88 in 2002. Annual percentage change, in Figure 2.2, lays out the case for this increase. Fourteen of the last 21 years indicated some positive level of change. Although not overwhelming, the direction belies many traditional arguments about the backwardness of the industry.

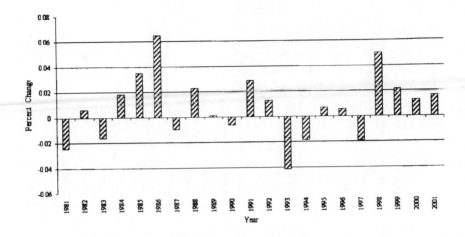

Figure 2.2 Annual percentage change of real construction GDP per production worker hours

Source: U.S. Department of Labor, Bureau of Labor Statistics.

Given the market structure and the historical development of the modern building industry, advancements in hourly output per worker need some explanation. As in any industry, the point of production is what attracts the greatest attention. It is here that the forces of technological innovation run headway into the traditions and past practices of a largely hand-tool, labor-intensive worksite. The response to the productivity challenge could be categorized in several ways. The first is the notion of a division of labor, both among trades and the employers of those trades, which improve output through specialization. With its roots traceable to the observations of Adam Smith, the skill levels and specific knowledge imbued in the workforce serve to produce a modern structural separation between installers. Although general handypersons exist, their applicability to any sizable project is highly unlikely. Thus, there is a focus on the immediate point of production and the skills and training linked to the process. For construction this presents two sub-issues. First, how to get the most value out of the individual laborer? Second, how to bypass or supplement that very same labor effort?

In a manufacturing plant, supervisors are faced with a permanent setting, repetitive operations, and readily predictable output levels. In a construction environment, foremen and managers operate in a scattered setting, with mobile crews and changing sets of installation requirements. Although output time should be predictable (jobs are bid based on labor hours and material prices), product completion is compromised by the fact that nearly every construction project is a custom designed installation which is being assembled on location. While both direct supervision and pay/wage inducements can coerce additional output, the marginal additions are constrained by coordination, logistics, and worker control.

A more encompassing response for increasing productivity is found in the ongoing development of prefabricated building components and improved tools and equipment. Prefabrication is simply the replacement or reduction of on-site hours for assembly and installation with off site labor units. There are two distinct forms of prefabrication. To a lesser extent, but of importance, is on-site prefabrication. This relates to management's decision to prepare parts of the job on location in near assembly line fashion. The semi-finished products are then moved to another area of the project for installation. Nippling by plumbers, conduit bending by electricians, and lathers' reinforcing rod assemblies fall into this category.

The more critical type of prefabrication however, is the off-site manufacturing and preparation of building segments. This process substantially reduces on-site labor time. Not only are items pre-built, but there is also a significant substitution of higher priced labor by cheaper, less skilled one. In some cases, skilled construction labor is employed in a factory, and there are in-house prefabrication departments such places as the sheet metal shops.

Although a construction project is filled with thousands of individual parts and installation efforts, the real thrust in prefabrication is in the off-site production of large portions of structural components. Walls, trusses, and concrete segments have all been reproduced in varying sizes and quantities in an effort to improve efficiency. A good example of large-scale prefabrication is the creation of prefabricated roadway piers for elevated highways, bridges, and rail lines. These segments were formerly created at the site and involved form work, lath work, and a final concrete pour. The materials all require specialized trades for the installation, and the hours of labor for the different trades can be considerable.

The pre-cast concrete sections allow for elemental 'just-in-time' scheduling. Concrete segments are now trucked in shortly before the scheduled installation time. The customized designs are factory built, avoiding weather issues, coordination delays, and most importantly, the need for load after load of ready-mix concrete.

Despite this growing trend toward off-site production, many construction employees have taken comfort in the fact that the building project must still be installed at a fixed location. Thus, the actual installation cannot be outsourced as if it was a computer company's customer service call center. That sense of job security is not well founded. The high speed internet transfer of data allows blueprints, computer assisted design drawings, and engineering to be outsourced to lower waged areas and then electronically sent to contractors or even jobsites. Of more significance than the back office work is the shifting of the prefabrication process to off-shore companies, where lower production costs make it economical to build and ship large finished building elements. For example, the 87,000 square-feet Salt Lake City Library façade was totally prefabricated in Mexico City and then trucked across the border to Utah (Millman, 2004).

Less dramatic forms of prefabrication are found within the smaller finished items that complete an installation. Lighting fixtures may be purchased pre-lamped and wired with only a flexible tail needed for connection. Ready to use kitchen equipment, with all of its plumbing in place, replaces the intricate on-site positioning and hookup of ranges, sinks, and basins. Of course, residential housing, even with semi-custom design is sold as a pre-fabricated unit and often advertised as such in the Sunday papers. Prospective buyers can select from a range of home types as shown in a catalogue. The home is then shipped in pieces and erected at a given location.

The effects of prefabrication are extended by the advancements in hand and power tool technology. Smart tools, embedded with processing chips, simplify calculations and improve accuracy. Light weight casings and parts have helped to shave time off of each skilled worker's hand movements while low tech improvements, such as ergonomically enhanced grips and handles, reduce worker stress and strain.

Tool technology is combined with materials and design to bolster cost savings. Consider the advantages of light weight materials: plastic pipe vs. metallic, composite and plastic forms as opposed to those made of plywood, or drop-in fluorescent fixtures instead of spline clip supported housings. These are the marginal improvements in the installation process that are akin to the saving of fractions of a second off a manufacturing process that occurs thousands of times a day.

Major changes in materials and products require certification and institutional approval. Design and material substitutions can be constrained by local building codes or any number of governmental regulatory agencies. However, market factors, competition, and ultimately, safety, are the real driving forces that can break down any type of opposition to innovation.

Up to this point, the discussion of the economic dimensions of the industry has focused on its historical development and attempts to improve efficiency and productivity. It is clear that the industry remains highly labor intensive. Yet it is not labor intensive in the way that agricultural hand pickers are somewhat frozen in time. It is also not immune from the historical de-skilling forces of industrial development. Nor is it the tightly controlled province of the skilled building trades, which, despite evidence to the contrary, are often accused of being the arbiters of technological advancement and regulatory control. It is in the public forum that these concerns reach a common ground in the debate on prevailing wage legislation.

The Public Sector

Throughout this chapter, the public sector has been woven into all of the major economic issues. It is clear that the fundamental paradigmatic shift during the mid 20th century moved government from a caretaker role to that of an active economic participant. In so doing, this political-economic change unleashed an extraordinarily large builder into the American construction market—the government. The pace of growth for the nation's construction markets have propelled the local, state, and federal building levels to the equivalent of nearly 25 percent of the entire construction sector's value put in place. Yet prior to this burst of public investment, there had been a consistent petition for governmental protections in terms of wages, safety, and economic security.

Early on, socio-economic issues led to worker agitation for statutory relief from oppressive working conditions. As the scope and scale of public works expanded, three particular concerns came to light. The first of these was focused on the hours of employment and, by extension, the level of a day's pay. State minimum wage guarantees were built into regulations prescribing the eight-hour day. For example, the Kansas Eight Hour law of 1891 held the workday to eight hours for any firms conducting business with the state (Philips *et al.*, 1995). Imbedded in the statute was a requirement to pay the local area daily wage. These forerunners of the modern prevailing wage laws waxed and waned in effectiveness over the early part of the last century.

Workers' compensation laws also developed in the latter part of the 19th century. Employees were faced with a series of common law hurdles that blocked their ability to file suit for jobsite injuries. 'Contributory negligence', 'the fellow servant doctrine', and 'assumption of risk' helped shift blame to the worker under many conditions (Marshall *et al.*, 1976). By 1911, the first workers' compensation legislation was enacted in Wisconsin to mitigate the harshness of the existing work place environment (Friedman, 1986). Public legislation that offered compensation for workplace injuries linked employer insurance premiums to injury rates in the hope that 'firms would have an incentive to lower costs by improving working conditions' (Burtt, 1979, p. 442). These were important innovations for construction workers since the industry has always rivaled mining for the distinction of being the country's most dangerous nonagricultural workplace.

At the same time, the Progressive era in American politics underscored certain moral and philosophical arguments about the nature of the state. Government became more involved as an adjudicator of labor issues, which culminated in the 1935 passage of the National Labor Relations Act (NLRA). Also known as the Wagner Act, after its sponsor, the federal law attempted to stabilize labor relations during a period of significant economic depression. While it set overall rules governing collective activity in the workplace, the act also established particular standards for the construction industry.

For example, the law requires the signing of union pledge cards by at least 30 percent of a company's eligible employees before a filing for election can take place (NLRA, Sec.9 e). The process is intensive and can require many hours of organizing at the production site. However, the NLRA provides the construction industry with an alternative methodology that is termed 'the pre-hire exemption'. The National Labor Relations Board (NLRB) determined that the large number of relatively small shops made the permanent site election process unwieldy and expensive for all parties. Thus, construction unions can enroll a contractor's employees by virtue of a pre-hire union/employer agreement that covers existing employees and future hires.

The original construct of the Wagner Act was, in part, to ensure union democracy. By requiring an election process and a majority vote, Congress was satisfied that the resulting agreements were not 'sweetheart deals' and that the collective voice of the workers would fairly determine representation. In construction, trade unions typically have jurisdiction over a limited geographic area. Although there are cases of alternative building unions attempting to organize or influence representation elections (jurisdictional disputes), the structure of the building trades limits the possibility of intra-union rivalries. In this respect, the NLRB has concluded that pre-hire agreements do not pose a threat to legitimate representation since the workers' choices are narrowly defined in the construction industry.

The underlying tenets of the American social contract, which is designed to protect 'life, liberty, and the pursuit of happiness', present themselves as a conundrum for government economic policy makers. On the one hand, government needs to take an active role in improving everyday life for its citizens. In this sense, public works projects are intended to enrich the entire spectrum of daily activities—from the social to the economic. On the other hand, internal revenue generation is confined to taxes, tariffs, and fees that constrain government enterprise and create a need for fiscal responsibility and budgetary caution. The public sector is then put in a position where it must balance costs with the public's interests. In economic terms, the federal, state, and local construction agencies have become extremely large purchasers of construction services with the potential to influence the prices of materials and labor. Building material prices fluctuate much in the same fashion as other commodity prices with supply and demand exacting their market tolls. Labor rates are only partially set by these factors and are subject to a number of social, political, and economic influences.

In certain markets where a purchaser of labor is so large that it has 'an observable effect on the local wage level, then it has a degree of monopsony power' (Marshall, 1976, p. 228). Thus, a situation of imperfect competition may lead to restricted employment and a wage below labor's marginal revenue product. In the traditional sense, economists view a wage below the laborer's marginal revenue product as exploitation—even if it is 'non-deliberate' (Cartter, 1975, pp.65-66). Private monopsonists behave in this fashion because they are concerned with profit maximization. Public sector institutions are driven by political developments and budget limitations so that this discrepancy between the wage and labor's marginal revenue product need not be so mechanical.

While this description of monopsony is more applicable to an open labor market with profit maximizing buyers, the wage bargain in the presence of trade union organization takes on some of the characteristics of a bilateral monopoly. In that type of monopoly scenario, the single buyer of labor adjusts the employment-wage level to a position consistent with its marginal expenditures on labor, but at a wage level based on the existing market supply curve. From the supply side, a single seller of labor units would ask for an employment/wage position that maximizes its returns based on the demand curve for labor and its marginal revenue curve. The resulting wage bargain is, to a large extent, indeterminate since it will eventually reflect the individual strengths of buyer and seller (Mansfield, 1979, p. 241). In the case at hand, the wage bargain on public projects is appropriately open to both market and political pressures in its final determination.

The precedents for government intervention in the economy are well established and have only grown in the latter half of the 20th century. The Taft-Hartley Act (1947), and the Landrum-Griffith Act (1959), were significant pieces of labor legislation that affected the building trades. The secondary boycott provisions of the Taft-Hartley Amendments weakened strike support. Landrum-Griffith provided ground rules for union democracy but required detailed financial reporting of union expenditures and salaries. The Employees Retirement Income Security Act (1974) opened the door for government oversight into the management of and payments from pension, benefit, and jointly administered trust funds. In more recent years, the issue of 'salting', which is a construction trade union organizing technique, has been challenged substantially by nonunion employers with only minimal success. In fact, the 1995 U.S. Supreme Court ruling on the *Town and Country Case*, which centered on the legal definition of an 'employee', legitimized the practice of sprinkling union members into the nonunion employers' workforce.

We have demonstrated that within the construction sector, the government has never been a neutral observer. It has been an active participant in the form of owner, purchaser, and builder, as well as a legislator and mediator. To the contrary, public sector purchases and expenditures on construction activity represent an important segment of the nation's gross domestic product. While this can be formally understood as part of the Keynesian identity for growth, it also presents government financed construction as an essential policy tool. With a $400 billion contribution to gross domestic output, it is in the public interest to ensure stability in both private and public construction programs.

For the general population, there are a number of contradictory views on the state's decision to build. While private construction projects are assumed to be undertaken by rational profit maximizers, public sector investment is very much a function of the political process. The beneficiaries of public improvements can be both firms and citizens. The same transportation additions that can facilitate the delivery of goods and supplies for businesses can also speed the personal commute for individuals.

The problem of public consensus with respect to government construction expenditure lies in the notion of citizens as consumers, wage earners, and taxpayers. As consumers, individuals derive a benefit from public construction by the overall improvements to daily life. New subways, bridges, or sewerage systems have positive impacts on the quality of life. In the role of wage earners, citizens may favor state expenditures because of temporary and long-term employment possibilities. The construction phase may be short term but the resulting structures and facilities need to be staffed and maintained on a long-term basis. The sticking point, in terms of public sector economics, occurs when 'citizens as taxpayers' are considered.

Public construction expenditure is a source of economic growth. As a significant addition to gross domestic product, a measure of the nation's economic well being, public investment benefits citizen consumers and citizen wage earners. Economic expansion in the public sector creates jobs, raises incomes, and ultimately sends revenues back to the government in the form of taxes. However, in the case of the citizen taxpayer, there is an ostensible concern with the cost of these investments.

In general, this concern seems to focus on one particular cost—that of the price of labor. In its simplest form, the argument states that government projects should be awarded to the lowest bidder, and that wage rates should be guided by the free market. The 'taxpayer' is led to the conclusion that cheaper must be better and that such cumulative savings are, in essence, a type of individual tax savings. In sum, public construction wage minimums are presented as a means to inflate costs while creating a form of exclusionary wage regulation that favors unionized (higher paid) workers. The arguments seldom include consideration of productivity, training, and product quality, while neglecting concerns for higher injury rates, lower consumption patterns, and reduced tax bases (Philips *et al.*, 1995).

This section has provided a rationale for direct government involvement in the construction industry in both practical and theoretical terms. The justification for this economic involvement stems from government's role as a buyer of services and as a guarantor of workers' rights. Prevailing wage legislation provides the state with a policy tool for ensuring that public investment receives a fair return with respect to efficiency and quality. At the same time, it stops government from operating as a discriminatory purchaser of labor by avoiding wage exploitation through standardized pay rates.

The Role of Prevailing Wage Regulations

In many ways, the federal Davis-Bacon Act and the state prevailing wage laws are a definitive expression of the institutional economic position. Established in 1931, the Davis-Bacon Act created wage floors for federally funded building projects. Political debate over provisions of the Act, if not the actual Act itself, has waxed and waned over its seventy plus years of existence, but the prevailing wage laws still remain in effect. The prevailing wage calculations are designed to capture the dominant wage in a defined geographic area. In this manner the nucleus of the wage benefit package is determined from a survey of the surrounding area. The results are weighted by the numbers of trades persons employed at a specified rate. Building trades unions consider this an important protection for the union wage scales established in the local labor market. Unionized employers argue that prevailing wages level the bidding field for all contractors. Opponents rely on free market arguments, which view union wages as the result of monopoly power in the labor market. The claim, then, is that any protections of such a wage artificially raise the wage costs of a publicly financed project.

Union wages are clearly higher than nonunion wages. The real issue is not the dollars per hour paid for public construction but rather the output per dollar. Union labor commands a premium because it is arguably more productive than its competition. In fact, higher costs in the public sector may result from legislated designs, standards, and the types of structures, rather than labor costs in general. In an analysis of the effects of state prevailing wage laws on school construction costs, Azari-Rad *et al.* (2003) show that these wage rules had no significant impact on public construction costs.

Government's public role is shaped by a political process, but lacks the underlying emphasis on private profit and accumulation. It extends itself into the infrastructure, commercial markets, utilities, and defense as well as land and waterway management. It can authorize millions of dollars for emergency construction or prioritize expenditures based on security reasons. In short, governmental reach is enormous and its economic implications are significant. The economic impact is similar to a private sector project with respect to the short term and long term effects. In the short-run, there are construction jobs and ancillary employment that generates local wealth during the construction phase. In the long-run, there is the permanence of the facility and its future employment/income additions.

Public construction expenditures can therefore be used in a traditional Keynesian model as a means of 'priming the local pump'. The affected region benefits through job stimulation and short-term growth. Although sustained expansion is dependent on a wider set of circumstances, there is usually strong regional voter support for public improvements during a downturn.

The passage of the Davis-Bacon bill predates the Roosevelt era Keynesian economic programs. Yet it is, in some ways, a localized economic stimulus plan in that it was created in part to keep wealth within a defined geographical area. During the 1931 House debates, opponents of the law continually cited the need to support the depressed wage earners of local economies (U.S. Congress, 1931, p. 6505-6521). In fact, Representative Mead of New York stated that 'with consumption falling far behind production ... it is our chief concern to maintain wages of our workers and to increase them ...' (U.S. Congress, 1931 p. 6513). The Act has served as a buffer in preventing the flow of spending power from moving to other areas of the country by reducing competition from migrant contractors and their workers.

Such provincial protections may not have a great impact on a vibrant national economy—such as the one at the turn of the 21st century. However, the impact of prevailing wages on local consumption, points to an important consideration. By preserving higher area construction wages, which have been determined in the local labor market, the law helps to ensure predictable incomes and spending levels, which are cornerstones of a local economy.

An alternative situation is the possibility of a publicly financed project foisted on an area that is experiencing an economic expansion. A saturated construction market adds to local inflationary pressures by raising prices. Not only will material prices be influenced, but also tight labor markets become even tighter. For these reasons, political concerns take precedence in the decision making process to permit or deny a project. In itself, this does not remove public spending from the business cycle factors that shape the private sector. It does, however, underscore the role of public policy in guiding expenditures

Prevailing wage restrictions are means to protect participants in the public sector from a single large buyer of construction services. As the sole developer and purchaser, government agencies can exert significant monopsonistic market power to drive down wages and prices. Conceptually, the prevailing wage law stops government from pushing down costs in a race to the bottom, thereby jeopardizing quality and sacrificing building standards. Opponents of such protections argue that free market mechanisms could adequately distribute work and employment opportunities.

The prevailing wage laws have established dollar value categories for applying these regulations. The dollar levels seemingly coincide with skill that, in turn, coincides with the higher paid and better-trained tradesperson. In the end, the public sector protects the taxpayer by using dollar value as a proxy for difficulty and matching it with the appropriate labor. The Davis-Bacon legislation presents one of the few areas, albeit in the public sector, where there is consistency in bidding practices, cost considerations, and installation requirements. With respect to market segmentation, the prevailing wage laws also reflect such divisions by establishing thresholds costs before the regulations apply.

As an aside, it should be noted that the history of federal prevailing wage legislation was ostensibly a protection from itinerant labor/employer competition. However, there was also concern expressed about the quality of construction. Without some regulatory structure, public projects across the country were at risk of inferior quality, materials, and methods. For example, in a House debate on a proposed amendment to the Davis-Bacon Act, a letter from United States Comptroller J.B. McCarl noted that the Treasury Department 'expects contractors to employ the best type of American mechanics and laborers on Federal work' (U.S. Congress, 1931, p. 6505-06). Further on in the debate, Rep. Clay S. Briggs of Texas claimed that the law would 'enable the Government to get better returns for its money in higher efficiency and greater skill' (U.S. Congress, 1931, p. 6513).[3] With the growth of national markets and codes, there is now less of a chance of inferior product substitution, but prevailing wage laws do not interfere with technological innovations. Labor saving devices and products are allowable, providing they do not compromise the job standards, specifications, and safety.

A related issue to these laws is the development of project labor agreements (PLAs). While these are found in both the public and private sectors, it is the PLA in the public sector that has proven most irksome to nonunion employers. These agreements are generally site specific and provide a *quid pro quo* for the government and the unions. The government gains access to a large pool of skilled trades-people, uniformity in insurance, standardized work times, and stabilized wage costs. In return, the government agrees to use only employers that are affiliated with the local building trades council or association. Unionized building trades have successfully rebuffed numerous challenges, such as in the Boston Harbor case, although nuances in the contract language have led to court rejections of some project labor agreements (e.g., the Wilson Bridge Project in Maryland).

In a similar manner, prevailing wage laws bolster the arguments favoring a project labor agreement. If the public project qualifies as a prevailing wage job, then the mix of employer bidders is constrained to those already paying or willing to pay the higher rate. Given the training and qualities of the various skilled workers, many nonunion employers cannot justify the prevailing wage rate based on the marginal productivity of their work forces, so they simply do not bid for this work.

Conclusion

The U.S. construction industry described in this chapter is one that is strongly connected to its past, shaped by the uniqueness of its products, and ultimately directed by the needs of the economy as a whole. The ancient swing of the stone-age hammer is imitated countless times a day by the carpenters and masons of the 21st century. Yet it is the form of that hammer and the treatment of its outputs that catapults this analysis into the modern era of market based construction. The tool's lightweight material, ergonomically correct grip, and smoothly machined head are designed for efficiency but run headlong into the limits of hand-tool production. The shift to power tools and the search for the means to replace that labor are the historical result of competition at all levels of the industry.

In a world where skill is king, technology strives to end its reign. Competitive forces in the industry dictate the direction but not always the pace of that change. Challenges and questions abound for the industry's participants. From apprentice to project manager, the issues of work opportunity, cost, and distribution of wealth are regularly contested. It is the sum total of all these relations that underlies the mechanical activity at the site itself. The cacophony of the construction job belies the ability of contractors and workers to operate in a productive and coordinated manner. The resulting profit and income that induce those efforts are anchored to construction productivity, which cannot be separated from the worker's skill or the supervisor's decisions.

Thus, it is not difficult to follow the logic of construction unions' political position favoring government wage minimums and special project agreements. Yet unions cannot dismiss the needs of a competitive market system that pushes firms to be efficient low cost producers. The NLRA, prevailing wage laws, and project agreements remain as significant issues behind the everyday installation of bricks and mortar.

As modern technology continues to make inroads into construction practices, organized workers will continue their reliance on their traditional sources of protection. Work opportunities, job conditions, and jurisdictional issues are important not only to the workers, but to their employers as well. Research and development in the manufacturing, tool and equipment industries has been combined with improved training and innovative management techniques to increase industry output over time. How such gains will be shared within this industry remains a critical question in both the union and nonunion sectors.

Issues surrounding the prevailing wage also fit with the arguments about public policy implications. If the intention of a public construction program is to satisfy a governmental need while stimulating a local economy, then wage and employment issues need to be reviewed in a much wider context. Does it make economic sense to substitute cheap labor for higher waged labor, thus, limiting any positive income effects gained from the proposed appropriations? Ultimately the debate is about time, productivity, and overall economic impact. For this reason, in both public and private construction, the industry continues to expand its productivity potential on three levels.

First, through training and skill development. Registered apprentice programs are the foundation for a unionized workforce and these are funded through collective bargaining agreements. Nonunion associations, such as the Associated Builders and Contractors (ABC), are funding a number of training programs and have followed the union model with its affiliation with institutions of higher learning, although to a far lesser extent. Many large corporate customers have inserted training funding into the job bid packages. The dividend from training relies heavily on the concepts of human capital theory and has, to a large degree, been institutionalized into the primary portions of the industry.

Second, through rapid advancement in technology. On-site and off-site prefabrication are directly related to the growth in tools, machinery, and design. In an industry traditionally viewed as a laggard with respect to research and development, smart tools, prefabricated structural elements, high output excavation equipment, hoists, cranes, and pumps have all moved to cut construction hours drastically.

Finally, through changes in the area of management and employee relations. Innovations, such as construction manager arrangements or design-build contracts, when coupled with fast track programs, are able to shrink labor hours while keeping projects on schedule. Each of these management methods can be employed in both union and nonunion settings. In addition, each can be used with a project labor agreement and are unaffected by prevailing wage laws. Unions, while traditionally wary of the threat from management-engineered changes, have found that these methods have certain advantages. For example, Washington, D.C.'s Blue Line transit was awarded as a 'design-build' joint venture, but under a union endorsed project labor agreement.

This helps to explain the attraction to project labor agreements, and the extensive political efforts behind them. Project labor agreements can provide public projects with an uninterrupted workflow, uniform scheduling, and an adequate labor supply. These arrangements can also provide a rationale for the role of prevailing wage legislation as an underlying economic support for a program of economic stimulation.

Notes

[1] This assortment of skills has created an industry wide division of labor. Although the trade separations are more stringently adhered to in the union sector, the entire industry is composed of approximately twenty major trades. These general and specialty craft workers provide an amalgam of skills that satisfy the needs of specific kinds of employers. The North American Industry Classification System (NAICS) provides some insight to the structure of the labor market. It lists nineteen areas of construction specialization and 6 additional groupings under heavy and civil engineering construction. The following list captures most of the typical employment categories and was produced from a review of NAICS, apprenticed trades noted in *The Construction Chart Book*, and *The Directory of U.S. Labor Organizations*.

1. Boilermaker	6. Elevator Constructor	11. Millwright	16. Plumber
2. Bricklayer	7. Glass and Glazing	12. Operating Engineer	17. Rigger
3. Carpenter	8. Ironworker	13. Painter	18. Roofer
4. Concrete and Masonry	9. Laborer	14. Pipe fitter	19. Sheet metal
5. Electrician	10. Lather	15. Plastering and Drywall	20. Tile and Terrazzo

Mirroring these trades are a similar set of apprentice programs registered with the Office of Apprenticeship Training. Formal and on-the-job training programs can be found in both the union and nonunion environments. Registered apprenticeships generally range from 3 to 5 years depending on the skill levels, collective bargaining agreements, and market conditions.

[2] As shown in table 2.1, a sample of general construction indices for April 2003 showed a quarterly range of percentage cost change from -0.1 to +0.8 and an annual rate change from +0.9 to +3.9.

Table 2.1 General purpose cost indices

Index	Percent Change	
	Quarter	Year
ENR 20 City: Construction Cost	0.8	2.4
Commerce Dept.: Price Deflator	0.6	3.7
Handy-Whitman: General Bldg.	0.0	1.1
Lee Saylor Inc.: Material/Labor	-0.1	3.9
Means: Construction Cost	0.4	2.4
Rider Hunt Levett & Bailey	0.0	0.9

Source: Engineering News-Record (2003).

[3] At another point Representative William Granfield of Massachusetts extolled the benefits of the legislation to the wider local community if general contractors would tend to use local sub-contractors. With respect to a post office project in his home state, he noted that the, 'vicinity of the construction work would receive the benefits that would accrue from the materials and accessories manufactured and used in the construction of the building (Congressional Record, 1931, p. 6514). Granfield went so far as to argue for the use of local granite over Midwestern limestone due to the climatic conditions in New England. With prevailing wages in place there would be a greater likelihood of the use of local sub-contractors and therefore the use of appropriate local materials.

References

Azari-Rad, Hamid, Philips, Peter, and Prus, Mark J. (2003), 'State Prevailing Wage Laws and School Construction Costs', *Industrial Relations*, vol. 42(3), pp. 445-457.

Allen, Steven G. (1994), 'Developments in Collective Bargaining in Construction in the 1980's and 1990's', in Paula Voos (ed.), *Contemporary Collective Bargaining in the Private Sector*, Industrial Relations Research Association, Madison, WI, pp. 411-445.

Allen, Steven G. (1995), 'Updated Notes On The Interindustry Wage Structure, 1890-1990', *Industrial and Labor Relations Review*, vol. 48(2), pp.305-321.

American Bridge Company (2003), 'Company History', http://www.americanbridge.net/company/history.php.

Boorstin, Daniel J, (1965), *The Americans, The National Experience*, Vintage Books, New York, N.Y.

Bureau of National Affairs (2002), *Construction Labor Report,* October, Washington, D.C.

Burtt, Everett J. (1979), *Labor in the American Economy,* St. Martin's Press, New York, NY.

Cartter, Allan M. (1975), *Theory of Wages and Employment,* Greenwood Press, Westport, CT.

Cassamatis, Peter (1969), *Economics of the Construction Industry, Studies in Business Economics, No.111,* The National Industrial Conference Board, Washington, D.C.

Chandler, Alfred J. (1959), 'The Beginnings of "Big Business", reprinted in *The Shaping of Twentieth-Century America,* Abrams, R. and Levine, L. editors, (1965), Little, Brown and Company, Boston, MA.

The Center to Protect Workers' Rights (2002), *The Construction Chart Book: The U.S. Construction Industry and Its Workers,* CPWR, Washington, D.C.

Dorman, Peter, and Hagstrom Paul (1998), 'Wage Compensation for Dangerous Work Revisited', *Industrial and Labor Relations Review,* vol. 52(1), pp. 116-135.

Engineering News-Record (2003), vol. 250 (22), 30 June.

Finkel, Gerald (1990), 'The Determination of Wages for Unionized Construction Electricians in New York City, 1953-1983', Ph.D. Dissertation, The Graduate Faculty of the New School for Social Research, New York, NY.

Finkel, Gerald (1997), *The Economics of the Construction Industry,* M.E. Sharpe, New York, NY.

Friedman, Lawrence M. (1986), *The History of American Law,* Simon & Schuster, New York, NY.

Foster, Howard G. (1973), 'The Labor Market In Nonunion Construction', *Industrial and Labor Relations Review,* vol. 26(4), pp.1071-1085.

Gifford, Court (2001), *Directory of U.S. Labor Organizations,* Bureau of National Affairs, Washington, D.C.

Gordon, David M. (1980), 'The Best Defense is a Good Defense: Towards a Marxian Theory of Labor Union Structure and Behavior', in Michael Carter and William Leahy (eds.), *New Directions In Labor Economics,* University of Notre Dame Press, South Bend, IN.

Gordon, David M. (1981), 'Capital-Labor Conflict and the Productivity Slowdown', *American Economic Association: Papers and Proceedings,* vol. 71(2), pp. 30-35.

Gordon, Robert J. (1968), 'A New View of Real Investment in Structures, 1919-1966', *Review of Economics and Statistics,* vol. 50, pp. 417-428.

Haven, Janet (2004), 'Canal Workers', University of Virginia, http://xroads.virginia.edu/~hyper/detoc/transport/workers.html.

Hirsch, Barry T., and Addison, John T. (1986), *The Economic Analysis of Unions: New Approaches and Evidence,* Allen & Unwin, Boston, MA.

Hofstadter, Richard, Miller, William, and Aaron, Daniel (1964), *The Structure of American History*, Prentice-Hall Inc., Englewood Cliffs, N.J.

Klein, Daniel B. and Fielding, Gordon J. (1992), 'Private Toll Roads: Learning From the 19th Century', *Transportation Quarterly*, vol. 46(3), pp. 321-341.

Lewis, H. Gregg (1963), *Unionism and Relative Wages in the U.S.. An Empirical Inquiry*, University of Chicago Press, Chicago, IL.

Lewis, H. Gregg (1986), *Union Relative Wage Effects: A Survey*, University of Chicago Press, Chicago, IL.

Lynch, Lisa M., and Black, Sandra E. (1998), 'Beyond the Incidence of Employer-Provided Training', *Industrial and Labor Relations Review*, vol. 52 (1), pp. 64-81.

Mansfield, Edwin (1979), *Microeconomics*, W.W. Norton & Co., New York.

Marshall, F. Ray, Cartter, Allan M., and King, Allan G. (1976), *Labor Economics, Wages, Employment, and Trade Unionism*, Richard D. Irwin, Inc., Homewood, IL.

Millman, Joel (2004), 'Blueprint for Outsourcing', *The Wall Street Journal*, 3 March, p. B1.

Monthly Labor Review (2000), 'Union Members Earn More In Most Industries', 2 February.

New York State Archives (2004), 'Erie Canal Time Machine', http://www.archives.nysed.gov/projects/eriecanal/ErieLinks.html.

New York Times (1872), 'The Brooklyn Steam Transit Company–The Underground Railroad from the Fulton Ferry to Flatbush', 10 November, p. 3.

Philips, Peter, Mangum, Garth, Waitzman, Norm, and Yeagle Anne (1995), 'Losing Ground: Lessons from the Repeal of Nine "Little Davis-Bacon" Acts', mimeo, Department of Economics, University of Utah, Salt Lake City, UT.

Sobotka, Stephen (1953), 'Union Influence on Wages: The Construction Industry', *Journal of Political Economy*, vol. 61, pp. 61-97.

The Center to Protect Workers' Rights (1997), *The Construction Chart Book: The U.S. Construction Industry and Its Workers*, CPWR, Washington, D.C.

U.S. 71st Congress (1931), *Congressional Record*, Government Printing Office, Washington, D.C.

U.S. Department of Commerce, Census Bureau (1964-2001), *County Business Patterns*, Government Printing Office, Washington, D.C.

U.S. Department of Commerce, Census Bureau (1997), *Economic Census, Table13*, Government Printing Office, Washington, D.C.

U.S. Department of Commerce, Census Bureau (2002), *Economic Census*, Government Printing Office, Washington, D.C.

U.S. Department of Commerce, Census Bureau (2000), *Economic Census, Occupation by Sex*, Government Printing Office, Washington, D.C.

U.S. Department of Labor, Bureau of Labor Statistics (2003), *Occupational Employment Statistics*, Government Printing Office, Washington, D.C.

Vincent, Jeff (1990), 'Indiana's Prevailing Wage Law: A Preliminary Analysis of Its Impact on the State's Construction Industry', *Labor Studies Journal*, vol. 15(3), pp. 17-31.

Chapter 3

Thoughtless Think Tanks: Sound Bite Thinking About the History and Intent of Prevailing Wage Laws

Hamid Azari-Rad and Peter Philips

Origin of the Factoid—Prevailing Wage Laws are Remnant Jim Crow Laws[1]

A Think Tank Factoid is Created

Scholarship discovers facts. But we are living in the world of think tank scholarship. Too often, think tank scholars do not see their jobs as discovering facts. They see their job as creating factoids. Factoids are not facts, but are treated like facts. They are presented as facts. They are packaged in sound bites and are promulgated to, and by a credulous media. In the hands of unscrupulous editorialists and lobbyists, they are better than facts. They are factoids, a modern, easy to swallow substitute for the truth. In the world of think tank research on prevailing wage regulations, the classic factoid of the 1990s is this:

> The original 'prevailing wage' law was dreamed up by a Long Island congressman who was shocked to learn local construction firms had been underbid for the contract to build a veterans hospital in his district by an out-of-state contractor. The contractor then proceeded to cut costs by bringing in black workers from the South, who were willing to work for less. The ensuing congressional oratory left no room for doubt that the new law, requiring any contractor on a federal construction project to pay the same high wages as the local white firms were paying, was specifically intended to block the importation of black labor.

> *Las Vegas Review Journal* (1997)

The federal law was intended to protect the high wages of union construction workers—predominately white Northerners—at the expense of Southern black, non-union workers. One congressman who supported Davis-Bacon actually made reference to the 'problem' of 'cheap colored labor' on the floor of the U.S. House.

Mark Fischer, Mackinac Center for Public Policy (1999)

The *Las Vegas Review Journal* did not create this factoid. Nor did Mark Fischer. They bought it, hook-line-and-sinker, second-hand, from a think tank in Washington. This is a story about factoids, and the facts they cover up. Where did this factoid come from? How did it spread? What are the facts it covered up?

Like Athena springing full-grown from the forehead of Zeus, in a modern act of parthenogenesis, the myth of prevailing wage laws being Jim Crow laws sprung full-blown from the head of one Scott Alan Hodge in a 1990 editorial in the *Wall Street Journal*. The charge that prevailing wage laws, in general, and the federal Davis-Bacon Act in particular were primarily and substantially racist laws was new. As Hodge put it in 1990:

> So far, debate on Davis-Bacon has focused primarily on its costs, the estimated $1.5 billion it costs U.S. taxpayers to pay union scale when qualified workers are available at lower rates. But that complaint avoids the real evil of Davis-Bacon: discrimination against black Americans (Hodge, 1990).[2]

Hodge's editorial deserves extended consideration because it is the source of this thesis. No scholarly work supported this position prior to Hodge's editorial that asserted this thesis.[3] In 1990, Hodge and other critics of prevailing wage laws had a problem. Between 1979 and 1988, nine states had repealed their state prevailing wage laws. But these states were the low apples on the tree. They were in the South or the Mountain West or New Hampshire. In short, the states that had repealed were, from a political perspective, the states most likely to repeal this regulation. Most of the nine were adjacent to the nine states that had never adopted this type of law. In 1988, advocates of prevailing wage law repeal reached for the top of the tree. They sponsored a ballot initiative in Massachusetts to repeal that state's law. This was a serious test for the political forces for repeal. Massachusetts was an early state to adopt these regulations, and it had a strong labor movement. Going head to head with the electorate as judge, the effort to repeal Massachusetts prevailing wage law failed (Erlich, 1988).[4]

Furthermore, the Massachusetts campaign created an intellectual crisis for advocates for repeal. As repeal became a political issue, the respected research organization located in Massachusetts, Data Resources (a division of McGraw-Hill, Inc.) analyzed the effects of a potential state repeal. The Regional Information Group of Data Resources concluded that there were no solid prospective taxpayer savings from repeal and that the only clear outcome of repeal would be lower wages for Massachusetts' construction workers. The concluding paragraph of the report summarized their analysis:

> While it does appear that some nominal tax savings can be attained by repealing the prevailing wage law, the 0.6 percent reduction in taxes indicated in the Most Likely scenarios would take place at the cost of increased instability in the construction labor market; fiercer competition for work from out-of-state contractors and workers, to the detriment of Massachusetts residents; and a lower standard of living for Massachusetts workers and their families. These costs would be incurred even in the event that the tax savings are less than indicated by the quantitative analysis, as increased contractor profits and decreased labor productivity would keep total cost reductions well below the amount indicated by the apparent savings in unit labor costs, while possible increases in state unemployment compensation and other social service expenditures would further offset the apparent initial savings. The only clear result of repealing the Massachusetts prevailing wage law would be lower wages for certain Massachusetts residents (Walls *et al.*, 1988).

So the campaign to repeal prevailing wage legislation was regrouping in 1990. If the cost argument was losing traction, another argument had to be found. That argument became the assertion that prevailing wage laws were left-over Jim Crow laws. One of the many ironies in this tactical move is the fact that when advocates of repeal were lobbying Southern legislatures in Alabama, Louisiana and Florida in the 1979-88 period, the Jim Crow argument was not used. As we will see, Davis-Bacon passed almost unanimously in both the House and Senate in 1931. In all the debate around Davis-Bacon (1931) and predecessor bills going back to 1927, the only smoking guns of racist legislative intent that Hodge and others could find came from three people—two southern congressmen and one border-state congressman (Alabama, Georgia and Missouri). Northern congressmen such as, the namesakes of the law, Senator John Davis (PA) and Robert Bacon (NY), and Northern supporters of Davis-Bacon such as Fiorello LaGuardia (NY), never once raised the race issue. Whatever smoking guns of Jim Crow intent came from voices from the South. Yet critics of prevailing wage laws never raised the race issue when seeking repeals in Southern states in the 1980s. From the perspective of prevailing wage critics, these laws were only labeled Jim Crow laws when the effort to repeal them left the South, the historical heart of Jim Crow legislation.

So the entire Jim Crow argument was omitted from repeal campaigns in Alabama, Louisiana, and Florida. But even when the Jim Crow argument was raised in 1990, it was necessary to leave much unsaid to make the argument work. Hodge argued in his 1990 *Wall Street Journal* editorial:

> The original Davis-Bacon Act was drafted in 1927 by New York Rep. Robert Bacon after an Alabama contractor won the bid to build a federal hospital in Bacon's district.[5] As Bacon reported at the first hearing on this bill, 'The bid ... was let to a firm from Alabama who brought some thousand non-union laborers from Alabama into Long Island, N.Y. into my congressional district'. What he meant, of course is that many of the workers were black—and willing to work for less than local building tradesmen.
>
> Bacon's complaints brought a knowing smile from Georgia Rep. William Upshaw, who commented: 'You will not think that a Southern man is more than human if he smiles over the fact of your reaction to the real problem you are confronted with in any community with a superabundance or large aggregation of Negro labor'.

Hodge does not report Bacon's response to Upshaw, which was:

> ... the contractor has also brought in skilled nonunion labor from the South to do this work, some of them negroes and some of them white, but all of them are being paid very much less than the wage scale prevailing in New York State ... (U.S. Congress, 1927, pp. 2-4).

For Bacon, the issue was not race. The issue was that both black and white workers from Alabama were being paid very much less than the wage scale prevailing in New York. Hodge and those who would repeat his argument try to characterize the Alabama contractor's labor force as entirely or primarily black. But this was not true. Hodge and his followers do not tell us that in the 1920s and 1930s, two-thirds of all Alabama construction workers were white. A typical Alabama general contractor of the time would have a white crew of carpenters, and a black crew of laborers.

But more on these facts later. We need to first understand the myth. Hodge went on to quote a second Southern congressman who supported the passage of the Davis-Bacon Act in 1931:

Four years later [in 1931] during the floor debate on the bill, Alabama Rep. Miles Allgood echoed Upshaw's sentiments: 'That contractor has cheap colored labor ... and it is labor of that sort that is in competition with white labor ... This bill has merit ... It is very important that we enact this measure'.

Hodge does not tell us that the Davis-Bacon Act passed the Republican House in 1931 by voice vote with only one Democratic Texas congressman arguing against the Act. Nor does he quote Northern voices such as that of New York Congressman Fiorello LaGuardia who spoke in favor of the Act. LaGuardia, in contrast to the Southern Democrats whom Hodge quotes, was a Republican as were both Representative Bacon and Senator Davis. He was from New York City near Bacon's Long Island district, and was personally familiar with the incident Bacon had mentioned. LaGuardia characterized the incident as follows:

A contractor from Alabama was awarded the contract for the Northport Hospital, a Veterans' Bureau hospital. I saw with my own eyes the labor that he imported there from the South and the conditions under which they were working. These unfortunate men were huddled in shacks living under most wretched conditions and being paid wages far below the standard. These unfortunate men were being exploited by the contractor. Local skilled and unskilled labor were not employed. The workmanship of the cheap imported labor was of course very inferior ... all that this bill does, gentlemen, is to protect the Government, as well as the workers, in carrying out the policy of paying decent American wages to workers on Government contracts [Applause] (U.S. Congress, 1931, p. 6510).[6]

Factoids are foreign to nuances. Myths require simplicity. The simple factoid that Davis-Bacon was a Jim Crow law cannot admit an awareness of Davis-Bacon supporters such as LaGuardia. It is too confusing. LaGuardia, for his time, was a progressive on race issues and supportive of African-American concerns. Harlem was part of his congressional district.[7] His prominent support for the Davis-Bacon Act, and the lack of racial references in his testimony do not square with the myth Hodge was trying to create. So LaGuardia is forgotten in the history Hodge writes on the editorial pages of the *Wall Street Journal* (1990).

Who is Scott Alan Hodge? What are his credentials as a historian? It turns out that Hodge was the Grover M. Hermann Fellow in Federal Budgetary Affairs at the Heritage Institute. According to the Heritage Institute web page, 'Hodge has authored over 60 Heritage Foundation studies on a wide range of issues, including the federal budget and spending policy, tax policy, 'reinventing government', privatization, and closing federal agencies. He holds a B.A. from the University of Illinois at Chicago'.[8] Hodge has recently become a Senior Fellow for Tax and Budget Policy at Citizens for a Sound Economy Foundation.[9] Hodge was not then, nor has he become a historian of any note.[10] Yet his historical take on the Davis-Bacon Act has become a widely accepted and repeated factoid in the media. The *Las Vegas Review Journal* and Mark Fischer of the Mackinac Center were neither the first nor the last to trumpet Mr. Hodge's viewpoint. For example, in 1994, the *Atlanta Journal-Constitution* wrote:

> U.S. Rep. Robert Bacon of New York was outraged. An Alabama contractor had won the bid to build a federal hospital in his district and minority workers were being used on the project. Rep. Miles Allgood of Alabama expressed regret for the 'bootleg labor' coming from his state: 'That contractor has cheap colored labor ... and it is labor of that sort that is in competition with white labor ... This bill has merit ... it is very important we enact this measure'.

> And so the Davis-Bacon Act of 1931 was made law. Its purpose was to squeeze out free-market workers, more often than not African-Americans, by mandating that the local prevailing wage—typically the union scale rate—be paid for work on public projects. The protectionist law worked splendidly. Davis-Bacon's effectiveness at keeping African-Americans from working on public projects was so impressive that states and cities enacted their own versions of the law. Georgia did not. Atlanta did in 1947 (*Atlanta Journal-Constitution*, 1994).

The *Atlanta Journal-Constitution* does not explain why legislation whose purpose was Jim Crow exclusion of minorities from construction met such resistance in the South in the 1930s. While Northern and Western States were passing state prevailing wage laws, Georgia, South Carolina, North Carolina, Virginia, and Mississippi all declined to do so. How did the *Atlanta Journal-Constitution* become so sure of itself, and so blind to its own local Jim Crow history? Why did the *Journal-Constitution* rely so heavily on the historical understanding of a non-historian with a B.A. writing for a Washington think tank? The answer is a common one. Repeat something often enough, and it becomes a factoid. In this case, conservative Washington think tanks played pass-the-baton with the Jim Crow thesis. What the Heritage Foundation asserted, the Cato Institute repeated. The Institute for Justice reasserted and the *Wall Street Journal* republished. Factoids became facts that irresponsible editorialists then promulgated to the public.

The Factoid Baton Gets Passed from
One Think Tank to Another

In January of 1993, David Bernstein of the Cato Institute wrote a briefing paper in which he revisited and repeated Hodge's thesis. In so doing, he added the only additional smoking gun quote from congressmen on the question of Davis-Bacon and race:

> The comments of various congressmen reveal the racial animus that motivated the sponsors and supporters of the bill [the Davis-Bacon Act]. In 1930, Representative John J. Cochran of Missouri stated that he had 'received numerous complaints in recent months about Southern contractors employing low-paid colored mechanics getting work and bringing the employees from the South'. [Alabama] Representative Clayton Allgood, supporting Davis-Bacon on the floor of the House, complained of 'cheap colored labor' that 'is in competition with white labor throughout the country' (Bernstein, 1993a, p. 3).

Neither Cochran nor Allgood were sponsors of Davis-Bacon. They were not even from the majority party. Of all those who spoke on Davis-Bacon in 1931. They are the only ones to mention the issue of race. David Bernstein was a recent law school graduate,[11] and he realizes that the Jim Crow thesis could not be sustained by these two passing remarks. So Bernstein emphasized a second thesis. He said that the real sponsors of the bill were indeed racist, but they spoke in code words. Rather than say 'colored' labor, they said 'cheap' labor. Rather than say 'Negro' labor, they said 'itinerant' labor. Bernstein states:

> Other congressmen were more circumspect in their references to African-American labor. They railed against 'cheap labor', 'cheap imported labor', men 'lured from distant places to work on this new hospital', 'transient labor', and 'unattached migratory workmen'. While the congressmen were not referring exclusively to African-American labor, it is quite clear that despite their 'thinly veiled' references, they had African-American labor primarily in mind (Bernstein, 1993a, p. 3).

Bernstein does not explain why proponents of Davis-Bacon felt compelled to speak in code in 1931. In a period in which Jim Crow institutions were widespread in the South and blacks were excluded from baseball, the national pastime. Bernstein does not explain why all the supporters of Davis-Bacon, except two, felt a need to completely hide their intentions in code words or why two congressmen felt no such compulsion. Bernstein does not consider the alternative hypothesis, that the congressmen actually meant what they said when they 'railed' against cheap labor, cheap imported labor and so on.

An extensive literature search does not show that Bernstein ever wrote on this topic before or after his one briefing paper. Nevertheless, Bernstein's views are quickly taken up by the press. His briefing paper was published on 18 January 1993. By 27 February, he had an editorial in the *Cleveland Plain Dealer* repeating the assertion of Hodge under the headline 'Davis-Bacon is a Jim Crow Labor Law':

> Appalled that blacks from the South were working on a federal project in his district, Rep. Robert Bacon of Long Island submitted a bill that was the antecedent of the Davis-Bacon Act (Bernstein, 1993b).

By July of 1993, Bernstein had a three-page spread in the *USA Today Magazine* (1993c).

The Factoid Becomes a Lawsuit
The Institute for Justice and Nona Brazier

On 12 January 1994, the Jim Crow thesis is repeated again in the *Wall Street Journal* in an editorial by one Nona Brazier. Under the headline 'Stop Law that Hurts My Minority Business', Brazier writes:

> The Davis-Bacon Act was passed in 1931 when migrant black workers competed with white union labor for scarce jobs. At the urging of unions, like the American Federation of Labor, Congress neutralized black labor competition by requiring that 'prevailing wages' be paid on all federal projects. In practice, 'prevailing wages' meant union wages. Well-capitalized companies could afford union wages, but their unions usually kept blacks out. Black businesses—which were often less well capitalized—could not afford to pay those prohibitive rates on labor (Brazier, 1994).

Brazier was identified by the *Wall Street Journal* as simply the co-owner of Brazier Construction. Brazier went on to argue that prevailing wage laws prevented her from offering employment opportunities to minorities:

> A few weeks ago, a local minister approached me asking if my company could hire ten gang members who wanted to escape the violence of the streets and learn a worthwhile trade. They were tired of living with bull's eyes on their backs. They needed jobs.

I had none to offer. The construction company my husband and I created to help rebuild Seattle and Tacoma, and provide jobs to the very kids I had just turned away, is now dormant. What is even more disheartening, however, is that our company did not withdraw from the market because of mismanagement or a general downturn in the construction industry.

Like many minority-owned construction firms, Brazier Construction no longer offers job opportunities because of artificially high labor costs that result from racist federal legislation enacted more than 60 years ago. This legislation is fulfilling its original, explicit intent: to keep black firms from competing for and winning federal construction projects.

What the *Wall Street Journal* did not say was that Brazier was, at the time, the Republican chair of King County (Seattle), Nor did the *Wall Street Journal* point out that Brazier had been approached by yet another Washington think tank—The Institute for Justice—to serve as chief plaintiff in a federal law suit to have the Davis-Bacon Act declared unconstitutional based on Hodge's thesis (Cohen, 1993). The lawsuit filed two months before on 9 November 1993 was to be called *Brazier, et al. vs. Reich*, Secretary of Labor.[12] Brazier asked the court to enjoin the act's enforcement by the Department of Labor on the grounds that it violated the equal-protection and other guarantees of the 14th and 15th Amendments.

The Nameplate for a Jim Crow Lawsuit
Who Was Nona Brazier

Nona Brazier's company started with one garbage truck in 1984. It quickly became a garbage collection and recycling business which by 1991 accounted for almost one-third of all Seattle's garbage collection and one-tenth of its recyclable materials collection (Strickland, 1991). In 1993, her garbage and recycling company employed 40 workers, majority of workers were African-Americans, and all but three were previously unemployed. She paid these workers up to $16 per hour with medical, dental, and some pension benefits (Tripling, 1993). However, one year later, Brazier's company was 'dormant'. Her business was fighting bankruptcy, she asserted, because prevailing wages prevented her from hiring unskilled minority workers at lower wages.

Brazier's complaint was not that prevailing wage laws prevented her from hiring African-Americans or other minority workers, because under prevailing wage regulations, she had indeed hired primarily African-Americans. What she wanted to do was to pay these workers less and perhaps hire additional unskilled minority workers (such as the gang members mentioned in her *Wall Street Journal* editorial).

In addition to opposing prevailing wage regulations, Brazier opposed affirmative action policies and other traditional civil rights initiatives.

> 'The civil-rights movement never made sense to me', she says. 'Why would you want to go to the counter for lunch where the man who fixed the meal had on a Klan robe the night before?' Eat someplace else. Better yet, start your own restaurant ...

> The idea of black people running around as whimpering little victims, unable to function in commerce and the social structure is an aberration to me (Large, 1995).

Among other civil rights programs publicly opposed by Nona Brazier were minority set-asides on public works. Indeed, during a failed attempt to attain the Republican nomination for governor in 1996, Brazier called affirmative action oriented public contracts 'the colored drinking fountain of 1996' (Serrano and Postman, 1996). However, this public position directly contradicted her own business behavior. Brazier's garbage collection company was built on, and grew rapidly because of minority set-aside contracts in garbage collection and recycling.

Starting with one garbage truck in 1982, Brazier applied for and received a Washington state certification as a minority owned business in 1984. Based on this certification, by 1991, her business had grown to 18 trucks and 35 employees earning $2.3 million from government minority set-aside contracts in Seattle and Fort Lewis, and only $60,000 from private sector work. During this period of prosperity, Brazier and family bought a 34 foot sail boat, ten acres of land and a gated home in an affluent, white suburb.

But also in 1991, according to a National Labor Relations Board ruling, Brazier's company illegally fired three of her employees for union organizing. By 1993, Brazier was failing to make payroll. Her company owed federal, state and local governments about $500,000 in unpaid taxes and workers compensation premiums. And the company pension fund was short a disputed amount of money ranging somewhere between $21,000 and $350,000.

Her company in trouble and dormant by 1994, Brazier argued two things at once. First, that prevailing wage laws were racist, preventing her from hiring minority workers and paying them lower than prevailing wages. Second, that minority set-asides of both public contracts and publicly available capital loans were appropriate because minority owned businesses 'have historically been discriminated against and deprived of numerous business opportunities'. She argued that Seattle's minority set-asides for public contracts 'recognize the difficulties and disadvantages experienced by minority members of the community seeking to start and maintain viable, competitive business operations' (Serrano and Postman, 1996).

Nona Brazier was not able to make a go of it in the garbage collection business. According to her, she would have been successful if she had not been forced to pay prevailing wages. Such a deregulation would not have increased minority employment in her business, but it would have allowed her to pay these workers less. But her business did require continued regulation of bidding. Brazier's company was competing only against other companies with female ownership or minority ownership, for public projects that were set aside for certified female or minority-owned businesses. Because Brazier's company was competing in the public sector against other minority owned businesses that also had to pay prevailing wages, it is not clear whether her business would have survived had the minority contractors she competed against been released from paying prevailing wages as well. The only clear outcome of releasing Nona Brazier from prevailing wage regulations would have been to lower the wages and benefits of her workers, the majority of whom were African-Americans.

Critics of prevailing wage regulations have attempted to portray the original federal regulation as racist. They tell a mythical story of an Alabama contractor who brought low paid workers into New York Representative Bacon's district. They assert without proof that these workers were primarily or entirely black. They assert without proof that Representative Bacon wanted these workers taken out of competition because they were black. They offer as an alternative story the case of Nona Brazier—a black contractor that has allegedly been run out of business because of prevailing wage regulations. They ignore the fact that under prevailing wage regulations, the majority of her workers were African-American. They ignore the fact that without prevailing wage regulations, Brazier intended to cut these workers' wages, pensions and health insurance. They ignore the fact that Brazier's business was built up under the shelter of minority set-aside regulations. And they offer her up as the nameplate on an effort to have the Davis-Bacon Act repealed as a Jim Crow law. As a paradigm for the Jim Crow thesis, the Nona Brazier case presents a contradictory and even hypocritical example of the argument that prevailing wage regulations are bad for minorities.

The Factoid Treated Like a Fact
Repeated in Many Editorials

Despite the lightweight scholarship standing behind the Jim Crow assertion and the seeming hypocrisy of Nona Brazier, editorials in the *Wall Street Journal,* a three page spread in the *USA Today Magazine,* and a filed federal lawsuit gave sufficient *gravitas* to the Jim Crow assertion for it to spread. Bob Dole, in the run up to his 1996 presidential campaign, adopted the argument in a *Wall Street Journal* editorial (Dole and Watts, 1995).[13] George Will adopted the argument in a nationally syndicated editorial just prior to congressional hearings on the Davis-Bacon Act in 1995.[14] He repeated the now widely circulated Southern congressmen Upshaw quote. But it is unlikely that Will read the testimony himself. While not a legal scholar, Will prides himself on his knowledge of baseball history. Had he read the congressional debate on Davis-Bacon, he could not have overlooked Fiorello LaGuardia's support of the Act. In baseball history, LaGuardia is known for his support and assistance to the Brooklyn Dodgers in bringing Jackie Robinson to the team and thereby integrating major league baseball.[15] Ignoring these facts, the assertion that Davis-Bacon was a Jim Crow law is repeated by the Greensboro, North Carolina, *News and Record* in 1996. 'The law was enacted in 1931 explicitly to keep Southern blacks out of government construction jobs in Northern cities, and it is the last significant surviving regulatory relic of the Jim Crow era' (*News and Record*, 1996). In 1997, a new think tank expert, William Maze of the Mackinac Institute in the *Detroit News* repeats the now familiar assertion (Maze, 1997).[16] The Jim Crow thesis has been repeated so often, it is worthwhile to carefully, and in detail, go through the real history of this legislation.

The True History and Intent of Prevailing Wage Laws

The *Las Vegas Review Journal* cited at the beginning of this essay, got its factoid patently wrong when it asserted: 'The original "prevailing wage" law was dreamed up by a Long Island congressman'. In fact, the first U.S. prevailing wage law was passed by the Republican Congress of 1868—the same 40th Congress that passed the 15th Amendment, one of the Constitutional principles used by the Institute for Justice as a legal bases to claim that prevailing wage laws are unconstitutional. We are now at a point where we should do a serious investigation of the original intent of these laws. We begin our investigation at the beginning by looking at the Congressional debate surrounding this first prevailing wage law.

Competition in post-Civil War construction labor markets segmented along racial lines. African-Americans outside the South tended to compete with immigrant labor for unskilled work and tended to be excluded from the skilled trades.[17] White unions in construction reinforced this pattern of racially segmented competition.[18] These same construction unions were also important supporters of the National Eight-Hour Day Act of 1868. Because this law not only restricted the hours of work on public construction projects to eight hours, but also required that contractors pay their workers the standard daily wage for construction workers in the area based on ten-hour day, this law became the country's first prevailing wage law.[19] Given that unions supporting this law also engaged in racially exclusionary membership practices, did Congress intended this law to be a barrier against African-American employment on public works? The answer is no.

The Congressional debate surrounding the National Eight Hour Day Law in 1868 was fought over class and not racial lines. For instance, the Abolitionist Republican Senator Wilson from Massachusetts argued in favor of the eight-hour day law by explicitly favoring the rights of labor over capital:

> In this matter of manual labor I look only to the rights and interests of labor. In this country and in this age ... capital needs no champion ... whatever tends to dignify manual labor or to lighten its burdens, to increase its rewards or enlarge its knowledge should receive our support (U.S. Congress, 1868, pp. 3424-3429).

Opponents of the eight-hour day law felt the market should be allowed to regulate the terms of employment and that the law violated the freedom of individuals to make contracts as they pleased. For instance, Abolitionist Maine Republican Senator Fessenden in opposing the law argued:

> Let men make contracts as they please; let this matter be regulated by the great regulator, demand and supply; and so long as it continues to be, those who are smart, capable, and intelligent, who make themselves skilled workmen, will receive the rewards of their labor, and those who have less capacity and less industry will not be on a level with them, but will receive an adequate reward for their labor (U.S. Congress, 1868, pp. 3424-3429).

Evaluating this debate historian David Montgomery concluded that the National Eight Hour Law was passed primarily with the support of Radical Republicans, the same political group that pushed the passage of the 13th, 14th and 15th Amendments to the Constitution (Montgomery, 1967).[20] There is no evidence in the Congressional debates that the first prevailing wage law in the United States intended to limit the labor market options of racial or ethnic minorities (Montgomery, 1967, p. 315).[21]

Early State Prevailing Wage Laws

The first three state prevailing wage laws, Kansas in 1891, New York in 1894 and Oklahoma in 1908, could not be construed as racially motivated laws. The Kansas and Oklahoma laws were similar to the National Eight Hour Law in mandating eight hours as the legal workday on public construction, and requiring that contractors pay the common daily wage. Both intended the shortening of the workday from 12 or ten to eight hours which did not result in a corresponding reduction in the daily wage. The Kansas Supreme Court identified the purpose of the Kansas Act as one of limiting 'the hours of toil of laborers, workmen, mechanics and other persons in like employment to eight hours, without reduction in compensation for the day's service' (*The Pacific Reporter*, 1899, p. 338).[22] The Oklahoma law, which was patterned after the Kansas act, had a wider purpose of improving the wages and hours not only on public works but in related labor markets.

> The eight hour law has been of inestimable value to the laboring men of this state ... The common laborer, who was heretofore employed ten and twelve hours per day, is now, under the provisions of this bill, allowed to work but eight hours ... The law has not only affected the laborers and those who are dependent upon this class of work for a living, but it has gone further, and in many localities has gradually force railroad companies, private contractors [i.e., private construction] and people of that class to pay a high rate of wages for unskilled labor (Oklahoma Department of Labor, 1910, p. 327).[23]

In neither case does the historic record mention issues of race.

Discussion of racial motivation is also absent from U.S. Supreme Court Justice John Marshall Harlan's review of the Kansas law. The eminent dissenter in *Plessey vs. Fergeson* (1890), Harlan's review of the plausible rationales for the Kansas law does not mention racial exclusion.[24]

> It may be that the state, in enacting the statute, intended to give its sanction to the view held by many, that, all things considered, the general welfare of employees, mechanics, and workmen, upon whom rest a portion of the

burdens of government, will be subserved if labor performed for eight continuous hours was taken to be a full day's work; that the restriction of a day's work to that number of hours would promote morality, improve the physical and intellectual condition of laborers and workmen, and enable them the better to discharge the duties appertaining to citizenship (*U.S. Reports*, 1903, pp. 207-224).

Harlan affirmed the law as a legitimate direction from the state to its agents including state contractors and their employees. Further, arguing that the law's 'constitutionality was beyond all question' he found:

> Equally without any foundation upon which to rest is the proposition that the Kansas statute denied to the defendant or to his employee the *equal protection* [author's emphasis] of the laws. The rule of conduct prescribed by it applies alike to all who contract to do work on behalf either of the state or of its municipal subdivisions, and alike to all employed to perform labor on such work (*U.S. Reports*, 1903, p. 224).

The New York Law: The First Modern Prevailing Wage Statue

The New York law presents somewhat different facts both in being closer to the current prevailing wage laws in construction and in explicitly excluding the use of low wage labor from public construction. New York's 1870 eight-hour law for government workers and public works contractors was amended in 1894 to require that these workers receive no less than the prevailing rate of wages in their respective trades in their locality. In all such employment, no one but citizens of the United States shall be employed (Groat, 1906, p. 416).

A primary concern of New York's prevailing wage law was the consequences of cheap, itinerant, foreign and non-local labor on local labor standards.[25] Unions complained of 'birds of passage' from England, Canada, Sweden and Denmark, often described as itinerant, spending little and remitting most earnings back home.[26] Local labor standards were also threatened by low wage domestic labor.[27] The citizenship clause of the New York law explicitly acted to exclude foreign labor. The prevailing wage provisions reduced the incentive for contractors on public projects to import labor from low wage labor markets. As such, it can be characterized as excluding low wage labor from the public construction market, just as the modern prevailing wage laws.

Was the prevailing wage component of the New York law intended to exclude racial minorities? To some degree this question is moot because the foreign and domestic construction workers who threatened labor standards in

New York in the 1890s were white. For instance a writer for the New York City Bricklayers and Masons International Union No. 34 noted in 1899:

> For some years what we term 'birds of passage' came over from Europe in the spring, worked here until fall, and then returned to the old country, but on account of the hard times they haven't been coming over lately. We are now affected by the flood of Westerners, and there is an overplus of bricklayers in the city ... (New York Bureau of Statistics of Labor, 1899, p. 1042).

Equally important, more direct means of excluding racial minorities were available had this been the purpose of the New York law.

Public Works Laws with the Explicit or Implicit Acts with Purpose of Racial Exclusion

Both Western and Southern states acted to exclude particular races from employment on public works projects. The Western states, primarily concerned with the large number of Asian laborers, acted to exclude Asians from such employment *per se*. Such direct approaches were unavailable to states which desired to exclude African-Americans because of the protections provided by the equal protection clause of the Constitution. Making employment condition on the payment of pole taxes was adopted as the means to exclude 'undesired' minorities. Neither used exclusion of non-citizens or imposition of a prevailing wage as a means to exclude their undesired group.

Several states excluded Chinese from public works employment in the time which prevailing wage regulations were being developed. Chinese came to California at the beginning of the Gold Rush. Cheap labor on the West coast was often seen as identical to Chinese labor and from the beginning they encountered racial hostility (Brown and Philips, 1986).

> The feeling is strong against permitting the thousands [of Chinese] flocking our shores to share the wealth of our mines untaxed, or without contribution to the support of the government and the property of the State ... In short, there is a strong feeling—prejudice it may be—existing in California against all Chinese, and they are nicknamed, cuffed about, and treated very unceremoniously by every other class (*Alta California*, 4 May 1852).[28]

In the 1881 floor debate over the American Federation of Labor's (AFL) stance towards a prospective Chinese Exclusion Act, Charles Burgman from San Francisco, representing the Assembly of the Pacific Coast Trades and Labor Unions presented a resolution stating:

... the presence of Chinese and their competition with free white labor, is one of the greatest evils with which any country can be afflicted; therefore be it resolved, that we use our best efforts to get rid of this monstrous evil (which threatens, unless checked, to extend to other parts of the Union) by ... [the] passage of laws entirely prohibiting the immigration of Chinese into the United States (Federation of the Organized Trades and Labor Unions of the United States and Canada, 1881, Reprinted 1905 p. 3).[29]

Unions that opposed Chinese immigration claimed that Chinese immigrants came as indentured slaves rather than free wage labor. They claimed that Chinese could not and would not assimilate the way European immigrants would.

A representative statement of this position is embedded in the preamble of the 1887 Nevada law that prohibited the employment of Chinese on public construction:

Whereas, all Chinese who come to this coast arrive here under contract to labor for a term of years, and all are bound by such contract, not only by the superstitions of their peculiar religions, but by leaving their blood relations ... as hostages in China for the fulfillment of their part of the contract; and whereas such slave labor and involuntary servitude is opposed to the genius of our institutions, opposed to the prevailing spirit of the age, as well as humanity and Christianity, and degrades the dignity of labor ... Therefore,

Section 4764. The immigration to this state of all slaves and other people bound by contract to involuntary servitude for a term of years, is hereby prohibited. [and]

Section 4947. From and after the passage of this act, no Chinaman or Mongolian shall be employed, directly or indirectly, in any capacity, on any public works, or in or about any buildings or institutions or grounds, under the control of this State (U.S. Commissioner of Labor, 1892, pp. 65, 305-6, and 409).[30]

On its face, this is essentially and substantially a racist law for the simple reason that Section 4947 restricts a people, regardless of whether or not they are bound or indentured. In some cases then subtle means of exclusion were not needed *de jure* or *de facto*. The omission of such exclusions from the New York law suggests a lack racial intent.

Citizenship Requirements for Public Works Jobs,
in General, Were Not Targeting Chinese

By 1894, four Northern and Western states (New York, Illinois, Idaho and Wyoming) had passed laws preferring or restricting employment on public works to citizens or those who had declared their intention to become citizens either of the U.S. or the particular state (U.S. Commissioner of Labor, 1892, pp. 119, 134, and 525). Of the four states that had citizenship requirements by 1894, two were Western states that had some Chinese immigrants and had experienced anti-Chinese agitation (Saxton, 1971, pp. 202-211). The Chinese Exclusion Act of 1882 prohibited Chinese from becoming U.S. citizens. The Chinese were caught in a catch-22. They could not declare their intention to become citizens. Therefore, they were automatically excluded from public works jobs. But does this mean that these regulations were primarily or substantially racist legislation targeted at Chinese?

In New York and Illinois the answer is clearly no simply because the percent of foreign born who were Chinese was negligible. In Idaho, however, in 1890, 12 percent of all foreigners were Chinese. In Wyoming, Chinese composed three percent of all foreigners (U.S. Department of the Interior, Census Office, 1892, pp. 468 and 470). However, if these Idaho and Wyoming laws were racially motivated, what accounts for the subterfuge? Chinese could be explicitly excluded legally, and there was no need to inconvenience the vast majority of foreign born to get at the Chinese if that was the intent. The parsimonious explanation is that these laws can be taken at face value. They were intended to limit the public employment prospects of non-citizens who were unwilling to become citizens in favor of citizens and would-be citizens. Thus, we can clearly distinguish between the California, Nevada and Oregon laws that had Chinese exclusively in mind and the Idaho and Wyoming laws that included Chinese in their restrictions but did not have Chinese primarily in mind. The fact that the New York and Illinois regulations were not considering Chinese at all supports the notion that citizenship requirements for public works employment were not Jim Crow laws.

Louisiana's Citizenship Requirement was
Implicitly Targeted at African-Americans

The issue of exclusion is somewhat more complex where the excluded groups are citizens, as the equal protection clause limits their direct exclusion. Louisiana passed a law in 1899 that gave preference in employment on public works in New Orleans to residents of that city. This law initially did not have a racial target. However, in 1908, that law was extended to all public construction in Louisiana giving employment preference to the citizens of the state over others. In this extended law a proviso was added that preference would not be given to Louisiana citizens who had not fully paid their poll taxes in the last two years. No racial group was explicitly targeted by this law, but African-American citizens in Louisiana were much less likely to have paid their poll taxes. Poll tax collections systematically fell short of their potential revenues. Little effort at increasing collections was made. Poll taxes outside the South had fallen into disuse by the beginning of the twentieth century.[31] Thus, most analysts today agree that the poll tax underlying purpose was revealed by its disproportionate impact on African-Americans. Its true general purpose was to keep African-Americans from voting and probably its specific purpose in being added to the Louisiana employment-preference bill was to prefer white Louisiana workers on public construction. California and Nevada could explicitly exclude Chinese because legally, as non-citizens, they were not protected from discrimination. African-Americans, as citizens, could claim equal protection. Thus, poll taxes proved a useful expedient in an effort to restrict public work jobs for whites in Louisiana.

Was the Davis-Bacon Act of 1931 Primarily Motivated by Racial Animus?

The New York case in the 1890s is of interest in part because it was a New York congressman, Robert Bacon, who was a prime mover for the passage of the Davis-Bacon Act (1931), the current federal prevailing wage law. Proponents of the Jim Crow thesis never quote Bacon directly. Indeed they do not quote any Republicans making any explicit racial comment associated with the Davis-Bacon legislative history.

In fact, direct reference to race by anyone in the debate over Davis-Bacon was rare. Of the 31 Senators and Representatives who spoke in favor of the Davis-Bacon Act in 1931, Alabama Representative Allgood is the only one to have explicitly mentioned the issue of race. Furthermore, only one of the thirteen witnesses who spoke at Senate and House hearings in that year mentioned the issue of race. To strengthen their Jim Crow thesis, advocates reach back to 1927 for an additional quote from Upshaw, again, a Southern Democrat. Thus, the view that Congressional debate demonstrates that the Davis-Bacon Act was motivated by racial animus relies primarily on the view that proponents of the Act hid their animus with racial code works. In this view, when proponents of the Davis-Bacon Act complained of cheap, itinerant, foreign, non-local labor undercutting local

Table 3.1 The role of out-of-state contractors in local construction activity in ten Northern states in 1929

Importing State	Average Construction Income	Percent of All Construction Activity in Importing State Accounted for by Contractors from:		
		North West Central	8 Southern	All Out of Region
NY	$2,254	7%	0%	28%
IL	$2,113	29%	1%	66%
NJ	$2,036	1%	1%	8%
MI	$1,921	12%	1%	55%
MA	$1,874	1%	0%	16%
CN	$1,842	0%	0%	2%
OH	$1,786	15%	3%	61%
RI	$1,774	0%	0%	7%
PA	$1,755	1%	5%	50%
IN	$1,581	10%	2%	35%
10 States		8%	1%	32%

Source: U.S. Census of Population, Construction (1930).

labor standards, these proponents were using these adjectives as code words for African-Americans.

A major problem with the code-word thesis is that racial and ethnic discrimination was accepted among white politicians in the 1920s and 1930s. Casting doubt on the notion that phrases such as 'cheap labor' in 1930 was primarily referring to 'African-American labor' is the fact that these phrases were explicitly used to refer to white labor in the case of New York in 1890s. One might argue that in the North, cheap imported African-American labor in the 1920s had replaced the cheap imported white labor of the 1890s. Even if this was the case, the parallel Northern opposition to cheap labor of either race would suggest the opposition was motivated by the issue of cheapness rather than race.

But it is not the case that cheap African-American imported construction labor had replaced cheap white imported labor by the 1920s. Most low wage itinerant labor coming into high wage states in the North in 1929 were not from the South, and even among itinerant Southern construction labor, most were not African-American. Table 3.1 shows the proportion of all construction activity in each of 10, high wage Northern states accounted for by contractors either from seven North-West-Central states or

Table 3.2   Black construction workers as a percent of all construction workers in Southern states in 1930

State	African-American as Percentage of All Construction Workers
South Carolina	39%
Georgia	31%
Mississippi	30%
Louisiana	28%
Alabama	25%
North Carolina	24%
Florida	17%
Virginia	15%

Source: U.S. Census of Population, Construction (1930).

eight Southern states. As a group, contractors from the North-West-Central states accounted for eight percent of the construction activity in these ten high wage states in 1929 while contractors from the Southern states accounted for one percent of the construction activity in these ten Northern states. The pattern of activity is partly determined by regional proximity. Illinois which is close to the Northwestern states has the highest involvement of contractors from North-West-central states. Pennsylvania which closest to the South has the highest Southern contractor involvement. Massachusetts, Connecticut and Rhode Island had little involvement from contractors of either the South or the West. Ohio and New York, states equally distanced from the South and the plains states had significantly greater involvement from plains state contractors compared to Southern contractors.[32]

Furthermore, when a Southern general contractor came North with a work crew, the crew would be composed of white and African-American workers. Construction occupations were racially segregated in the South. A Southern crew requiring the craftsmen from a variety of construction occupations would include workers of both races. Thus, the Southern general contractor would bring African-American laborers, hod-carriers, and perhaps brick masons. But the same contractor would probably bring white carpenters. If the Southern firm was a mechanical subcontractor, it might bring African-American laborers, but it was likely to bring white plumbers, gas fitters and sheet metal workers. If a Southern contractor came North with an integrated crew at the proportions typical of the racial composition of the Southern construction labor force, the majority of Southern workers coming North would have been white, as shown in Table 3.2.

A Southern contractors going North might however not look like the typical Southern construction firm. The traveling contractor was probably larger and might have a disproportionately African-American labor force. One of the two Southern contractors working outside the South that were explicitly mentioned in the Davis-Bacon congressional record was the Virginia Engineering Company. The name of the company suggests that it was from Virginia, and it might have been either a general or a mechanical contractor. (The word 'engineering' is often used by mechanical contractors). In 1910, the last year for which we have firm level data for Virginia, 125 mechanical contractors together employed 557 white plumbers, fitters and sheet metal workers, 77 white laborers and 270 African-American laborers. The largest Virginia mechanical contractor employed 30 white plumbers and fitters, eight white sheet metal workers and five African-American laborers. Thus, if the Virginia Engineering Company was a mechanical contractor working outside the South but bringing with it Virginian workers, it was likely to have been a firm employing primarily white workers.

General contractors in Virginia in 1910 employed a variety of trades including in order of importance—carpenters, laborers, bricklayers, helpers, plasterers, painters, stone masons, and plumbers. As a group, these general contractors employed 23 percent African-American workers. Table 3.3 compares the five largest general contractors with the average general contractor. On average, the five largest contractors employed 214 construction workers compared to the 22 workers employed by the average contractor. Again, on average, the five largest firms employed 29 percent African-Americans compared to 23 percent for all firms. But this disguises a wide variation. Two of the five largest general contractors employed more than 64 percent African-American workers while the other three employed 21 percent or fewer African-American workers. While two of the five largest general contractors employed relatively few African-Americans and were relatively high wage firms, the largest general contractor in Virginia employed only 13 percent African-Americans and was a very low-wage firm. In short, if large general contractors traveled from Virginia, they might have left with a disproportionately African-American labor force, or they might have not. In either case, they would have traveled with at least 36 percent white workers. The vast majority of African-Americans were employed as construction laborers in these five large firms. Some were hired as bricklayers, painters, plasterers and lathers. However, none hired African-Americans as carpenters, plumbers or stone masons.

Table 3.3 Five largest general contractors compared to the average general contractor in Virginia in 1910

	Firm 1	Firm 2	Firm 3	Firm 4	Firm 5	Weighted Average of 5 Largest General Contractors	Weighted Average of All 224 General Contractor
Average Wage	$1.35	$1.78	$2.08	$2.45	$2.87	$1.95	$2.29
Average White Wage	$1.38	$3.07	$3.04	$2.75	$3.10	$2.05	$2.52
Average Black Wage	$1.16	$1.25	$1.53	$1.37	$1.81	$1.41	$1.52
Percent Black of All Workers	13%	71%	64%	21%	18%	29%	23%
Percent Black of All Laborers	15%	100%	95%	53%	27%	55%	60%
Total Construction Workers	351	154	275	159	131	214	22

Source: U.S. Census of Population, Construction (1930).

Segregation prevented general contractors from integrating these occupations, ironically forcing traveling general contractors to use integrated crews. Table 3.4 shows that there were too few African-American carpenters to staff the work crews of traveling contractors in Virginia in the 1920s. In occupations such as hod-carriers and laborers, where African-Americans were the majority, African-American-white wages were similar. Thus, firms which did not employ disproportionate numbers of African-Americans such as numbers one, two and five shown in Table 3.3 could compete with firms such as numbers two and three.

In sum, there is no statistical reason to conclude that companies such as the Virginia Engineering Company were necessarily traveling with majority African-American work crews. And there is nothing in the historical record that says they did. The code word hypothesis requires that when proponents of Davis-Bacon Act spoke of cheap labor or Southern labor they meant African-American labor and when they referred to Southern contractors they meant the employers of African-American labor. The statistical picture of the Southern construction labor force of the time describes integrated work crews typically segregated by occupation. While some larger contractors had disproportionately African-American work forces, other large contractors did not. Even contractors

Table 3.4 **Average wage by occupation and race for Virginia construction workers in 1919 to 1928**

Occupation	Race	Avg. Wage	Wage Gap	% Black
Carpenter	White	$5.78	67%	3%
	Black	$3.89		
Apprentices	White	$3.37	84%	10%
	Black	$2.85		
Bricklayers	White	$9.44	87%	17%
	Black	$8.26		
Helpers	White	$3.59	88%	29%
	Black	$3.17		
Plasterers	White	$8.35	93%	32%
	Black	$7.80		
Cement Masons	White	$6.29	78%	37%
	Black	$4.89		
Lathers	White	$5.65	94%	45%
	Black	$5.30		
Hod Carriers	White	$4.28	95%	68%
	Black	$4.08		
Laborers	White	$3.25	97%	69%
	Black	$3.15		

Source: U.S. Census of Population, Construction (1930).

employing disproportionate numbers of African-American unskilled labor had to employ typical numbers of whites in the skilled trades, especially in carpentry and the mechanical trades.

The Paradigmatic Example

As mentioned above, proponents of the Jim Crow interpretation of the Davis-Bacon Act rely strongly on the story of an Alabama contractor coming into Representative Robert Bacon's Long Island district around 1926 to build a veterans hospital. This Jim Crow view assumes that this contractor brought a primarily African-American labor force with him. Bernstein argues this was a coded complaint against the employment of African-American workers in Bacon's district (Bernstein, 1993a, p.3).

Bernstein relies on a memorandum written by U.S. Commissioner of Labor Ethelbert Stewart in 1928 that characterized the Alabama contractor's crew as primarily or essentially African-American.[33] However, as pointed out earlier, in hearings for a predecessor bill, Rep. Bacon indicated that the Alabama contractor had brought an integrated crew and that the issue was not race, in any case, but rather the undercutting of local labor standards (U.S. Congress, 1927, pp. 2-4).[34]

If this contractor hired no local labor to build a veterans hospital, then the skilled labor would very likely have been white Southerners. Table 3.2 shows that in 1929, only 25 percent of the Alabama construction labor force was African-American. In any case, Bacon explicitly stated that the issue was not whether the outside labor was African-American but rather whether the outside labor undercut local union wages and working conditions. When Georgia congressperson Upshaw suggested that the problem was created by the presence of African-American labor, Bacon responded:

> The same thing would be true if you should bring in a lot of Mexican laborers or if you brought in any nonunion laborers from any state (U.S. Congress, 1927, pp. 2-4).

This response is consistent with the debate around the New York state prevailing wage law 30 years before that sought to reduce the employment prospects of European whites and cheaper labor from Western states.

We now revisit Representative Fiorello LaGuardia's presentation to the House in 1931.[35] Given LaGuardia reputation as a progressive on race issues and supportive of African-American concerns, his prominent support for the bill, and the lack of racial references in his testimony suggests that the race was not an issue in his support of the Davis-Bacon Act. The Jim Crow factoid has not been constructed from the statements of either Robert Bacon or Republican Senator from Pennsylvania, John Davis, the sponsors for whom the Act was named. It has not been constructed from the statement of close allies such as fellow New York Republican Fiorello LaGuardia. It has been constructed from the statement of Southern Democrats, that are few in number and in proportion to those who spoke in favor of the Act.

Although a small number of racial references can be found in the Davis-Bacon debate, the principal issue of the debate is the protection of labor standards.[36] The Davis-Bacon Act was supported by Southern politicians who also favored racial segregation. But it was also supported by progressive politicians such as LaGuardia who had liberal positions regarding race. The Act was supported by construction unions many of which at the time were Jim Crow institutions, themselves. But these same unions supported a variety of legislation in the 1930s such as workers compensation and factory inspections, Social Security and the Fair Labor Standards Act, which are not, by dint of labor union support alone, considered racist laws. No, the Jim Crow thesis cannot stand on a handful of quotes from Southerners outside the party and the region from which this law emerged. Nor can it stand on tarring the Act with the fact that construction unions at the time often practiced racially exclusionary membership policies. Labor unions were not alone in their racism. Business, religious organizations and higher education, among others, share in this guilt. What law of the time cannot be connected in some fashion with the racism of the time? The code word argument founders on the very fact that the America of the 1920s and 1930s was comfortable with its own racism. Why use code words to hide your central racist intent when such intentions were common and accepted?

Conclusion

This is not a story about Jim Crow laws. It is a story about factoid production. Critics of prevailing wage regulations were stymied by the failure to win repeals at the ballot box. The 1988 ballot initiative failure in Massachusetts followed by a similar failure at the ballot box in Oregon in 1994 called for a new strategy. Critics were concerned that their claims of substantial taxpayer savings from repeal were beginning to appear false. In any case, prevailing wage regulations had already been swept out of the South in the 1980s with repeals in Alabama, Florida and Louisiana. A new argument was needed that might work in the rest of the country. The Jim Crow factoid was invented to serve this purpose.

The Jim Crow factoid was never based on scholarly research. The argument has never been published in respected academic or scholarly outlets. No qualified economic, legal or labor historian has ever asserted that prevailing wage laws were essentially or fundamentally Jim Crow legislation. This is because the major premises of this argument are false.

Davis-Bacon (1931) was not the original prevailing wage law. The first national prevailing wage law was enacted in 1868, and the first state law (Kansas) was enacted in 1891. There is not a scintilla of evidence that either of these laws or the half dozen other state laws passed before Davis-Bacon were Jim Crow laws. Furthermore both England (1890) and Canada (1900) passed similar laws without any tradition of slavery or Jim Crow.

Finally, of the nine states which never passed prevailing wage laws, five were in the South (Virginia, North Carolina, South Carolina, Georgia and Mississippi). If prevailing wage laws were Jim Crow laws, why were they least common in the heart of Jim Crow country?

The sponsors of Davis-Bacon did not proclaim any racial intentions in their arguments favoring the law. Indeed, the Republican sponsor Robert Bacon, explicitly rejected such arguments when they were proffered by non-sponsoring Southern Democrats.

The vast majority of supporting arguments for the law involved maintaining labor standards not excluding African-American workers. So the Jim Crow thesis must and does assert that the sponsors, while not mentioning race, were nonetheless talking in code about their racist intentions. But why in 1931 would legislators feel the need to talk in code? And why if code words were necessary for almost everyone, did three congressmen feel no need to talk in code about their racist outlook? A simpler explanation is that no one was talking in code, and three Democratic supporters of the law—one from Georgia, one from Alabama and one from Missouri—were true blue segregationists who personally saw the law through that racist lens. It is unfair and inaccurate to tar Northern Republicans Fiorello LaGuardia, Robert Bacon, and others with the statements of Southern Democrats.

This essay has shown a woeful willingness of credulous or unscrupulous editorialists to spread factoids as facts. It has shown that slipshod scholarship at think tanks has replaced careful research as the resource relied upon by opinion makers. The real story here is not one of an archaic Jim Crow law somehow left on the books. The real story here is one of the debasement of political discourse through the spread of factoids by thoughtless think tanks.

Notes

[1] Parts of this paper was published in an article in the *Review for Radical Political Economics*. We would like to thank *RRPE* for permission for long quotations.

[2] Hodge does not cite the source for his claim that Davis-Bacon costs the taxpayer $1.5 billion. In any case, $1.5 billion is a small percentage (around 1-2 percent) of overall expenditures regulated by Davis-Bacon.

[3] In 1975, Armond Thieblot, a vigorous critic of prevailing wage laws, in a book of 239 pages, devoted only one paragraph to the issue of race. In it he stated:

> Behind the fear of itinerant workers may have been some feelings colored by racial bigotry. This issue is mentioned explicitly only once during the House

debate, but the allusions to it in other speeches—including Congressman Bacon's—are thinly veiled ... As for 'itinerant contractors', it should be noted that all contractors are mobile to some degree, moving about to find work. Much opposition to 'outsiders' is expressed in all business fields by those who desire to monopolize local work (Thieblot, 1975, p. 9).

4   The only other repeal though the ballot box ever tried was in Oregon in 1994. It failed.

5   In fact, the 1927 bill was not a prevailing wage regulation. Rather it was a regulation giving preference in employment on public works in a state to citizens of that state. This is an important distinction. Critics of prevailing wage laws claim that they intend to keep minorities off public construction by requiring high wages that exclude low-skilled workers. The argument asserts that minorities are low-skilled and therefore are excluded from public construction. But Bacon's original proposal would have allowed any New York citizen to work on public construction at any wage rate. Thus, it would not have excluded the many blacks that had migrated to New York during the great migration of the World War One-1920s period. Critics bring Upshaw's 1927 remark into the Davis-Bacon debate simply because there is a scarcity of smoking guns in the 1931 debate, itself.

6   The '[Applause]' is in the Congressional Record itself and is not added by authors.

7   Greenberg (1991, p. 85) comments: 'LaGuardia prided himself on championing the underdog. He steadfastly defended the rights of ethnic groups to receive the full range of opportunities America had to offer. While less consistent on racial issues (his [subsequent] anti-Japanese sentiment is startlingly out of character in this regard), [as mayor] he did support the equal access of African-Americans to municipal benefits. Unlike earlier administrations, LaGuardia enforced strong civil service protections against racial discrimination. Because private industry had no such standards, the city government became the largest employer of white-collar African-Americans in the New Deal period'.

8   See http://www.heritage.org/staff/hodge.htm

9   See http://135.145.55.74/csefhome/bioscsef.htm#Scott Hodge. Mr. Hodge's bona fides as presented by the Citizens for a Sound Economy Foundation describe his work subsequent to his 1990 *Wall Street Journal* article. 'Prior to joining CSE Foundation, Mr. Hodge spent ten years at The Heritage Foundation, including eight years as the Senior Budget Analyst. While there, he edited three books on balancing the budget and streamlining the federal government and authored over 60 studies on government spending and fiscal policy. Mr. Hodge also has extensive media experience. He has conducted over 400 radio and television interviews including appearances on the "NBC Nightly News with Tom Brokaw', the 'CBS Evening News with Dan Rather", CNN, Fox News, and C-SPAN. He has also authored dozens of editorials and opinion pieces for publications such as the *Wall Street Journal*, the *Washington Post*, *USA Today*, the *New York Post*, and the *Washington Times*'.

[10] It may be asked what this author's bona fides are in history. Peter Philips specializes in economic history and has published in the *Journal of Economic History*, *Historical Methods*, and *Business History Review*. Azari-Rad and Philips specialize in labor economics and regularly teaches American Economic History.

[11] He was described in the Briefing paper as follows: 'David Bernstein, a recent graduate of the Yale Law School, and clerk on the U.S. Court of Appeals for the Sixth Circuit, practices law with the Washington, D.C., law firm of Crowell and Moring'.

[12] Bernstein (1993b) indicated that he was aware that there were plans afoot to file this suit.

[13] Dole and Watts (1995) assert that 'we should immediately repeal the discriminatory Davis-Bacon Act, which was passed in the 1930s with the explicit aim of keeping low-wage blacks out of the labor market for government construction contracts'.

[14] 'Why was Davis-Bacon enacted? Because in 1931, the second year of the Depression, the federal government was engaged in pump-priming spending on construction, and blacks were competing successfully for jobs that whites wanted. Four years earlier, Rep. Robert Bacon, a Long Island Republican, had been distressed because the low bidder to build a veterans' hospital in his district was an Alabama contractor using black labor. When the Depression made federal construction money hugely important, and the law bearing Bacon's name was enacted, Rep. William Upshaw, a Georgia Democrat, was amused, saying to his Northern colleagues that he hoped they would not think ill of a Southerner 'if he smiles over the fact of your reaction to that real problem you are confronted with in any community with a superabundance or large aggregation of Negro labor'. Such labor was willing to work for lower wages than whites could get as members of unions, most of which excluded blacks. The Davis-Bacon congressional debate was replete with references to 'itinerant labor' or 'cheap bootleg labor' or 'labor lured from distant places' for 'competition with white labor throughout the country' (Will, 1995b). Will indicated that he was aware of the *Brazier vs. Reich* suit that had been filed a year earlier. This editorial was syndicated across the country under various headlines (See, for instance, Will, 1995a).

[15] See, for instance, Tygiel and Thorn (1997).

[16] 'The federal law was intended to protect the high wages of union construction workers—predominantly white and from the North—at the expense of black, nonunion workers from the South. Citing congressional remarks on Davis-Bacon at the time of its passage, the Sixth Circuit Court in its recent decision stated that the prevailing wage law was intended 'to combat the practice of certain itinerant, irresponsible contractors, with itinerant, cheap, bootleg labor, (who) have been going around throughout the country 'picking' off a contract here and a contract there'. 'Itinerant, cheap, bootleg labor' were 1930s code words for black and

immigrant workers. Davis-Bacon's co-sponsor, Rep. Robert Bacon, actually referred to the problem of 'cheap colored labor', and Congressman William Upshaw said during House hearings on Davis-Bacon that 'you will not think that a Southern man is more than human if he smiles over the fact of your reaction to that real problem you are confronted with in any community with a superabundance or large aggregation of Negro labor' (Maze, 1997). The argument gets repeated a month later by another Mackinac writer, Robert P. Hunter in 'Union Racial Discrimination is Alive and Well', a posting on the Center's website. http://www.mackinac.org/article.asp?ID=325. Interestingly, prior to 1997, the Mackinac, while critical of prevailing wage regulations, was silent on the Jim Crow thesis. For instance, see Barnier (1991), where he criticized Michigan for subsidizing high paid labor while slashing welfare spending. This critique of prevailing wage law focusing on issues of the poor entirely omitted the Jim Crow thesis.

The Mackinac Center for Public Policy keeps the myth alive today. See Mark Fischer's writings cited above. These Mackinac Center position papers on prevailing wage regulations are short—usually one page. They are not typically original works of scholarship. In the case of the Jim Crow thesis, they are entirely derivative, relying on the scholarship or lack thereof found elsewhere. Nonetheless, these position papers on the web and in op-ed pieces play a crucial role in factoid diffusion. What use is a myth if it is not sincerely repeated? The Mackinac pieces are nothing if not sincerely repetitive.

[17] Only 14 African-American masons and bricklayers were reported working in New York City in 1870. African-Americans in construction tended to be construction laborers. A African-American newspaper reported: 'The [black] longshoremen and common laborers [in New York City] are outnumbered by foreign competition; but as a general thing, their services as good honest laborers are preferred, and to a certain extent when business is brisk, get their share of employment' (*The [San Francisco] Elevator,* 1870).

[18] For instance, in 1869, the National Labor Convention of Colored Men complained: 'the exclusion of colored men and apprentices from the right to labor in any department of industry or workshops in any of the States and Territories of the Unties States by what is known as 'Trades Unions' is an insult to God and an injury to us' (*The [Washington] Evening Star,* 1869).

[19] This law met with bureaucratic resistance requiring President Grant to issue orders in 1869 and 1872 insisting that its provisions be enforced. After 1874, the law fell into disuse when the Supreme Court held that its provisions did not apply to the employees of government contractors.

[20] The 14th Amendment guaranteeing equal protection under the law regardless of race was proposed by the 39th Congress and the 15th Amendment guaranteeing the right to vote was proposed by the 40th Congress. The National Eight-Hour Day Law was a law of the 40th Congress (Montgomery, 1967).

[21] In California in the mid-1860s, labor unions had two main legislative goals—the exclusion of Chinese immigrants and the eight-hour day. California Republican U.S. Senator John Conness distanced himself from Chinese exclusion but led the fight for the National Eight Hour law (Montgomery, 1967, p. 315).

[22] Inre Ashby, Kansas Supreme Court decision, 10 December 1898.

[23] Similar to Kansas, the historical record for Oklahoma is replete with hours and wage regulatory issues but includes no mentions of issues of race. The primary concern in both states with using public works hours and wage policies to set and improve local labor standards. A typical enforcement case in Oklahoma as reported by the Labor Commissioner follows:

> [Anadarko. May 10. 1908] We were advised that the O'Neill Construction Company had cut the wages on public works at Anadarko from twenty-five cents to seventeen and one-half cents per hour ... [C]ontract was taken with the understanding that twenty-five cents per hour should be paid. The work was not progressing as rapidly as necessary to keep the cost within the estimate, hence the contractors tried to take advantage of the situation by reducing pay. After thoroughly discussing the matter before the [city] council and contractor, the wages were restored to twenty-five cents (Oklahoma Department of Labor, 1909, p. 320).

[24] This case established the legality of racial segregation based on the principle of separate but equal public accommodations and services.

[25] The link between cheap foreign labor and cheap domestic labor from other regions of the country was made by a writer from the New York City Bricklayers and Masons' International Union Local No. 47:

> The only difficulty the bricklayers have is the influx of members of their craft from other States and countries to this city which is almost impossible to overcome (New York, Bureau of Statistics of Labor, 1896, p. 387).

George D. Gaillard of New York District Council of the United Brotherhood of Carpenters similarly stated:

> I think there should be something done about foreigners coming here in the spring and working during the summer and then again returning to Europe in the fall. They come over here and work for less money than the native American, thus depriving him of work (New York, Bureau of Statistics of Labor, 1896, p. 388).

[26] For example, Edward F. O'Brien, the Secretary of the Bricklayers and Masons' International Union No. 32 said:

> ... when business in our trade is brisk, the crowd of masons that come here to work from England is awful. They work during the summer here, live poorly, bank all they get, fill our positions and take all they earn back to England, to come again next summer (New York, Bureau of Statistics of Labor, 1896, p. 387).

[27] Mervyn Pratt of the United Tin and Sheet Iron Workers' Association of New York City emphasized that:

There should be some law which would prevent foreign contractors—I mean contractors from other States—from coming here and taking contracts, as it brings on many troubles. The wages in other places than New York City are certain to be lower than here and they only want the wages and work the hours of the places from which they came (New York, Bureau of Statistics of Labor, 1896, p. 535).

[28] Quoted in Cross (1935, p. 316, fn 12).

[29] This organization changed its name to the American Federation of Labor in 1886.

[30] The 1885 California law prohibiting Chinese employment on public construction contained a similar rationale as well as provisions legalizing the ghettoizing of Chinese resident in California.

The presence of foreigners ineligible to become citizens of the United States is declared to be dangerous to the well-being of the State, and the legislature shall discourage their immigration by all the means within its power. Asiatic coolieism is a form of human slavery, and is forever prohibited in this State, and all the contracts for coolie labor shall be void ... The legislature shall delegate all necessary power to the incorporated cities and towns of this State for the removal of Chinese without the limits of such cities and towns, or for their location within prescribed portions of those limits ... (U.S. Department of Labor, Bureau of Labor Statistics, 1914, p. 261).

[31] The poll tax is one of the oldest taxes in the United States and throughout the colonial period, it was the major source of government revenue. While some states outlawed the poll tax during the Revolutionary era, roughly half the states retained poll taxes into the Twentieth Century. The origins of the poll tax were not generally racist in intent, but in Southern states during the time of slavery, poll taxes were clearly racially discriminatory. For example, in Mississippi prior to 1865 a higher poll tax was charged to free males of color compared to white males. After the Civil War, this discriminatory pricing scheme was dropped, but as an observer in 1900 noted:

No concealment need be made of the fact that the poll tax is used in Mississippi as a means of disqualifying the Negro in national elections and controlling his vote in local elections. That the poll tax is more important in the state as an adjunct of suffrage than as a source of revenue is revealed by the fact that in 1897 out of a capitation of $529,694, only $250,057 was collected.

In contrast to Mississippi and elsewhere in the South where the poll tax was bent to a racial regulation of voting, such a pattern was not clear outside the South. Several Northern states had outlawed the tax and others such as Wisconsin did not enforce the tax. Not all poll taxes entailed voting rights. At least one municipality in Kansas in 1898 had a 'poll' tax or head tax requiring that all males between the ages of 21 and 45 either pay $3 each or work for two ten hour days on public construction. The Kansas Supreme Court held that this violated the Kansas Eight Hour Law. The court argued it was a violation of the law for a ... man who, either from necessity or choice, works out his own tax ... [to be] forced to do four hours more service to discharge his tax than the man employed by the city to render two days service for three dollars.

Given that minorities may have been more likely to work out their tax rather than pay it, this interpretation of the law protected minorities along with other less-wealthy males (Ely *et al.*, 1920, p. 734; Brough, 1900, pp. 165 and 213; The *Pacific Reporter*, 1899, p. 338).

[32] The two regional groupings, eight Southern states and seven plains states, had similarly sized construction industries at the time. The labor force in the Southern states earned on average around $1,200 per year and were roughly 20 percent African-American. The plains states workers earned roughly $1,450 per year and few were African-American. Workers in the Northern states selected earned around $1,800 per year and employed few African-Americans.

[33] Stewart wrote:

[The Alabama contractor] brought with him an entire outfit of Negro laborers from the South, housed them in barracks and box cars, permitting no one to see them, that he employed no local labor whatsoever (Quoted in Bernstein, 1993a, p. 4).

[34] Repeating Bacon's statement:

... the contractor has also brought in skilled nonunion labor from the South to do this work, some of them negroes and some of them white, but all of them are being paid very much less than the wage scale prevailing in New York State (U.S. Congress, 1927, pp. 2-4).

[35] Repeating LaGuardia's statement:

A contractor from Alabama was awarded the contract for the Northport Hospital, a Veterans' Bureau hospital. I saw with my own eyes the labor that he imported there from the South and the conditions under which they were working. These unfortunate men were huddled in shacks living under most wretched conditions and being paid wages far below the standard. These unfortunate men were being exploited by the contractor. Local skilled and unskilled labor were not employed. The workmanship of the cheap imported labor was of course very inferior ... all that this bill does, gentlemen, is to protect the Government, as well as the workers, in carrying out the policy of paying decent American wages to workers on Government contracts [Applause] (U.S. Congress, 1931, p. 6510).

[36] The New York Times characterized the Davis-bacon House debate as follows:

The Davis-Bacon maximum wage scale bill, provides that the maximum wage scale prevalent in any community where public works are undertaken under Federal contract, be paid to all laborers and mechanics ... While the [voice] vote against the measure was negligible, the fight on it was bitter during the forty minutes of debate. Representative Blanton, Democrat, Texas, staged a virtual one-man opposition, declaring that the bill would do away with the right of free contract, and furthermore represented a further surrender to organized labor (*New York Times*, 1931, p. 6).

References

Atlanta Journal and Constitution (1994), 'City Prevailing-Wage Law Needs to be Terminated', 28 June, p. A8.

Barnier, Brian G. (1991), 'Prevailing Wage Act Harms the Poor', http://www.mackinac.org/article.asp?ID=198.

Benton, Elbert J. (1900), 'Taxation in Kansas', in Hollander, J. H. (ed.) *Studies in State Taxation*, Johns Hopkins University Studies in Historical and Political Science, Series XVIII, No. 1, Baltimore, MD, pp. 115-176.

Bernstein, David (1993a), 'The Davis-Bacon Act: Let's Bring Jim Crow to an End', *Cato Briefing Paper No. 17*, Cato Institute, 1000 Massachusetts Avenue, N.W., Washington, D.C., 18 January.

Bernstein, David (1993b), 'Davis-Bacon is a Jim Crow Labor Law', *Cleveland Plain Dealer*, 27 February, p. B7.

Bernstein, David (1993c), *USA Today Magazine*, vol. 122(2578), July.

Brazier, Nona (1994), 'Stop Law that Hurts My Minority Business', *Wall Street Journal*, 12 January, p. A10.

Brazier Construction Co., Inc., *et al.*, Plaintiffs, vs. Robert Reich, Secretary of Labor, *et al.*, Defendants, Civil Action No. 93-2318 WBB, United States District Court for the District of Columbia.

Brough, Charles H. (1900), 'Taxation in Mississippi', in J. H. Hollander (ed.) *Studies in State Taxation*, Johns Hopkins University Studies in Historical and Political Science, Series XVIII, No. 1, Baltimore, MD, pp. 177-216.

Brown, Martin, and Philips, Peter (1986), 'Competition, Racism and Hiring Practices Among California Manufacturers, 1860-1882', *Industrial and Labor Relations Review*, vol. 40(1), pp. 61-74.

Brown, Tony (1995), *Black Lies, White Lies: the Truth According to Tony Brown*, William Morrow and Company, Inc., New York, NY.

Cohen, Julie (1993), 'Minority Entrepreneurs Wage War on Wage Law', *New Jersey Law Journal*, 13 December, p. 13.

Cross, Ira B. (1935), *A History of the Labor Movement in California*, University of California Press, Berkeley, CA.

Dole, Bob, and Watts, J. C. (1995), 'A New Civil Rights Agenda', *Wall Street Journal*, 27 July, p. A10.

Ely, Richard T., Adams, Thomas S., Lorenz, Max O., and Young, Allyn A. (1920) *Outlines of Economics*, The MacMillan Company, New York, NY.

Erlich, Mark (1990), *Labor at the Ballot Box: the Massachusetts Prevailing Wage Campaign of 1988*, Temple University Press, Philadelphia, PA.

Federation of the Organized Trades and Labor Unions of the United States and Canada (1881), *Proceedings of the American Federation of Labor, 1881 to 1888*, Original Printing Pantograph Printing, Bloomington, Illinois, Reprinted 1905, Washington, D.C.

Fischer, Mark (1999), 'Michigan's Prevailing Wage Act: Will Common Sense Prevail?', http://www.mackinac.org/article.asp?ID=2461.

Groat, George G. (1906), 'The Eight Hour and Prevailing Rate Movement in New York State', *Political Science Quarterly*, vol. 21(3), pp. 414-433.

Greenberg, Cheryl L. (1991), *'Or Does It Explode?' Black Harlem in the Great Depression*, Oxford University Press, New York, NY.

Heywood, John S., and Peoples, James (1994), 'Deregulation and the Prevalence of Black Truck Drivers', *Journal of Law and Economics*, vol. 37(1), pp. 133-156.

Hill, Herbert (1987), 'Race, Ethnicity and Organized Labor', *New Politics*, vol. 1(2).

Hodge, Scott A. (1990), 'Davis-Bacon: Racist Then, Racist Now', *Wall Street Journal*, 25 June, p. 14.

Large, Jerry (1995), 'Politics as Usual? Not if Nona Brazier has a Say', *Seattle Times*, 7 August, p. A1.

Las Vegas Review Journal (1997), 'Time to Get Rid of the "Prevailing Wage" Law', 30 March, p. E2.

Kansas Supreme Court (1899), In re Ashby, 1898, *The Pacific Reporter*, vol. 55, p. 338.

Maze, William J. (1997), 'Wage Law Return Makes Mockery of Fair Play', *Detroit News*, 10 August, p. B7.

Montgomery, David (1967), *Beyond Equality, Labor and the Radical Republicans, 1862-1872*, Alfred A. Knopf, New York, NY.

New York, Bureau of Statistics of Labor (1899), *Sixteenth Annual Report, 1898, vol. I*, Albany, New York, NY.

New York, Bureau of Statistics of Labor (1896), *Thirteenth Annual Report, 1895, vol. I*, Albany, New York, NY.

News and Record, (1996) 'Jim Crow Needs No Survivors', 23 July, p. A7.

New York Times (1931), 'Maximum Wage Bill is Passed by House', 1 March, p. 6.

Oklahoma, Department of Labor (1910), *Third Annual Report*, Oklahoma City, OK.

Oklahoma, Department of Labor (1909), *Second Annual Report*, Oklahoma City, OK.

Roediger, David R. and Philip S. Foner (1989), *Our Own Time*, Verso Press, New York, NY.

Saxton, Alexander (1971), *The Indispensable Enemy: Labor and the Anti-Chinese Movement in California*, University of California Press, Berkeley, CA.

Serrano, Barbara A. and David Postman (1996), 'Brazier, Businesses Owe $500,000 for Workers Comp, Taxes—Though a Critic of Affirmative Action, Candidate Sought Race-Based Contracts', *Seattle Times*, 18 July, p. A1.

Strickland, Daryl (1991), 'South Business Snapshot', *Seattle Times*, 11 September, p. E9.

The [San Francisco] Elevator (1870), 'Labor in New York', vol. 5(50), 18 March, p. 4.

The [Washington] Evening Star (1869), 'The National Labor Convention of Colored Men', vol. 34(5224), 8 December, p. 4.

Thieblot, A.J. (1975), *The Davis-Bacon Act*, Industrial Research Unit, Report No. 10, Wharton School, University of Pennsylvania, Philadelphia, PA.

Thieblot, A.J. (1999), 'Prevailing Wage Laws and Black Employment in the Construction Industry', *Journal of Labor Research*, vol. 20(1) pp. 155-159.

Tripling, Sherry (1993), 'Peeling Back the Labels—Through their Republican Affiliations, Two African-Americans Defy Pigeonholing—Nona Brazier: On the Fast Track', *The Seattle Times*, 17 January, p. K1.

Tygiel, Jules, and Thorn, John (1997), 'Jackie Robinson's Signing: The Untold Story', in Tygiel, Jules (ed.), *The Jackie Robinson Reader,* Dutton, New York, New York, pp. 81-94.

U.S. 40th Congress, 2nd Session (1868), *The Congressional Globe, Senate Debates,* 24 June, Government Printing Office, Washington, D.C.

U.S. 69th Congress, 2nd Session (1927), *Hearings before the Committee on Labor, House of Representatives,* H.R. 17069, 18 February, Government Printing Office, Washington, D.C.

U.S. 71st Congress, 3rd Session (1931), *Congressional Record-House,* 28 February 28, Government Printing Office, Washington, D.C.

U.S. Bureau of the Census (1930), *Census of Population, Construction,* Government Printing Office, Washington, D.C.

U.S. Bureau of the Census (1930), *Census of Population, Occupations,* Government Printing Office, Washington, D.C.

U.S. Commissioner of Labor, Carroll D. Wright, Commissioner, (1892), 'Labor Laws of the Various States, Territories and the District of Columbia', *Second Special Report*, Government Printing Office, Washington, D.C.

U.S. Department of the Interior, Census Office (1892), *Compendium of the Eleventh Census, 1890, Part I., 'Population'*, Government Printing Office, Washington, D.C.

U.S. Department of Labor, Bureau of Labor Statistics (1914), 'Labor Laws of the United States', *Bulletin 148, Part I*, Government Printing Office, Washington, D.C.

U.S. Reports (1903), 'Atkin vs. Kansas', vol. 191, October, pp. 207-224.

Vedder, Richard, and Gallaway, David (1995), *Cracked Foundation: Repealing the Davis-Bacon Act*, Center for the Study of American Business, Policy Study Number 127.

Walls, Donald, Poutasse, Douglas, and Devol, Karen (1988), *The Impact of the Repeal of the Massachusetts Prevailing Wage Law*, Data Resources (McGraw-Hill, Inc.), Regional Information Group, Lexington, MA.

Will, George (1995a), 'It is Time to Repeal the Davis-Bacon Act', *Desseret News*, 5 February, p. V8.

Will, George (1995b), 'Davis-Bacon and the Wages of Racism', *Washington Post*, 5 February, p. C7.

Chapter 4

Prevailing Wage Laws, Unions, and Minority Employment in Construction

Dale Belman

The Davis-Bacon Act, which requires that federal construction contractors pay their workers 'prevailing wages' was passed by Congress in 1931 with the intent of favoring white workers who belonged to white-only unions over non-unionized black workers. The act continues to have discriminatory effects today.

David Bernstein (1993)

Introduction

Until the mid-1970's debate over prevailing wage laws in construction was limited to its effect on project costs and taxpayer expenses. In 1975 Armond J. Thieblot introduced a new argument, that the Davis Bacon Act was, at least in part, motivated by racial bigotry. Thieblot noted that the issue of race was mentioned explicitly only once during the House debate on Davis Bacon by a Southern Congressman, but asserted that thinly veiled allusions to race could be found in other speeches including those of Congressman Bacon (Thieblot, 1975, p. 9).

In recent years, Thieblot's initial assertion has been refined and advanced by several conservative think tanks, notably the CATO Institute, Heritage foundation, and the Institute for Justice. [1] They argue that prevailing wage statutes acted to exclude African-American workers because the higher wages on public projects inclined contractors to pass over lesser skilled workers, such as African-Americans. They also allege that such exclusion was not an unintended by product of the law, but reflected the purpose of the supporters of the Davis-Bacon Act. This interpretation of prevailing wage laws in general and the Davis-Bacon Act in particular has received favorable attention from the media and in congress (Hodge, 1990; Will, 1995; Brown, 1995).

This paper examines the first of these issues and provides new empirical work estimating the effect of state prevailing wages on minority employment. Consistent with the claims of Thieblot and others, we find a simple negative correlation between state prevailing wage legislation and minority employment. This disappears once we control for the racial composition of state's non-construction labor force. More complete models of the racial composition of the construction work force also do not support the exclusion hypothesis. We conclude that the evidence typically cited in support of current prevailing wage laws negatively affecting African-American employment is derived from naive models that do not adequately account for factors beyond prevailing wage laws that may impact the racial composition of the construction labor force.

Theoretic Views: Can Prevailing Wage Laws Act to Exclude African Americans

Critics of prevailing wage laws suggest that African-American workers are disadvantaged both by the higher wage required by prevailing wage laws and by the lack of low wage entry occupations other than apprentice. The higher wage makes less skilled and less productive employees unattractive to contractors because the wage level cannot be adjusted to conform to the productivity of such employees. Contractors will prefer higher skilled workers, workers who are overwhelmingly white due to hiring and training practices, and will avoid hiring the lower skilled African-American workers. In addition the only type of employee who can be paid at less than the journeyman rates under current administrative practice is an apprentice. The lack of alternative lower wage positions, such as 'helper' or 'trainee', precludes less skilled workers from being hired onto jobs where they could develop the skills needed to qualify as a journeyman. This restriction on the ports of entry for lower skilled workers acts to exclude African-Americans in particular. Both arguments premise that African-Americans in the building trades and related fields have lesser skills than other workers in construction occupations. This might be due to discrimination in entry to apprenticeship programs, in hiring into jobs for which there is union representation, or a lack of family background in the building trades. [2]

Prevailing wage laws may also act to exclude African-Americans from construction by facilitating the discriminatory preferences of construction employers (Vedder and Gallaway, 1995). In a theoretic model of a competitive market, employer tastes for discrimination cannot be exercised without deleterious consequences for employers who choose to discriminate. Suppose that wage discrimination exists in a competitive market, a group of workers with skills and abilities comparable to those of other workers are paid less because of traits unrelated to economic performance. The lesser wage of discriminated group provides an opportunity for employers who are unconcerned with discrimination to hire the disadvantaged group at its lower wage. This becomes a competitive advantage for those employers who, in the extreme, can drive those who refuse to use disadvantaged groups from the market. The operations of the market are beneficial to the disadvantaged group because rising demand for their services raises their wage toward that of the majority group. A prevailing wage law arrest such market dynamics. The high wage established by prevailing wage laws causes construction workers to queue for such jobs. Employers who wish to discriminate can pick those workers, in this view non African-American workers, from the queue. Prevailing wage laws prevent competitors who are willing to hire minority employees from undercutting discriminatory employers and so such employers from the economic consequences of their practices.

Empirical research on this issue is scarce. Richard Vedder and David Gallaway (1995) find that federal and state prevailing wage laws increased African-American unemployment and that the proportion of African-Americans employed in construction occupations declined relative to the proportion of white workers in such occupations between 1930 and 1980. The supporting evidence is fundamentally descriptive. As such, its persuasiveness is lessened by the possibility that intervening factors not incorporated in the analysis might be the source of the declining role of African-Americans in construction.

Thieblot (1999) takes an additional step in comparing the racial composition of state construction labor force under different prevailing wage law regimes relative to the racial composition of the overall state labor force. Dividing the 50 states into those with no prevailing wage law, a weak prevailing wage law, average prevailing wage laws and strong prevailing wage laws, Thieblot concludes that the racial composition of the construction labor force is considerably more like the racial composition of the overall workforce in states without prevailing wage laws. The author relies upon simple comparison of the outcomes across the different legal regimes and does not perform statistical tests to validate the conclusions.

Using data provided in the article, we find his conclusion is supported for states with weak and strong laws but is not supported in a comparison of states with average laws and those with no laws. Thieblot's conclusions are further weakened by the aggregation of data on the 50 states into four broad legal categories. This presumes, rather than tests, that the underlying conditions and effects of strong prevailing wage law on racial composition are similar in New York State, which has a large African-American community and Minnesota which has a small African American community. Similarly, it assumes that the consequences of not having a prevailing wage law are similar in Mississippi and Louisiana and Wyoming. Finally, the article does not investigate whether factors other than the racial composition of the state labor force affect the racial composition of the construction labor force.

The Current Research

The current research investigates whether such statutes reduce African-American representation in the construction labor force. Our strategy for investigating this issue is to first use descriptive statistics to illustrate the inter-relationship between statutes and the racial composition of the labor force. We supplement this with estimates of five progressively more complete multi-variate models of the racial composition of the construction labor force. These models include factors such as union membership, individual characteristics and occupation that may influence employment in construction. The descriptive statistics illuminate the central features of the relationship of interest; the multi-variate models assure that the effects of statutes have been isolated from those of correlated factors as well as provide statistical tests of the relationship between statutes and racial composition.

Our research finds no relationship between prevailing wage statutes and the racial composition of the construction labor force. There is a simple negative correlation between prevailing wage laws and the probability of observing an African-American in the blue-collar construction labor force. Although this is consistent with the views of the critics of prevailing wage laws, it neglects the role of the racial composition of labor supply on the characteristics of the construction labor force. Many of the states that lack prevailing wage laws are in the South and have a large proportion of African-Americans in their labor force. Once we allow for differences in the labor supply between states, there is no evidence of a relationship between state prevailing wage laws and the proportion of African-Americans in construction. This pattern is apparent in our descriptive statistics and across all specifications of the multi-variate models.

This analysis focuses on the effect of state prevailing wage laws on the racial composition of the construction labor force. Analysis of the Federal Davis-Bacon Act is difficult as there is little cross sectional or inter-temporal variation in provisions and application of the Act. In contrast, there is considerable variation between states with respect to both the presence and provisions of state prevailing wage statutes. In 1994, 33 states (including the District of Columbia) had prevailing wage statutes that applied to construction, 18 did not. Among the 33 states with laws there were considerable differences in projects subject to the laws and the formula used to determine the prevailing wage. In some states all construction financed by state and local government is subject to prevailing wages, in other states only state financed construction is subject to this legislation, other states exempt specific types of construction such as schools. Laws also vary in the formula used to determine the prevailing wage: in some states the prevailing wage is the wage paid at least 30 percent of the construction workers in an occupation and type of work, others use a 50-percent rule and still others used a mean wage rule. The diversity of 'Little Davis-Bacon Acts' suggests that a simple distinction between states that have some law and those that do not is overly restrictive. Further disaggregation of the statutes will better capture the effects of prevailing wage laws on minority employment. Thieblot classifies states according to whether their prevailing wage law is 'strong', 'average' or 'weak' and we adopt this approach.[3]

If the critics of prevailing wage laws are correct, the presence of prevailing wage laws should be associated with a reduced probability of observing an African-American in the blue-collar labor force of the construction industry. One approach to measuring this proposed relationship is to examine the relationship between legal regimes and the proportion of African Americans in the construction labor force by state. A complementary approach is to estimate a micro data model for a sample of construction workers in which the dependent variable is whether the individual is African-American and the explanatory variables include the legal regime. Treatment of race as endogenous is unusual, as it has been described as one of the few factors that can dependably be treated as exogenous. Although race is exogenous to the individual, it can be explicit or implicit criteria for being chosen into a particular occupation or industry, as is the case in the current study. Heywood and Peoples (1994) have considered a similar issue, the effect of deregulation in trucking on the racial composition of the driver labor force, and estimated a model in which race is determined by individual characteristics and legal regimes.

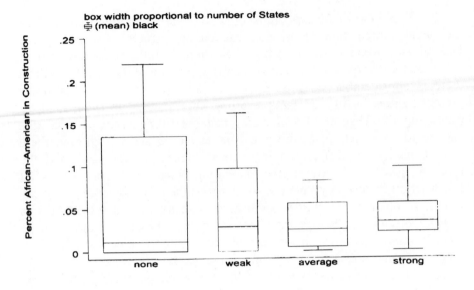

Figure 4.1   **Percent of African-Americans in the construction labor force by state**

Note: The construction labor force of the District of Columbia is 78 percent African-American. This observation has been removed to prevent excessive compression of the scaling.

Data for this analysis is taken from the 1994 Outgoing Rotation File (ORG) provided by the Bureau of Labor Statistics (BLS). These files include individuals who are in the last month of their Current Population Survey (CPS) rotation and who are asked questions about their wages, hours of work, and union membership. We include all individuals who report being employed as a 'precision production' (craft), operative, transportation operative or laborer in the construction industry from the 1994 ORG files of the BLS. There are 5,886 observations in the data set, 5.96 percent of the employees self report as African-American.

Turning first to our descriptive statistics, we calculate the proportion of African-Americans in the blue collar construction labor force for 50 states and the District of Columbia, group this data according to the strength of the prevailing wage law, and rank the states from those with the fewest African Americans in the labor force to those with the greatest proportion. The relationship between the strength of prevailing wage statute and the proportion of African-Americans in the construction labor force is summarized in the box plot in Figure 4.1 and the data in the upper panel of Table 4.1. The box and whiskers plot is defined so that the center line in the box is the median of the distribution (the proportion of African-Americans in the middle state of the particular legal regime), the lower boundary of the box is the proportion African-American for the state at the 25th percentile, the upper line is the proportion at the 75th percentile. The upper and lower ends of the whiskers show the proportion African-American for the state that is closest to 1.5 times the inter-quartile range from the 25th and 75th percentiles.[4]

Figure 4.1 depicts the proportion of African-Americans in the construction labor force by state. Although the proportion of African-Americans for the median state is similar across legal regimes, the proportion of African-Americans at the 75th percentile and whisker-end is higher for the states without statutes than for the states with such statutes. The proportion of African-Americans for the median state ranges from 2.9 percent in weak law states to 3.4 percent in strong law states with the median state without laws (3.3 percent) falling close to the upper end of the range. States with strong laws have a larger proportion of African-Americans in construction in the state at the 25th percentile than do states without laws, but the difference is modest—0.7 percent for states without laws against 2.6 percent for strong law states.

The more dramatic difference, a difference consistent with the views of critics of the statute, is apparent at the 75th percentile. Where the state at the 75th percentile has a construction labor force which is 5.6 percent African-American in strong law states, 6.2 percent in average law states, and 9.7 percent in weak law states, the state at the 75th percentile of states without laws has a construction labor force which is 14.1 percent African-American. This pattern is also found for the states at the 90th percentile (see Table 4.1), where the proportion of African-Americans in construction in no law states is more than double the percent in average and strong law states. There is then a simple negative relationship between prevailing wage statutes and the proportion of African-Americans in construction.

But states vary greatly in the proportion of African-Americans in their population and labor force and we do not expect to observe as many African-Americans in construction in Maine, where only 3 percent of the labor force is minority, as in Mississippi. All else equal, we would expect the proportion of African-Americans in construction to mirror the proportion of African-Americans in the states' labor force. The second panel of Table 4.1 depicts the proportion of African-Americans in states non-construction labor force by strength of prevailing wage law. Again, although the proportion of African-Americans in the labor force for the median state is similar across statutory regimes, the proportion of African-Americans in the state labor force is substantially higher for the state at the 75th and 90th percentile for the no law regime states than for the average or strong law regime states. Southern states, states which have a large proportion of African-Americans in both their non-construction and construction labor forces, are particularly unlikely to have prevailing wage laws. And it is these states that compose the 75th and 90th percentiles for the no law regime states in the first panel of the table and the box plot.

We can examine this issue more carefully by taking the ratio of the percent African-Americans in the construction labor force to the percent of African-Americans in the non-construction labor force by state. If the proportion of African-Americans in construction mirrors the proportion in the non-construction labor force, the ratio will be one. If African-Americans are 'over represented' in construction the ratio will be greater than one, less if they are 'under represented'. If state prevailing wage laws reduce African-American representation in construction, this ratio should be systematically lower in states with laws than in states without prevailing wage laws (see Figure 4.2). What is most striking about Figure 4.2 (and the lower panel of Table 4.1) is, first, the larger variance of the ratio for the no law states relative to the other three regimes and second, the similarity of the ratio at 50th, 75th and 90th percentiles for no law, average law and strong law states. The no law states not only include states with the highest ratio of African- Americans in construction to African-Americans in the non-construction labor force, they also include the states with the lowest ratios. More apropos to the present question, the ratio for the median strong law state (0.70) lies slightly above that for states without laws (0.64), while the strong law state at the 75th percentile has a ratio (0.92) only slightly below that of its counterpart among the no law states (1.0). Comparison of the average and no law box plots also indicates little systematic difference in the relative representation of African-Americans between these two legal regimes. There is also only a small difference in the ratio between the no law, average and strong law regimes at the 90th percentile.

This analysis suggests that although African-American employees are more prevalent in construction in states without prevailing wage laws, this reflects the larger proportion of African-Americans in those states labor force rather than any favorable influence of legal regime. States in the deep South do not have prevailing wage laws and this resulted in a simple if spurious correlation between the proportion of African-Americans in construction and the lack of prevailing wage laws. Why might these states

Table 4.1 The racial composition of the construction labor force by strength of prevailing wage law

	Percent African-Americans in construction labor force			
	No Law	Weak Law	Average Law	Strong Law
10th Pct	0%	0%	0%	1.7%
25th Pct	0%	0%	1.0%	2.1%
Median	3.3%	2.9%	3.1%	3.4%
75th Pct	14.1%	9.7%	6.2%	5.6%
90th Pct	21.9%	16.1%	8.2%	8.5%

	Percent African-Americans in non-construction labor force			
	No Law	Weak Law	Average Law	Strong Law
10th Pct	0.2%	0.1%	1.7%	1.9%
25th Pct	0.7%	1.7%	2.3%	2.6%
Median	4.4%	5.3%	4.8%	6.4%
75th Pct	20.9%	13.4%	6.8%	11.0%
90th Pct	29.2%	25.8%	15.3%	11.3%

	Percent African-Americans in construction/ percent African-American in non-construction labor force			
	No Law	Weak Law	Average Law	Strong Law
10th Pct	0	0	0	0.24
25th Pct	0	0	0.41	0.50
Median	0.64	0.42	0.56	0.70
75th Pct	1.0	0.75	0.82	0.92
90th Pct	1.25	0.90	1.21	1.16

Source: Current Population Survey Outgoing Rotation Files (1994).

lack such laws? In the era when social regulatory laws such as prevailing wage laws were being considered by state legislatures in 1880 to 1960, African-Americans were disenfranchised throughout the South. The denial of the voting rights to such a large proportion of the working class of these states may have been an insuperable barrier to the passage of prevailing wage laws as well as other progressive labor legislation.

Descriptive statistics are, in the end, not decisive because we do not believe that prevailing wage laws and the racial make up of the labor force are the only factors affecting African-American representation in construction. Other factors may influence employment in construction and

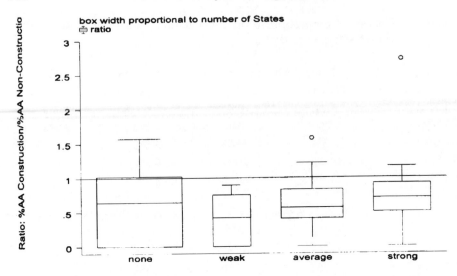

Figure 4.2 Ratio of the percent of African-American construction to African-American in non-construction labor force by state

may, if not controlled for, mask the true effect of prevailing wage statutes. We address this by estimating five multi-variate models, working from a simple model that allows only for the influence of prevailing wage statutes, to models that better reflect the complexity of the employment decision. Parallel to our descriptive statistics, the initial model includes only the three prevailing wage indicators: strong law, average law, and weak law, as explanatory variables (Model I). Individuals are assigned values for the prevailing wage variables according to their reported state of residence. Again paralleling our descriptive statistics, the next model adds a control for the percent of African-Americans in the non-construction labor force of the state (Model II).

The third model includes two variables related to unionization, union membership and union density by state, for the construction industry (Model III). Some construction unions have historically acted to exclude African-Americans from membership and from their trade. Although such practices have been determined to be illegal by the courts, unions may still engage in practices that de facto serve to exclude African-Americans from employment in construction. These two measures of unionization control for and measure the effect of construction unionization on African-Americans employment independent of the effects of state prevailing wage laws. Individual characteristics, such as age, education, place of residence and gender may influence the suitability of individuals for employment in construction. The fourth model follows the work of Heywood and Peoples (1994) in adding controls for demographic characteristics and educational attainment (Model IV).

The final estimate, Model V, provides controls for three-digit occupation. The argument for racial hiring consequences of prevailing wage laws suggests that such laws systematically favor more skilled, and hence more productive, workers. African-American workers are on the lower end of the skill distribution, so prevailing wage laws act to exclude them from the industry. But skills in construction are, for the most part, specific to occupations. Those excluded by prevailing laws are excluded because they are on the lower end of the skill distribution for their occupation. To this point coefficients have been estimated without regard to occupation and, as such, combine 'within' occupation and 'between' occupation effects. This might veil the racial effects of prevailing wage laws if such effects occur entirely within occupations. The addition of controls for occupation resolves this as 'between' occupation effects are accounted for by the occupational controls and the non-occupational coefficients capture only 'within' occupation effects. Although most econometric research control for occupation at the level of major occupation (23 categories) or, less frequently, detailed occupational (45 classifications) controls, this research uses three digit occupational controls to better delineate the craft structure of the industry.

The models are estimated using probit, but as the error term has both individual and state error components, consistent estimation is more complex than the typical probit. The two-component error structure, an implication of inclusion of state level variables in the model, results in an n.i.i.d. error that is correlated across individuals within states. If this were a linear model, OLS estimates would be consistent but inefficient.[5] The implications for estimation of a maximum likelihood model are more serious; coefficient estimates are no longer consistent. This can be corrected with a model that allows for a random state error component. There are several methods of estimating such a model; we utilize Butler and Moffitt's (1982) approach.[6] We illustrate the issue of random components by estimating Model I with a conventional probit and the random effects corrected estimator used throughout the balance of the paper. Estimates of the derivatives of the likelihood functions, the non-linear counterpart of regression coefficients, are provided in Table 4.2.[7]

Estimates of Model I derived from a conventional probit are found in the first column in Table 4.2, estimates for a model which allows the state error term are in the second column. The derivatives of the

The Economics of Prevailing Wage Laws

Table 4.2 The effect of prevailing wage laws on minority employment

	Models					
	I	Ia	II	III	IV	V
Weak Law	-0.033	-0.0377	-0.0032	-0.0029	-0.0065	-0.0058
	(-1.75)	(-4.44)	(-0.308)	(-0.277)	(0.659)	(-0.643)
Average Law	-0.034	-0.0296	-0.0030	-0.0021	-0.0023	-0.0019
	(-1.38)	(-2.90)	(-0.315)	(-0.197)	(-0.225)	(-0.209)
Strong Law	-0.038	-0.0090	0.0094	0.011	0.0050	0.0066
	(-2.32)	(-1.27)	(1.112)	(0.799)	(0.381)	(0.562)
Percent African American			0.5002	0.5003	0.4471	0.3946
			(13.94)	(13.92)	(13.110)	(12.913)
Union				0.0045	-0.0011	0.0007
				(0.468)	(-0.175)	(0.128)
Percent Union				-0.0096	-0.0089	-0.0147
				(0.264)	(-0.262)	(-0.479)

Notes: Demographic, Education, and Occupational Controls are omitted. Percent black is the proportion of African Americans in the non-construction labor force by state. Demographic controls include age and its square, gender, marital status and urban residence. Education variables are qualitative measures of educational attainment indicating some high school high school degree, associate of arts, B.A., M.A., professional degree or Ph.D. Occupation is controlled for with dummies for three digit blue-collar occupations.

Coefficients Reported as Derivatives of the Likelihood Function at Sample Means; t-statistics for coefficients in parentheses.

* significant in a 10-percent one tailed test
** significant in a 5-percent one tailed test
*** significant in a 1-percent one tailed test

(All tests against of null of zero or positive coefficient).

coefficients from the conventional probit are similar across the three classifications of prevailing wage laws. The presence of a law reduces the likelihood of observing an African-American employee by approximately 3.5 percent without regard to the strength of the law. The coefficients are statistically significant at conventional levels, but the level of significance varies widely, from significant in a 1 percent one tailed test for strong laws, to 5 percent in a one tailed test for weak laws, to 10 percent for average laws. Despite such differences—but parallel with the descriptive statistics—the conventional probit estimates of Model I may be taken as supporting the racial exclusion theory.

These results are, however, misleading both with regard to coefficient estimates and statistical significance. Correction for random state effects (column two) has little impact on the estimated effect of the coefficients on weak and average laws; African-American employment is reduced between 3 percent and 3.8 percent in the presence of such laws. The standard errors for these two variables are substantially smaller than those in the conventional probit, both coefficients are significance at better than a 1 percent level. The more striking change is the decline in the estimated effect of strong laws, to one third the level indicated by the conventional probit, and its consequent loss of statistical significance in any conventional test.[8] The result for the strong law coefficient is at variance with the racial exclusion theory, as strong laws should have a more marked exclusionary effect than average or weak laws. The random effects estimates might be interpreted as providing partial support for the racial exclusion theory, but it more clearly illustrates the need to use an appropriate estimator.

Model II adds a variable for the proportion of African-Americans in the states' non-construction labor force, a critical determinant of the proportion of such workers in construction. The derivative of the coefficient on the proportion of African-American in the non-construction labor force is 0.5002 with a t-statistic of 13.9; a state with 10 percentage points more African-American workers in its labor force will have a five percentage points higher level of African-American employment in its construction labor force. As with the descriptive statistics, inclusion of this variable in the model eliminates the relationship between prevailing wage laws and African-American employment in construction. The coefficients on the prevailing wage variables become smaller in magnitude, the point estimates of the derivatives range between −0.003 and +0.0094; the decline in magnitude causes the coefficients to become non-significant. This result also carries through models III - V, prevailing wage coefficients are never significant in models that include the proportion of African-Americans.

Addition of controls for union membership and union density, Model III, do not alter any the estimates. The coefficient on the proportion of African-Americans in the state labor force remains large and statistically significant, those on the prevailing wage law variables continue to have small, non-significant coefficients and the coefficients on union membership and union density by state are also small and non-significant. This outcome, which is maintained in all further estimates, is unexpected given the historic and legal record of some building trades unions with regard to employment of African-American workers. It may reflect the success of legal and institutional efforts to end discriminatory practices. Whatever the source, this research suggests that construction employees who are union members are no less likely to be African-American than those who are not African-American. Further, that the increased bargaining power provided by greater union organization of construction labor markets is not being used to exclude African-Americans from employment in construction.

Model IV, which controls for factors such as age, education and residence, which might influence the suitability of individuals for employment in construction, does not alter the relationship between prevailing wage laws and minority employment. The effect of the proportion of African-Americans in the state labor force remains large; the effects of prevailing wage laws and of union membership and density remain small in magnitude and non-significant. Other important determinants of African-American employment are age and its square, metropolitan residence, marital status and holding a college degree, as shown in Table 4.3. Older employees are more likely to be African-American, although the relationship is convex. Considering the effect of age alone, a 20 year old has an 8 percent probability of being African-American, a 30 year old has a 10.6 percent probability, at 40 the probability is 12.3 percent, at 50 it is 13.1 percent. The probability to decline between 50 and 60 and at 60 it is 12.9 percent. One source of this pattern may be recent shifts in minority employment in construction, with Hispanics increasingly competing with African-American workers over the last 20 years. Older African-American construction workers, who have ties to the industry, would have remained employed at relatively high rates. But fewer young African-Americans would find employment in construction as Hispanics have moved into the industry (Belman and Bilginsoy, 1997). In addition to age, residence in a metropolitan area increases the probability of an employee being African-American by 1.7 percent. Being married and holding a college degree both decrease the likelihood of observing an African-American, by 2.3 percent and 4.2 percent respectively. Educational

Table 4.3 Model IV estimates of the effect of prevailing wage laws on African-American employment

Weak Law	-0.00652 (0.657)	Female	0.003944 (0.228)
Average Law	-0.002270 (-0.225)	Metro Resident	0.017332*** (3.417)
Strong Law	0.004977 (0.381)	Married	-0.023039*** (-3.844)
Percent African American	0.447090*** (13.110)	Separated, Widowed or Divorced	-0.010232 (-1.330)
Union Density	- 0.008926 (- 0.262)	Some High School	-0.000554 (-0.083)
Union Member	-0.001057 (-0.175)	High School Degree	-0.006667 (-1.209)
Age	0.004916*** (3.735)	AA Degree	0.007785 (0.753)
Age^2	-0.000046*** (-2.934)	College Degree	-0.041692** (-2.483)
		More than College	0.044863 (1.446)

Number of obs = 5883
Model chi2(17) = 161.33
Prob > chi2 = 0.0000
Log Likelihood = -1096.96

Notes: t-statistics for coefficients in parentheses.
*** significant in a 1 percent two tailed test
** significant in a 5 percent two tailed test
* significant in a 10 percent two tailed test

attainment other than a college degree has little effect on the racial composition of the construction labor force, a result in keeping with the importance of occupation specific rather than general skill training in the industry (Belman and Bilginsoy, 1997).

Model V, the final model in this series, differs from prior estimates in controlling for a fixed effect by three-digit occupation. Again, by removing the effects of inter-occupational factors including skill related factors, this model eliminates the masking of the effects of prevailing wage laws by occupational factors, as shown in Table 4.2. The thrust of prior results remains. The cardinal explanatory variable is the proportion of African-Americans in the state labor force; the effects of prevailing wage laws and unionization are small in magnitude and non-significant. Model V suggests varied patterns of racial employment by trade. There are 34 distinct trades in this data set including three grades of mechanic, carpet layers, ironworkers, electricians, apprentices, and bricklayers. There is evidence that African-Americans are significantly less likely to be observed in occupations such as construction supervisor, heating-ventilation-air-conditioning, carpenter, electrician, painter, plumber, ironworker, sheet-metal, welder, operating engineer or material moving operative. Although no simple pattern is apparent in this set of occupations, it appears that African-Americans are less likely to be employed in licensed occupations (such as plumbing and electrical) and occupations which require formal training (such as operating engineer, electrician and plumber). But, carpenters and welders, occupations that are often self-taught or learned on the job, are also less likely to be African-Americans. The estimates also indicate that apprentices are no less likely to be African-American than other construction workers. This cuts against the argument that such positions do not provide ports of entry to construction for African-Americans and is consistent with Bilginsoy's research on apprenticeships. The small number of apprentices in the sample argues against putting too much weight on this result.[9]

Conclusion

Prevailing wage laws have come under increasing criticism for allegedly reducing the employment of African-Americans in the construction industry. This premise has been supported by evidence from legislative records and theoretic arguments about administered wages role as a bar to the employment of the lesser skilled African-American worker. The argument was further buttressed with evidence on discrimination against

African-American employees by buildings trades unions.

The empirical evidence developed in this research does not support the premise that prevailing wage laws act to exclude African-Americans from employment in the construction industry. Utilizing a conventional data source and a procedure incorporating a state and individual error component, we find a moderate negative simple correlation between state prevailing wage laws and minority employment in blue-collar construction. This correlation is, however, the product of the lack of such laws in the South, the region with the largest proportion of African Americans in its labor force. Once adjusted, the association between prevailing wage laws and minority employment disappears.

The debate surrounding the Davis-Bacon Act will continue on other grounds. How the Act effects the cost of public construction, the quality of work done, the amount of training that takes place in construction, the extent to which the law promotes labor standards and encourages collective bargaining, all remain open for debate. However, the proposition that the Davis-Bacon Act acts to limit African American access to construction employment is not consistent with current racial patterns of employment in the industry.

Notes

[1] Institute for Justice lawyers presented arguments on behalf of plaintiffs in seeking the constitutional overturning of the Davis Bacon Act as a racially discriminatory law. Brazier Construction Co., Inc., *et al.*, Plaintiffs, v. Robert Reich, Secretary of Labor, *et al.*, Defendants, Civil Action No. 93-2318 WBB.

[2] As noted previously in this paper, there is historic evidence of discrimination in acceptance into apprenticeship programs. More recent work by Bilginsoy suggests that such practices have largely been ended (1998). Further, apprenticeship programs provide only half of the trained journeymen in the industry. Other important sources include training in the military, community colleges and on the job training.

[3] Thieblot (1993), uses a 2 to 17 point system in another work (Thieblot, 1995).

[4] The box defines the inter-quartile range of the distribution (IQ). The horizontal lines at the end of the whiskers are the upper and lower observation which is closest to being 1.5 times the inter-quartile range beyond the 25th and 75th percentile.

[5] The standard errors obtained from the OLS routine in a typical software package would, however, be wrong, as they are calculated under the assumption of independence of error terms. The correct OLS errors can be obtained by methods typically referred to as robust or White-Huber corrections.

[6] Estimation with this procedure can be sensitive to the procedures used for estimation, such as the number of quadratures used, but estimates with this data were stable across variations on the routine.

[7] The complete estimates are available from the authors.

[8] The divergence in the effect of strong laws from that of other laws can be tested by comparing this model to one in which the strong, average and weak coefficients are constrained to be the equal. The hypothesis of equality between the coefficients on the three prevailing wage variables can be rejected in a one-percent Wald test.

[9] The helper classification is of interest as opponents of prevailing wage legislation suggest that the helper category is utilized by African-Americans as a point of entry to the construction labor force. The relationship between employment as a helper and racial status could not be tested as there were few helpers in the data set and since none were African-American it could not be included in the model.

References

Belman, Dale, and Bilginsoy, Cihan (1997), *An Analysis of the Labor Force of the Construction Industry: 1979 – 1995*, report to the Construction Alliance.

Bernstein, David (1993), 'The Davis-Bacon Act: Let's Bring Jim Crow to an End', *Cato Briefing Paper, No. 17*, Cato Institute, 1000 Massachusetts Avenue, N.W., Washington, D.C., 18 January.

Bilginsoy, Cihan (1998), 'Apprenticeship Training in the U.S. Construction Industry', mimeo, University of Utah, Salt Lake City, UT.

Brazier Construction Co., Inc., *et al.*, Plaintiffs, v. Robert Reich, Secretary of Labor, *et al.*, Defendants, Civil Action No. 93-2318 WBB.

Brown, Tony (1995), *Black Lies, White Lies: the Truth According to Tony Brown*, William Morrow and Company, Inc., New York, NY.

Butler, J.S., and Moffitt, Robert, (1982), 'A Computationally Efficient Quadrature Procedure for the One-Factor Multinomial Probit Model', *Econometrica*, vol. 50(3), pp. 761-764.

Heywood, J.S., and Peoples, J. (1994), 'Deregulation and the Prevalence of Black Truck Drivers', *Journal of Law and Economics*, vol. 37(1), pp. 133-156.

Hodge, S. A. (1990), 'Davis-Bacon: Racist Then, Racist Now', *The Wall Street Journal*, 25 June, p. A14.

Thieblot, Armond J. (1995), *State Prevailing Wage Laws, An Assessment at the Start of 1995*, Associated Builders and Contractors, Inc., Rosslyn, VA.

Thieblot, Armond J. (1975), *The Davis Bacon Act, Industrial Research Unit, Report No. 10*, Wharton School, University of Pennsylvania, PA.

Thieblot, Armond J. (1993), 'Impact of Prevailing Rates on Black Employment in the Construction Industry', in Brazier Construction Co., Inc., *et al.*, Plaintiffs,

v. Robert Reich, Secretary of Labor, *et al.*, Defendants, Civil Action No. 93-2318 WBB.

Thieblot, Armond J. (1999), 'Prevailing Wage Laws and Black Employment in the Construction Industry', *Journal of Labor Research,* vol. 20(1), pp. 155-159.

Vedder, R., and Gallaway, D. (1995), *Cracked Foundation: Repealing the Davis-Bacon Act,* Center for the Study of American Business, Policy Study Number 127.

PART II
PUBLIC POLICY:
COSTS, SKILLS, AND SAFETY

Chapter 5

Prevailing Wage Laws and Construction Costs: Evidence from British Columbia's Skills Development and Fair Wage Policy

Kevin Duncan and Mark J. Prus[1]

Introduction

Prevailing wage laws have been a part of public policy toward labor in North America for over a century. Prevailing wage laws at the state and federal level in the United States, as well as at the provincial and federal level in Canada remain controversial because of the belief, supported by several empirical studies, that the costs of these policies exceed the benefits. For example, in March of 1992 the Province of British Columbia introduced the Skills Development and Fair Wage Act (SDFW) which mandated that prevailing wages be paid on provincially funded construction projects.[2] One goal of this policy was to arrest the decline in apprenticeship participation in the B.C. construction industry with additional benefits related to larger local economic impacts from public construction and an award process based on expertise, efficiency and quality instead of wage costs.[3] However, the Quantity Surveyors Society of British Columbia (1993) estimated that the SDFW cost taxpayers $100 million (CAN) annually. Concern over the cost of this policy resulted in the Skills Development and Fair Wage Repeal Act of 2001.

The Davis-Bacon Act of 1931, the prevailing wage law that governs wage determination for federally funded construction projects in the U.S., is viewed as sharing many of the benefits of the SDFW.[4] But, estimates of the cost of Davis-Bacon suggest that this act adds as much as 35 percent to the cost of federal construction, relative to the cost of comparable private structures (see Fraundorf et al., 1983). Concern over the cost of the Davis-Bacon Act has motivated many, including the

Government Accounting Office, to call for its repeal (Government Accounting Office, 1979).

More often than not, the primary line of attack on prevailing wage laws is the contention that they artificially raise the cost of public construction, and hurt taxpayers in the process. Consequently, the costs of prevailing wage laws are inevitably seen as out-weighing any potential benefits. Proponents of prevailing wage laws argue that these regulations promote the development of a skilled labor force in construction, improve work place safety, encourage quality construction, increase apprenticeship training, and provide career opportunities in construction for local citizens. Additionally, they emphasize that prevailing wage regulations also induce contractors to provide health insurance and pension coverage that otherwise would be absent.

In contrast, critics of prevailing wage laws have long argued that these regulations raise construction costs on public works and cost taxpayers money. They anticipate considerable cost savings from the repeal of prevailing wage laws. Typical estimates of the cost impact of prevailing wage laws expressed in public policy debates range from 15 to 25 percent.

Before policy makers can reach informed decisions about fair and prevailing wage legislation, it is important that the cost estimates of these policies are accurate. However, the studies cited above by the Quantity Surveyors and Fraundorf, *et al.* suffer from the methodological error of assuming away the concomitant input substitution that affects costs, or confuse the cost differential between public and private construction projects with the cost of prevailing wage laws. In this paper we estimate the impact of the SDFW on the cost differential between private and public construction in British Columbia. Specifically, we find that construction projects funded by the Province of British Columbia prior to the SDFW were more expensive than privately funded projects. However, our results indicate that there was no statistically significant change in the public-private cost differential after the introduction of the SDFW. Our findings suggest that, in the case of British Columbia, the benefits of the fair wage policy were enjoyed at an insignificant monetary cost.

The remainder of this paper is organized along the following lines. In the next section we survey the literature addressing the cost of fair and prevailing wage laws. We discuss in further detail the data and methodological problems that have limited previous research. We also provide a simple example that illustrates how construction cost data collected before and after the introduction of the SDFW avoids the limitations faced by previous researchers and provides a more accurate estimate of the impact of fair wage requirements. In section three we describe, in greater detail, the construction cost data from British Columbia that covers the period before and after the introduction of the SDFW. In section four we describe the regression model used to estimate the cost differential between provincial and private construction projects. We also explain how the model can be used to determine if the cost differential was affected by the requirements of the SDFW. In section five we present and discuss model estimates. We conclude with a discussion of implications for policy and future research.

Empirical Cost Estimates of Fair and Prevailing Wage Policies

In 1993 the Quantity Surveyors Society of British Columbia concluded that the SDFW increased construction costs from six to seven percent and cost taxpayers $100 million annually. The Quantity Surveyors Society study is based on an examination of seven of the 109 provincial construction projects awarded between March of 1992 and June of 1993 to nonunion contractors who were subject to the fair wage act. The Surveyors estimated the added cost of complying with the SDFW by calculating total labor costs using rates from the SDFW wage schedule and wage rates under open shop conditions, holding labor utilization constant. These labor costs were then adjusted to reflect the ratio of labor costs to total costs to arrive at the final estimate of the percentage increase attributed to the SDFW. While this methodology provides a measure of the impact of a prevailing wage law on labor costs (given fixed labor usage), it does not provide an accurate measure of the total cost of such a policy because it ignores any changes in labor hours that might result from increased productivity due to managerial efficiency, the substitution of capital for labor, or employing labor with more training. Specifically, if any of these changes occurred with the introduction of the SDFW, the cost estimate provided by the Quantity Surveyors Society is too high. Because the introduction of a fair wage law may alter input utilization and the total input bill, it is important to examine the effect of fair and prevailing wage laws on total construction costs since total costs include any adjustments management has made.

The study by Fraundorf *et al.* was the first to use a multivariate regression approach to estimate the total cost impact of a prevailing wage law. The authors collected data on 215 buildings constructed in rural areas of the U.S. in 1977 and 1978. Approximately half of these buildings (113) were federally funded construction projects built under Davis-Bacon regulations while the remaining projects (102) were private buildings constructed without these regulations. The authors predict the log of total construction costs based on the square foot size of the building, dummy variables for a variety of building materials and regional dummy variables indicating where the building was constructed. The focus variable is a dummy variable indicating whether or not the building was federally or privately financed. The authors find that, after controlling for other factors, the total cost of a federal building is 26 percent higher than the cost of a comparably sized private structure (other reported estimates range as high as 35 percent). The authors ascribe this cost differential to the impact of the Davis-Bacon Act.

    This finding is substantially higher than the impact reported by other studies that have estimated the cost of the Davis-Bacon Act. The bulk of these studies indicate that the wage requirements of the Davis-Bacon Act increase construction costs from 1.5 to 3 percent (Gujarati, 1967; GAO, 1979, 1981; Goldfarb and Morrall, 1978, 1981; Gould, 1971; Gould and Cittlingmayer, 1980; Keller and Hartman, 2001). On the other hand, Bourden and Levitt (1980) fail to find a cost effect of this law. These studies share the approach of estimating the cost of prevailing wage laws by calculating the difference between the federal or state determinations of the prevailing wage and the researcher's survey estimate of the 'true' prevailing wage of an area, holding labor utilization constant. As mentioned above, cost estimates based on the assumption of constant labor utilization may be biased. However, even when Allen (1983) adjusts his cost estimate for factor substitution, he still finds a modest Davis-Bacon cost impact of 0.3 to 0.4 percent. Thieblot (1975) pursues a unique approach by taking advantage of President Nixon's temporary suspension of the Davis-Bacon Act in 1971. Thieblot's examination of the re-bids allowed during the suspension suggests that the absence of the Davis-Bacon wage requirements reduced costs on federal projects by 0.63 percent. Thieblot's re-examination of the data indicates that a repeal of the Act would result in a cost savings of 4.74 percent (see Thieblot, 1986, 105-106). In sum, the results of these studies, based on a variety of techniques, yield cost estimates of the Davis-Bacon Act that are surprisingly lower than the estimate obtained by Fraundorf *et al.*

    The result reported by Fraundorf *et al.* is also surprising given that construction-worker labor costs, including wages, benefits and payroll taxes, as a percent of total construction costs, including materials and labor, but excluding land purchases and architect fees, in the United States in 1982, was 30 percent (Census of Construction, 1982).[5] It is unlikely that the total cost of construction would fall from 26 to 35 percent from a regulatory change that is hypothesized to primarily affect a cost component that accounts for only 30 percent of total costs. The above suggests that the

Fraundorf *et al.* estimate of the cost differential between federally and privately funded construction is too high to be entirely attributed to the wage changes required by the Davis-Bacon Act. A better explanation of this high estimate is that the dummy variable used by Fraundorf *et al.* captures the effect of the prevailing wage law and other regulations and practices that influence the cost of projects funded by the U.S. federal government. For example, the fittings and components in public buildings may be more expensive. Quality and workmanship specifications may be higher. In general, the fact that public owners are under different economic and political pressures compared to private owners may lead to higher costs associated with public buildings, independent of prevailing wage regulations. Unfortunately, the data used by Fraundorf *et al.* do not allow for the kind of distinctions necessary to separate other influences from the effect of the prevailing wage law.

Subsequent studies that have relied on regression analysis to measure the cost impact of prevailing wage laws have taken advantage of distinctions in more recent data to overcome the limitation faced by Fraundorf *et al.* For example, Bilginsoy and Philips (2000) conduct a before and after test of the impact of the SDFW on the total construction costs of a fairly homogenous sample, elementary and secondary public schools. They fail to find a statistically significant difference in the total construction cost of public schools built after the introduction of the SDFW. In addition, Azari-Rad, Philips and Prus (2003) estimate the impact of state level, or 'little Davis-Bacon Acts', on school total construction costs. These authors observe a significant construction cost differential between private and public schools, holding state prevailing wage laws constant. However, they fail to find a statistically significant difference in public school construction costs between states with and without little Davis-Bacon Acts.

Both of these studies avoid the problem encountered by Fraundorf *et al.* of confusing public/private costs differentials with the costs of fair wage laws. However, these recent studies are not without limitations. For example, Bilginsoy and Philips do not fully control for fluctuations in the state of the industry that may affect construction costs before and after the introduction of the SDFW. In an early estimate of the cost impact of this fair wage law, Casselton (1992) reports that construction projects came in under budget during depressed conditions in the spring of 1992. Consequently, it was difficult for Casselton to assess the impact of the SDFW by comparing costs before and after March of 1992 because of changing industry conditions at the time the law became effective. Similarly, changes in the state of the industry may also affect the school construction cost differential reported by Bilginsoy and Philips. In addition, the empirical results obtained by Bilginsoy and Philips rely on the accuracy of the price index used to measure changes in construction costs over the period. Just as substitution behavior on the part of consumers creates a difference between measured inflation and the actual price increases that households experience, the non-residential construction price index used by Bilginsoy and Philips may overstate the actual price increases experienced by builders. For example, between 1989 and 1995 construction cost in British Columbia may have increased because of the combined effect of the general increase in prices and the wage requirements of the SDFW. However, if inflation measured by the price index overstates experienced cost increases, the price index may be picking up, and consequently masking, some of the cost effect of the SDFW. If this is the case, the SDFW cost estimate from Bilginsoy and Philips is too low.

On the other hand, Azari-Rad, Philips and Prus rely on differences within and between states with and without prevailing wage legislation using a fixed effects model. State dummy variables are introduced to control for differences in state construction costs while year dummies are used to control for business cycle variations (in one model state unemployment rates replace year dummies for this purpose). Some may not find these controls satisfactory and prefer to focus strictly on jurisdictions that have changed their prevailing wage regulations.

Our data allow us to improve on the methods employed by previous researchers. Using construction data for British Columbia before the introduction of the SDFW, we are able to determine if a cost differential between government and private construction projects exists in the absence of the fair wage policy. We then determine if the SDFW altered the cost differential between government and private construction projects by examining data after the introduction of the SDFW. Since our cost estimate is based on the change in the public-private cost differential, it avoids the problem encountered by Fraundorf *et al.* Our data also allow us to avoid the kinds of problems associated with the before and after test used by Bilginsoy and Philips. Since we focus on changes in the cost differential between public and private projects, our results are not influenced by changes in the state of the industry, as long as conditions are the same for private and public construction activity. Since contractors are qualified and licensed to build public or private versions of the types of buildings included in our sample, there is no barrier that would distort a public-private cost differential if one or both of the sectors were depressed. For example, if the private segment of hospital construction was depressed, the number of projects and the level of bids would fall. Competition for

Table 5.1   Private and public average real construction costs per square foot before and after SDFW

Before SDFW	After SDFW
Private Square Foot Cost	Private Square Foot Cost
$96.24 (CAN)	$97.10
(56.30)	(57.70)
N=173	N=201
Public Per Square Foot Cost	Public Per Square Foot Cost
$142.97	$157.90
(60.40)	(88.58)
N=136	N=213

Note: Standard deviations in parentheses.

public hospital construction would increase with the bid price falling in a manner that would tend to preserve the cost difference between public and private hospital construction. Since private and public hospital construction costs are adjusted by the same price index, the results are free from the kind of deviations between measured and experienced inflation that may affect the results reported by Bilginsoy and Philips. In addition, by also taking advantage of measuring the impact of a policy change within a province, we avoid the difficulties associated with the cross sectional comparisons used by Azari-Rad *et al.*

The construction cost data reported in Table 5.1 can be used to illustrate the approaches used by Fraundorf *et al.* and by Bilginsoy and Philips, as well as our suggested method. In Table 5.1 we report the number of public and private construction projects built in British Columbia before and after the introduction of the SDFW. Our overall sample of 723 projects consists of 173 private and 136 public projects built prior to the SDFW (from 1989 to 1992). Between March of 1992 and the end of 1995, there were 201 private projects and 213 public projects. All of the public projects started after 1992 were covered by the SDFW. Table 5.1 also reports real square foot construction costs in British Columbia before and after the introduction of the SDFW for public and private construction.

The approach used by Fraundorf *et al.* estimates the cost impact of wage legislation by comparing private and public construction costs during the period when the prevailing wage law is in effect. Applying this method to the cost data for British Columbia reported in Table 5.1 indicates that after the SDFW, the difference between public and private real square foot costs is $60.80 ($157.90-$97.10), or 63 percent. These figures would provide an accurate estimate of the cost of the SDFW if the wage requirements of this law were the sole determinant of the cost differential between private and public construction. However, the data for the period before the SDFW indicates a real square foot cost difference between public and private construction of $46.73 ($142.97-$96.24), or 48.6 percent, in the absence of the fair wage law. This finding suggests that the method used in the Fraundorf *et al.* study provides an estimate of a prevailing wage law that is too high because factors other than the wage law contribute to the cost differential between public and private construction.

The study by Bilginsoy and Philips measures the impact of the SDFW by comparing public construction costs before and after March of 1992. This method, applied to the data reported in Table 5.1, suggests that real public construction costs increased from $142.97 to $157.90, or 10.4 percent per square foot, with the introduction of the SDFW. However, as stated above, construction costs after 1992 may have been influenced by the SDFW and by changes in the state of the industry. If Casselton's observation is correct, that construction projects came in under bid in a depressed construction industry after 1992, then the SDFW cost estimate of 10.4 percent is too low. This method also relies on the price index to accurately measure the inflation experienced by contractors over the period. If inflation measured by the price index is greater than the inflation experienced by contractors, the price index may be masking a portion of the cost impact of the SDFW. This problem would also contribute to a cost estimate of the SDFW that is too low.

Finally, these data allow us to examine changes in the public-private cost differential with the introduction of the SDFW. For example, the data discussed above indicate that the difference in real square foot cost between public and private construction increased by $14.07 (from $46.73 to $60.80), or by 30 percent, with the introduction of the SDFW. With this approach we have controlled for a pre-existing public-private cost differential and, if the state of the industry is the same in both sectors, this method is free of the methodological problems encountered by the other approaches. However, while the average cost data reported in Table 5.1 can be used for illustrative purposes, they do not provide for an accurate estimate of the cost of the SDFW because they do not control for other factors, such as changes in the distribution of building types before and after the law that can affect relative square foot costs. In the following sections we describe a method of examining the effect of the SDFW on construction costs, holding many other factors that affect costs constant.

Construction Data for British Columbia, 1989 to 1995

The results of this study were derived from information obtained from Canadata, an organization that collects and disseminates data on construction projects to the industry. These are the most comprehensive data available for analyzing construction costs in British Columbia. These data provide information on construction costs at the start of the project, or bid price, for approximately 13,000 projects built between 1989 and 1995. Since the Skills Development and Fair Wage Act came into effect in March of 1992, we are able to measure the cost difference between government and private projects before and after this date. However, since the cost data are based on the bid price, not the final cost of the project, we are unable to control for differences in add-on cost submissions that low-ball bidders may use as a means of padding artificially deflated bids.

Using the bid price as a measure of total cost, Fraundorf *et al.* find a significant Davis-Bacon effect. However, these authors report less robust results when the square foot of the bid price is used as the dependent variable. Similarly, Bilginsoy and Philips fail to find a significant fair wage effect based on square meter costs. These findings suggest that the empirical effect of a prevailing wage law may be sensitive to the specification of the dependent variable. To avoid this kind of confusion concerning the effect of the SDFW on construction costs, we report results of estimates based on total and square foot bid prices.

These construction data contain information on detailed structure type, project scale, date the project started, technical characteristics of the project such as number of stories above and below ground, and heating type. In contrast to the data used by the Quantity Surveyors, the information provided by Canadata makes it possible to compare construction costs on a large number of similar projects built for the private and public sectors. These sample characteristics are essential if one is to accurately sort out the cost differences associated with the fair wage policy from cost differences associated with other factors.

To focus on the changes in the cost differential caused by the SDFW, we included only those projects funded by private companies and by the Province of British Columbia (projects funded by the Canadian government are not included). We also omitted all projects with a value less than $1.5 million (CAN) since projects under this value were not initially affected by the SDFW.[6] As a consequence of these limitations, and after removing observations with missing values; we are left with a sub sample of less than 13,000 observations.

We use two extracts from the data set described above to estimate the empirical results reported below. The first, relatively large extract (n=723) has the advantage of a large number of construction projects funded by private companies and by the Province of British Columbia. This sample is the basis for the data reported in Table 5.1 and consists of 309 private and 414 publicly funded construction projects. This large extract also allows us to control for a variety of factors, including heating and exterior wall type, which influence construction costs. We use OLS to obtain the model estimates reported below (see Tables 5.2 and 5.3). However, since approximately 25 percent of the project owners (the cross-sectional units) in this sub-sample purchased more than one construction project between 1989 and 1995, the assumption of a constant intercept and slope, particularly among this 'pooled' component of the sample, may be unreasonable.[7]

We created a second extract, consisting of only the pooled component of the sample, by deleting, from the overall sample, those project owners that purchased fewer than two construction jobs over the period. This unbalanced panel extract has 308 observations of which 44 are privately funded projects (25 were started before the SDFW and 19 started after the law). We use this panel extract to compare OLS with one and two way fixed and random effects estimates.[8] However, the specification test statistic developed by Hausman (1978) indicates that the random effects model is favored over the fixed effects model. Furthermore, the Lagrangian multiplier test statistic developed by Breush and Pagan (1980) argues in favor of OLS (with no group specific effects) over the fixed or random effects models. Regardless of the estimation technique, or sample extract employed, the results reported below consistently indicate that the SDFW did not significantly increase the cost of public construction relative to the cost of private projects.

To be able to estimate the cost differential between public and private construction requires some heterogeneity with respect to building type. While our sample contains only building types common to public and private construction, there is not a sufficiently large sample of a single building type to compare public and private costs. In this sense, our data are similar to that employed by Fraundorf *et al.* That is, the data allow for the comparison of costs across building types. As mentioned above, the advantage of the Bilginsoy and Philips study is the homogenous nature of the sample with respect to building type, public schools in their case.

However, the construction of private schools during the period of their study was too small for a significant analysis of the impact of the SDFW on the relative costs of private and public school construction. We face the same limitation with respect to sample size. Considered individually, the number of any building type is too small for the purposes of the comparative question, but collectively this heterogeneous sample, with respect to building type, provides a suitable size to allow for a comparison between public and private construction costs. Using the data in this way we can focus on how the SDFW affected relative costs and are able to improve on the before and after test employed by Bilginsoy and Philips.

Estimating the Impact of the Skills Development Fair Wage Act

The following model applies to the estimation techniques and data extracts described above:

$$\ln TC = \alpha + \beta_1 BCProject + \beta_2 SDFW + \beta_3 BCProject \times SDFW + \beta_4 X + \beta_5 Z + \mu \qquad (5.1)$$

where ln TC is the natural log of total project cost in constant 1995 dollars. The Non-Residential Building Cost Price Index, available from Statistics Canada, is used to adjust project costs.[9] BCProject is equal to one if the provincial government of British Columbia funded the project and this variable is equal to zero if the project is privately funded. SDFW is equal to one if the provincial project was started after March 1992 and covered by the Skills Development and Fair Wage Act. SDFW is equal to zero for all private projects and for those public projects started before the enforcement of the policy. BCProject $\times$ SDFW is the product of the BCProject and SDFW variables. X is a vector of building types common to both of the public and private projects included in our sample. Z is a vector of variables that also affect building costs such as square footage, number of stories above and below ground, method of heating, industry trends associated with time and whether the project was new or an addition. The X and Z vectors of independent variables are similar to those used in the Fraundorf *et al.* study that also employs the log of total costs as the dependent variable. The error term is μ which contains cross-section and time-series components.

With this specification we can examine several issues relevant to the literature addressing the effect of prevailing wage laws on total construction costs. For example, the coefficient for BCProject (β_1)

measures the cost differential between government and private projects, independent of the fair wage policy (holding SDFW constant). The prevailing wage policy may have a direct effect on costs (through SDFW), or (and) the policy may affect the public-private cost differential (measured by the interaction term, BCProject × SDFW). However, since the SDFW dummy variable has a time aspect, the coefficient for this variable may be influenced by the cost impact of the fair wage legislation and by the state of the industry after 1992. Problems associated with changes in the state of the industry can be avoided by relying on the coefficient for the interaction term (β_3) as a measure of the cost impact of the fair wage policy. This coefficient measures the change in the cost differential between public and private construction projects after the introduction of the SDFW (if SDFW and BCProject both equal one). However, given the possibility of period sensitive results, we report results from several specifications with and without measures of time. We also report, or discuss, the estimates of models with SDFW interacted with all independent variables as well as models with the log of real square foot costs and nominal total costs as dependent variables.

Empirical Results

Regression results, with the natural log of real total construction costs as the dependent variable, are reported in Table 5.2.[10] This table contains the results of three specifications that include different time and wage policy variables. Regardless of the specification used, the results for BCProject indicate that the costs of publicly funded construction projects, holding SDFW constant, are from 40 to 43 percent higher than privately funded projects in British Columbia.[11] The results for the interaction between the BCProject and SDFW dummy variables indicate that the cost differential between public and private projects is not significantly affected by the introduction of the fair wage law. Once again, this is the case regardless of the specification employed.

It is possible that the effect of the SDFW on construction costs varies with the size of the project. That is, larger, more costly projects may have greater flexibility in adjusting to the cost impact of the prevailing wage law than smaller projects. To address this possibility, we also estimated the models with the interaction of SDFW and Ln (Square Feet) as an additional explanatory variable. The value of the coefficient for this

Table 5.2 OLS regression results for total construction costs in British Columbia 1989-1995

		Dependent Variable: ln(Real total costs)		
Dummy Variable Reference Category	Variable	Spec. 1 Coefficient	Spec 2 Coefficient	Spec. 3 Coefficient
Funding:	BCProject	0.358** [43.0%]	0.338** [40.2%]	0.339** [40.4%]
Private Project		(7.47)	(6.25)	(6.00)
SDFW:	SDFW Project	---	---	0.01
Not SDFW Project				(0.13)
(Interaction)	BCProject × SDFW	0.025 [2.5%]	0.059 [6.1%]	0.057 [5.9%]
		(0.61)	(1.05)	(0.90)
Census Sub. Div.:				
Not Vancouver	Vancouver	-0.059	-0.057	-0.057
Exterior Walls:				
Reinforced	Concrete Block	0.062	0.068	0.069
Concrete	Wood Frame	-0.031	-0.032	-0.032
	Concrete	0.076	-0.079	-0.079
	Steel	0.045	0.043	0.043
Heating Type:	Electric	-0.012	-0.023	-0.023
Unheated	Gas	-0.005	-0.015	-0.015
	Steam	0.017	0.039	0.038
Building Type:	Recreation	0.273**	0.282**	0.282**
Parking Garage	Clinic	0.274**	0.273**	0.273**
	Assembly	0.298**	0.320**	0.320**
	School (K-12)	0.247**	0.253**	0.253**
	Hospital	0.343**	0.358**	0.358**
Construction Type:				
New Construction	Addition	-0.072	-0.073	-0.074
Year:	1990	---	0.038	0.0370
1989	1991	---	0.020	0.020
	1992	---	-0.061	-0.068
	1993	---	0.014	0.005
	1994	---	-0.018	-0.028
	1995	---	-0.028	-0.0037

Continued on next page

Table 5.2 OLS regression results for total construction costs in British Columbia 1989-1995 (continued)

Dependent Variable: ln(Real total costs)

Dummy Variable Reference Category	Variable	Spec. 1 Coefficient	Spec. 2 Coefficient	Spec. 3 Coefficient
Continuous Variables:	ln(Square Feet)	0.651**	0.650**	0.650**
		(20.46)	(20.34)	(20.34)
	#Stories Above	0.090**	0.091**	0.011**
	Ground	(8.58)	(8.44)	(8.41)
	# Stories Below	-0.002	-0.003	-0.003
	Ground	(-0.54)	(-0.08)	(-0.08)
Constant:		8.012**	8.027**	8.025**
		(23.6)	(22.83)	(22.77)
Adjusted R^2		70.00%	69.90%	69.90%
F		89.62	68.05	65.3
N		723	723	723

Notes: t-statistics in parentheses for selected variables, percentage impact of selected dummy variables in brackets.
** significant at 1 percent level two-tailed test
* significant at 5 percent level two-tailed test

interaction term, based on specification three, is negative (-0.011) suggesting that the cost impact of the SDFW diminishes as size increases. However, this coefficient is not statistically significant (t-value = -0.23), suggesting that the effect of the SDFW is uniform across project size. We also interacted SDFW with all of the other independent variables listed in model 1. The results from this estimate are consistent with those reported in Table 5.2.[12]

Other results reported in Table 5.2 indicate that the SDFW did not have a significant direct impact on costs (the SDFW coefficient from specification three). Construction costs are not significantly different in the Vancouver census subdivision. Nor are the different exterior walls, heating types, or additions more expensive than the reference categories. However, the building types common to private and public construction are significantly more expensive than the reference category. Though, not statistically significant, signs of the coefficients for the year dummy variables (from specifications two and three) are generally consistent with a depressed industry after the introduction of the SDFW in March of 1992.

Building size, measured by square feet and the number of stories above ground, significantly affect costs. Yet, adding stories below ground does not have the same effect. The cost elasticity with respect to project square footage (coefficient for ln Square Feet) is similar to that reported by Fraundorf *et al.* suggesting economies of scale with respect to total costs.

As mentioned above, Fraundorf *et al.* report a statistically significant public cost effect based on total construction costs. However, their results are less robust when square foot costs are the dependent variable. To determine if the estimates from British Columbia are sensitive to the measure of construction costs employed, we also report results (in Table 5.3) from a model with the log of real square foot costs as the dependent variable. Results reported in Table 5.3 are consistent with those reported in Table 5.2 indicating a higher cost for public projects (ranging from 26 to 29 percent, based on the log of real square foot costs).[13] But, there is no significant increase in the public-private cost differential after the introduction of the prevailing wage law (indicated by the t-values of the coefficients for the interaction between BCProject and SDFW). To be consistent with the square foot and square meter cost specifications used by Fraundorf *et al.*, and Bilginsoy and Philips, we also omit measures of project size from the results reported in Table 5.3. However, we also estimated the log of square foot costs with ln (Square Feet) as an independent variable. The coefficient for ln(Square Feet), based on specification three, is -0.349 indicating an inelastic relationship (t-value = -10.89). The negative coefficient verifies economies of scale with respect to per foot costs. Including ln(Square Feet) improves the fit of this estimate (R^2 = 0.48), but did not significantly alter the results with respect to BCProject and BCProject × SDFW. The remainder of the results reported in Table 5.3 are similar to those from the estimate of real total cost with respect to significance levels for heating and building types and time variables. However, with respect to square foot costs, construction in Vancouver and additions are significantly more expensive. In addition, concrete walls (from specifications one, two and three) and concrete block walls (from specifications two and three) have significantly higher square foot costs.

It is possible that the lack of a significant increase in the costs of public projects after the introduction of the SDFW is an artifact of price deflator used in the transformation to real costs. To avoid potential problems associated with the use of the price index, we also estimated the model using the log of nominal construction costs as the dependent variable. The results from the estimation of nominal construction costs are

Table 5.3 OLS regression results for total construction costs in British Columbia 1989-1995

Dummy Variable Reference Category	Variable	Dependent Variable: ln(Real total costs per square foot)		
		Spec. 1 Coefficient	Spec. 2 Coefficient	Spec. 3 Coefficient
Funding:	BCProject	0.255**	0.237**	0.248**
		[29%]	[26.7%]	[28.1%]
Private Project		(4.97)	(3.97)	(3.92)
SDFW:	SDFW Project	---	---	0.076
Not SDFW Project				(0.78)
(Interaction)	BCProject × SDFW	0.029	0.048	0.028
		[2.9%]	[4.9%]	[2.8%]
		(0.62)	(0.72)	(0.38)
Census Sub.Div.:				
Not Vancouver	Vancouver	-0.132**	-0.129**	-0.129**
Exterior Walls:				
Reinforced	Concrete Block	0.114	0.126*	0.128**
Concrete	Wood Frame	0.053	-0.049	-0.049
	Concrete	-0.215**	-0.219**	-0.218**
	Steel	0.048	0.043	0.0042
Heating Type:	Electric	0.067	-0.005	-0.01
Unheated	Gas	0.064	0.058	-0.061
	Steam	-0.071	0.063	-0.072
Building Type:	Recreation	0.273**	0.276**	0.276**
Parking Garage	Clinic	0.298**	0.295**	0.294**
	Assembly	0.394**	0.400**	0.400**
	School (K-12)	0.331**	0.337**	0.337**
	Hospital	0.314**	0.326**	0.328**
Construction Type:				
New Construction	Addition	0.125**	0.126**	-0.124**
Year:	1990	---	0.084	0.082
1989	1991	---	0.083	0.080
	1992	---	0.028	-0.024
	1993	---	0.088	0.021
	1994	---	0.057	-0.001
	1995	---	0.017	-0.05

Continued on next page

Table 5.3 OLS regression results for total construction costs in British Columbia 1989-1995 (continued)

Continuous Variables:				
# Stories Above	Ground	0.051**	0.052**	0.052**
		(5.10)	(5.15)	(5.15)
#Stories Below	Ground	0.002	-0.001	-0.001
		(-0.04)	(-0.001)	(-0.001)
Constant:		4.25**	4.200**	4.191**
		(36.03)	(30.86)	(30.96)
Adjusted R^2		32.30%	31.90%	31.90%
F		20.09	15.12	14.53
N		723	723	723

Notes: t-statistics in parentheses for selected variables, percentage impact of selected dummy variables in brackets.
** significant at 1 percent level two-tailed test
* significant at 5 percent level two-tailed test

consistent with those reported in Tables 5.2 and 5.3 indicating the SDFW did not increase the relative costs of public construction. For example, results based on specification three, with total nominal construction costs as the dependent variable, indicate a coefficient for the interaction term (BCProject × SDFW) equal to 0.053 (t-value = 0.84) and a parameter estimate for the BCProject equal to 0.341 (t-value = 6.02). These coefficients and significant levels are comparable to those reported for the same specification in Table 5.2.[14]

We used the panel extract to estimate one way (group only) and two way (group and time) fixed and random effects models. In the one way estimates the panel groups are defined as the cross-sectional units, or, the project owners in our case. That is, the one way specification is similar to specification one from Tables 5.2 and 5.3, but estimated for groups of project owners. The two way estimates include the cross-sectional units as well as time variables. The two way estimates are similar to specifications two and three from Tables 5.2 and 5.3, but are estimated for groups of project owners. While not presented below, the results from the two way estimates are consistent with the one way results reported in Tables 5.4 and 5.5. We report random effects and OLS estimates below because the Hausman specification test statistic indicates that the one way random effects model is preferred to the one way fixed effects estimate.[15] Furthermore, the Lagrangian multiplier test developed by Breush and Pagan (1980) indicates that OLS is preferred to either one way effects

Table 5.4 OLS and REM regression results for total construction costs in British Columbia. Panel data extract 1989-1995

Dummy Variable	Independent	OLS	REM (One Way)
		Dependent Variable: ln(Real total costs)	
Reference Category	Variable	Estimate	Estimate
Funding:	BCProject	0.329**	0.312**
		[39.0 %]	[36.6 %]
Private Project		(3.66)	(2.92)
Interaction	BCProject × SDFW	0.016	0.01
		[1.6 %]	[1.0 %]
		(0.34)	(0.19)
Census Sub.Div.:			
Not Vancouver	Vancouver	-0.035	-0.016
Building Type:	Clinic	0.123	0.097
Assembly	School (K-12)	0.280**	0.293**
	Hospital	0.428*	0.453
Construction Type:			
New Construction	Addition	-0.039	-0.034
Continuous Variables:	ln(Square Feet)	0.692**	0.747**
		(13.72)	(19.76)
	# Stories Above	0.149**	0.150**
	Ground	(4.20)	(4.81)
	# Stories Below	-0.027	-0.069
	Ground	(-0.47)	(-0.98)
Constant		7.461**	6.888**
		(15.25)	(17.56)
N		308	308
		$R^2 = 0.73$	LM Stat. = 0.46
		F = 83.71	Hausman Stat. = 0.05

Notes: t-statistics in parentheses for selected variables, percentage impact of selected dummy variables in brackets.
** significant at 1 percent level two-tailed test
* significant at 5 percent level two-tailed test

models, suggesting that there is no significant group effect in our sample.[16] Still, the random effects estimates reported below have the advantage of increased parameter efficiency in a pooled sample. As mentioned above, the one way random effects and OLS estimates reported in Tables 5.4 and 5.5 are based on a model similar to specification one from Tables 5.2 and 5.3 (including measures of project ownership, BCProject, and of the effect of the SDFW on the private-public cost differential, BCProject × SDFW). This smaller sample does not include parking garages and recreation buildings among the building types. Also, due to the high number of missing values, we are not able to control for exterior wall types.[17] Despite the differences in sample composition, model specification and estimation technique, the results reported with respect to total costs and total costs per square foot yield comparable conclusions to those discussed above. For example, the coefficients for the focus variables BCProject and BCProject × SDFW with respect to OLS and random effects estimates of total cost, reported in Table 5.4, are lower than comparable OLS coefficients reported in Table 5.2. Results reported in Table 5.4 indicate that provincial projects are from 36.6 percent (according to random effects) to 39 percent (based on OLS) higher than privately funded projects. However, the t-values of the coefficients for the interaction term (BCProject × SDFW) from either model reported in Table 5.4 fail to indicate that the fair wage policy significantly increased relative costs. Other results reported in Table 5.4 such as those related to location (Vancouver), additions, project size (ln Square Feet) and stories below and above ground, are consistent with those reported in Table 5.2. Since there are no parking garages or recreation buildings in the panel extract, the new reference category is assembly buildings. Schools and hospitals (OLS only) are significantly more expensive than assembly buildings. The random effects model estimates indicate that only schools are more expensive than the reference category.

The results from the panel-based estimate of real square foot costs are reported in Table 5.5. The coefficients measuring the additional expense of public projects (BCProject) from OLS and random effects models are slightly higher than the estimates reported in Table 5.3. The remarkable difference between the results reported in the two tables is the negative sign of the coefficients for the interaction term (BCProject × SDFW) reported in Table 5.5. This negative coefficient is consistent with the view (espoused by many proponents of prevailing wage laws) that these laws motivate management to employ more productive construction labor to the extent that the substitution effect is associated with lower costs. This hypothesis is supported only by the coefficients for the estimate of real

Table 5.5 OLS and REM regression results for total construction costs in British Columbia. Panel data extract 1989-1995

Dependent Variable: ln (Real total costs per square foot)

Dummy Variable	Independent	OLS	REM (One Way)
Reference Category	Variable	Estimate	Estimate
Funding:	BCProject	0.283**	0.312**
		[32.7 %]	[36.6 %]
Private Project		(2.71)	(2.59)
Interaction	BCProject × SDFW	-0.076	-0.087
		[-7.3 %]	-0.087
		(-1.56)	(-1.49)
Census Sub.Div.:			
Not Vancouver	Vancouver	-0.092	-0.065
Building Type:	Clinic	0.074	0.047
Assembly	School (K-12)	0.307**	0.292**
	Hospital	0.385*	0.277
Construction Type:			
New Construction	Addition	0.171**	0.116*
Continuous Variables:	# Stories Above	0.051	0.064*
	Ground	(1.34)	(2.04)
	# Stories Below	0.019	-0.057
	Ground	(0.25)	(-0.73)
Constant:		4.431**	4.407**
		(33.34)	(32.61)
N		308	308
		R^2 = 0.20	LM Stat. = 1.54
		F = 9.33	Hausman Stat. = 6.64

Notes: t-statistics in parentheses for selected variables, percentage impact of selected dummy variables in brackets.
** significant at 1 percent level two-tailed test
* significant at 5 percent level two-tailed test

square foot costs and implies that the t-test for the coefficient of the interaction term is two-tailed. However, the coefficients for the interaction terms from the OLS or random effects models fail to achieve conventional levels of significance. Other results reported in Table 5.5 differ from those reported in Table 5.3. Based on the panel extract, construction in the

Vancouver Census subdivision and stories above ground (for OLS) are not significantly related to costs (except for stories above ground in the random effects estimate). With the new reference category for building type, schools (for OLS and random effects) and hospitals (OLS only) are significantly more expensive than assembly buildings.

While not reported here, one way fixed effects estimates indicate that the interaction of BCProject and SDFW are not significantly related to real total construction costs, or to real costs per square foot. Results from two way fixed and random effects are consistent with those discussed above. Hausman specification tests indicated that two way random effects is preferred to two way fixed effects. Regardless, the results from either approach, using different specifications, failed to find a significant interaction between BCProject and SDFW, based on a two-tailed test.[18]

The Lagrange multiplier statistics reported in Tables 5.4 and 5.5 can be used in a test of the one way effects models against a homoskedastic, nonautocorrelated classic regression model with no group specific effects. Large values of the Lagrange multiplier argue in favor of one of the one way effects models over OLS. However, the computed Lagrangian multiplier statistics from either the real total, or real square foot cost estimates (see LM Stat. in Tables 5.4 and 5.5) fail to achieve conventional levels of significance (the critical Chi-square test statistic is 3.84 at the 5 percent level with one degree of freedom). These results indicate an absence of significant group effects in our sample. Regardless of the estimation technique or sample employed, our results fail to find a significant cost impact associated with the SWFD.

Conclusion

The study by Fraundorf *et al.* was the first to use regression analysis to estimate the cost impact of fair wage policies on construction costs. As a consequence, this study has received considerable attention in the debate regarding the cost of fair wage policies. However, the conclusions of the Fraundorf *et al.* study are based on a comparison of public-private construction costs, rather than a direct test of the impact of these policies. Ours is the third in a series of recent studies that have conducted more direct tests of the cost impact of fair and prevailing wage laws. These more recent studies have employed different data sets and statistical tests to estimate the cost of these polices in Canada and the U.S. Despite these differences, these studies all share the common finding that fair and prevailing wage laws are not associated with higher construction costs.

Globerman, Stanbury and Vertinsky (1993) argue that the SDFW raised the cost of public construction and, consequently, reduced the total amount of public construction undertaken. Our results suggest that the policy did not affect costs in such a way as to reduce the number of projects. However, the policy did increase the wage rates paid on provincial projects. Our data do not allow us to answer the question of why higher wage rates are not associated with higher total costs. The wage effects of the SDFW may have been substituted away as more productive construction labor was employed. Or, the wage increase may have been absorbed by a margin enjoyed by non-union contractors. Such a margin is implied in the Labour Minister's announcement of the introduction of the SDFW Act when he observed that, ' ... in terms of costs to government there is not much difference between union and non-union companies. Non-union companies bid within a few percent of the union companies but pay their workers in the neighborhood of 20 to 30 percent less'.[19] The introduction of the SDFW may have erased this two-tier system and non-union builders of public projects may have seen their labor costs rise, and their margin erode, with the new wage requirements. But, competition would prevent the higher labor costs from being reflected in the bids of non-union contractors. The degree that the wage costs of the SDFW were substituted away, or absorbed, is a question for future research.

Notes

[1] The authors would like to thank Hamid Azari-Rad, Kathleen Burke, Sharmila Choudhury, Lisi Krall, Dennis Maki, Paul Miller, Gigi Peterson, Peter Philips and Gerald Surette for insightful comments. Thanks also to Vasanthi Peter for valuable research assistance. We are responsible for remaining errors. We would also like to acknowledge the financial support of the Construction Labour Relations Association of British Columbia.

[2] The SDFW established the Schedule for Fair Wage Minimum Hourly Rates for specific construction occupations. The initial Schedule covered the period from 30 March 1992 to 19 August 1993 where the hourly wage rate under the Fair Wage Schedule was typically 88 percent, but ranged from 82 to 94 percent, of the corresponding building trade union rate as of 1 May 1992. Changes to the SDFW with respect to the types of projects covered were made in August 1993, but the fair wage schedule described above was not revised and remained unchanged over the period of this study. The Skills Development and Fair Wage Repeal Act was passed on 26 September 2001

[3] The benefits of, and motivation for, the SDFW are based on comments made by Moe Sihota, Minister of Labour, British Columbia, at the time of the

introduction of the policy (see Ministry of Labour and Consumer Services News Release, 1992).

4 The Davis-Bacon Act provides for workers on federally subsidized construction projects to be paid the 'prevailing wage' which is determined by the Department of Labor. For more detail on this act see Allen (1983) and Thieblot (1975).

5 Also, the 1992 Census of Construction indicates that labor costs as a proportion of total cost in 1992 were 26 percent.

6 Initially, the SDFW wage standards applied to provincial building construction contracts of $1.5 million or more. In August the threshold was lowered to $250,000 or more. For consistency, and to avoid having the changing threshold drive the empirical results, we include only those contracts over $1.5 million before and after the SDFW. Based on an overall Canadata sample of 13,114 projects from 1989 to 1995, the threshold of $1.5 million (CAN) eliminates 81.3 percent of the sample. The remaining sample of 2448 observations (18.7 percent) has a mean contract value of $5.81 million.

7 Many private owners purchased only one project between 1989 and 1995. However, others such as school districts purchased a project in each year over the period.

8 See Kmenta (1986, pp. 616 to 635) for a discussion of the estimation techniques appropriate for pooled data.

9 This price index measures contractor's selling price changes of non-residential construction (commercial, industrial and institutional). The index excludes land costs and real estate fees, but includes equipment, material and labor costs, overhead, profits, federal and provincial taxes. The labor cost measures included in this price index are based on changes in the union wage scale. As a consequence, the price index will not control for the legislative wage changes that affected the costs of non-union contractors. Instead, this effect will be captured by the variables in the model. The index is available for seven Canadian cities. We use the index for Vancouver. For more details see Statistics Canada.

10 Kmenta (1986) suggests a cross-sectionally heteroskedastic and time wise autoregressive model as a method for combining the assumptions regarding the regression disturbances from estimates based on pooled data (see page 618). However, a balanced panel (containing the same number of observations for each individual) is required for the estimation of Kmenta's model. Since these results are not based on panel data, we conduct separate tests for heteroskedasticity and autocorrelation. For example, the results reported in Table 5.2 have been corrected for heteroskedasticity using the technique developed by White (1978) and Breusch and Pagan (1979) (the Breusch-Pagan Chi-squared are 99.4, 108.5 and 108.6 for specifications 1, 2 and 3, respectively). We also use the Ljung-Box Q-Statistic to test for different orders of autocorrelation. For example, based on specification one, the Q-statistics for preselected orders of autocorrelation (in parentheses) are: Q(1) = 0.035 (significant at the 0.850 level), or Q(2) = 0.263 (significant at the 0.877 level). We tested up to Q(12) = 1.909

(significant at the 0.999 level) and failed to find evidence of significant autocorrelation within the time-series aspect of our data.

[11] According to Kennedy (1981) the correct interpretation of the percentage change for a coefficient for a dummy variable in a semi-log estimate is given by the transformation: ($e^{\beta i}$ -1).

[12] The coefficients of the interaction of SDFW with all of the independent variables from Specification 1 are statistically insignificant, with the exception of concrete block exterior walls. This wall type was significantly more costly after the SDFW (interaction coefficient value = 0.493, t-value = 3.23). The results from the complete interaction model are not different from those reported in Table 5.2. BCProject is positive and statistically significant while the interaction between SDFW and BCProject remains statistically insignificant.

[13] The regression results reported in Table 3 have also been corrected for heteroskedasticity using the technique developed by White (1978). The Breusch-Pagan chi-squared statistics are 61.4, 74.7 and 73.6 for specifications one, two and three, respectively.

[14] The complete results from this estimate are available from the authors upon request.

[15] The computed Hausman specification test statistic is 0.05 with a critical value of 18.71 and ten degrees of freedom at the 5 percent level, based on the estimate of real total cost. For the estimate of the log of real square foot cost, the critical Chi squared value is 16.92 at the 5 percent level with nine degrees of freedom.

[16] The critical Chi squared value is 3.84 at the 5 percent level with one degree of freedom. The computed Lagrangian multiplier statistics for the total and square foot cost estimates are 0.46 and 1.54, respectively.

[17] Due to the exceptionally high number of missing values for exterior wall type, we are unable to control for these factors without further significant reductions in our sample. For example, to include controls for exterior walls would reduce the sample to 52 observations for 22 distinct groups. This significantly reduces the degrees of freedom, particularly for the fixed effects estimate. There are no parking garages and recreation buildings among the building types in the panel extract. Further, all but three of the observations have gas heating. When we delete the two observations with electric heating and the single observations with steam, we have results that are comparable to those reported in Tables 5.4 and 5.5.

[18] These results are available from the authors upon request.

[19] See Ministry of Labour and Consumer Services News Release, p. 1.

References

Azari-Rad, Hamid, Philips, Peter, and Prus, Mark J. (2003), 'State Prevailing Wage Laws and School Construction Costs', *Industrial Relations*, vol. 42(3), pp. 445-457.

Allen, Steven (1983), 'Much Ado About Davis-Bacon: A Critical Review and New Evidence', *Journal of Law and Economics*, vol. 6, pp. 707-736.

Bilginsoy, Cihan, and Philips, Peter (2000), 'Prevailing Wage Regulations and School Construction Costs: Evidence from British Columbia', *Journal of Education Finance*, vol. 24, pp. 415-432.

Bourdon, Clinton C., and Levitt, Raymond E. (1980). *Union and Open Shop Construction*, Lexington Books, Lexington, MA.

Breusch, T., and Pagan, A. (1979), 'A Simple Test for Heteroskedasticity and Random Coefficients Variation', *Econometrica*, vol. 47, pp. 1287-1294.

Breusch, T., and Pagan, A. (1980), 'The Lagrange Multiplier Test and Its Application to Model Specification in Econometrics', *Review of Economic Studies*, vol. 47, pp. 239-254.

Casselton, Valerie (1992), 'No Concrete Fair-Wage Results Yet', *Vancouver Sun*, 22 December, p. D1.

Fraundorf, Martha, Farrell, John P., and Mason, Robert (1983), 'The Effect of the Davis-Bacon Act on Construction Costs in Rural Areas', *The Review of Economics and Statistics*, vol. 66, pp. 142-146.

Globerman, Steven, Stanbury, W.T., and Vertinsky, Ilan B. (1993), 'Analysis of Fair Wage Policies: British Columbia and Other Jurisdictions', Unpublished.

Goldfarb, Robert S., and Morrall, John F. (1981), 'The Davis-Bacon Act: An Appraisal of Recent Studies', *Industrial and Labor Relations Review*, vol. 34, pp. 191-206.

Goldfarb, John, and Morrall, John F. (1978), 'The Cost Implications of Changing Davis-Bacon Administration', *Policy Analysis* vol. 4, pp. 439-453.

Gould, John P. (1971), *Davis-Bacon Act: The Economics of Prevailing Wage Laws*, American Enterprise Institute for Public Policy Research, Washington, D.C.

Gould, John P., and Cittlingmayer, George (1980), 'The economics of the Davis-Bacon Act: An Analysis of Prevailing-Wage Laws', *American Enterprise Institute Studies in Economic Policy*, No. 278, American Enterprise Institute for Public Policy Research, Washington, D.C.

Gujarati, D.N. (1967), 'The Economics of the Davis-Bacon Act', *Journal of Business*, vol. 40, pp. 303-316.

Hausman, J. (1978), 'Specification Tests in Econometrics', *Econometrica*, vol. 46, pp. 1251-1271.

Keller, Edward C., and Hartman, William T. (2001), 'Prevailing Wage Rates: the Effects on School Construction Costs, Levels of Taxation, and State Reimbursements', *Journal of Education Finance*, vol. 27, pp. 713-728.

Kennedy, Peter (1981), 'Estimation with Correctly Interpreted Dummy Variables in Semilogarithmic Equations', *American Economic Review*, vol. 71(4), p. 801.

Kmenta, Jan (1986), *Elements of Econometrics*, Macmillan, New York, NY.

Ljung, G.M., and Box, G.E.P. (1978), 'On a Measure of Lack of Fit in Time Series Models', *Biometrika*, vol. 65, pp. 297-303.

Ministry of Labour and Consumer Services News Release (1992), 'Government Announces Fair Wage and Skill Development Policy', Province of British Columbia, 30 March.

Quantity Surveyors Society of British Columbia (1993), 'Analysis of the Impact on Construction Costs of British Columbia's Fair Wage and Skills Development Policy', Unpublished manuscript August.

Statistics Canada, *Construction Price Index*, Price Division, First Quarter, 1993 and Third Quarter, 1995.

Thieblot, Armond J. (1986), *Prevailing Wage Legislation: The Davis Bacon Act, State 'Little Davis-Bacon' Acts, The Walsh-Healey Act, and The Service Contract Act*, Industrial Research Unit, The Wharton School, University of Pennsylvania, Philadelphia, PA.

Thieblot, Armond J. (1975), *The Davis Bacon Act*, Industrial Research Unit, Report No. 10, Wharton School, University of Pennsylvania, Philadelphia, PA.

U.S. Government Accounting Office (1979), *The Davis-Bacon Act Should Be Repealed*, Government Printing Office, Washington, D.C.

U.S. Government Accounting Office (1981), *Modifying the Davis-Bacon Act: Implications for the Labor Market and the Federal Budget*, Government Printing Office, Washington, D.C.

White, H. (1978), 'A Heteroskedasticity Consistent Covariance Matrix and a Direct Test for Heteroskedasticity', *Econometrica*, vol. 46, pp. 817-838.

Chapter 6

Wage Regulation and Training: The Impact of State Prevailing Wage Laws on Apprenticeship

Cihan Bilginsoy[1]

Introduction

Prevailing wage laws require contractors to pay workers the prevailing wage in state or federal projects in order to prevent wage-based competition in the bidding for contracts. Currently, the prevailing wage in a trade is defined roughly as the wage received by 50 percent of workers in the local market. The prevailing wage laws have been a controversial topic. Critics see it as an intervention that distorts the labor market, rewards union contractors at the expense of open-shop contractors, and inflates government outlays on construction projects. Supporters, on the other hand, argue that prevailing wage laws help create and maintain a more productive and efficient labor force—a benefit that, ultimately, offsets any drawbacks. In this chapter, I contribute to policy debates by addressing a topic that has attracted limited attention in these debates: apprenticeship training. Construction workers learn their craft through a variety of methods ranging from informal 'catch-as-catch-can' training on the job to highly structured formal apprenticeships that combine on-the-job practical training with in-class theoretical instruction. The latter aims to turn out workers that have all-around knowledge of a particular craft, and it has been the traditional port of entry into the trades. It is critical to evaluate whether the regulatory environment facilitates or impedes apprenticeship programs because dividends of training and skill acquisition are expected to accrue both to individual workers in terms of higher life-time earnings, and the society, which would reap the benefits of higher productivity.

This chapter is a statistical inquiry into the variations in recruitment, retention, and the ethnic/racial composition in apprenticeship programs across states with and without the prevailing wage law. The prevailing wage law may affect the recruitment and retention of apprentices through several channels. First, contractors are permitted to pay apprentices in registered programs less than the prevailing wage, creating an incentive to hire apprentices where substitution for skilled workers is feasible. Thus, the relative share of apprentices in the labor force is expected to be higher in the prevailing wage law states. Secondly, and more importantly, the prevailing wage law may affect apprenticeship programs via its effect on trade unions whose participation in apprenticeship training is extensive. If the weakening of the prevailing wage law adversely affects union strength, it could also reduce the volume of training, unless the open-shop sector can make up for the emerging gap by expanding its own training programs.

The issue of ethnic/racial composition is of special interest because the most passionate criticism of prevailing wage laws has been that it is a Jim Crow law. According to this argument, the original motivation of the law was to inhibit wage competition among workers by excluding the Southern black workers from the unionized Northern labor market. It is still claimed that the removal of the law would enhance the participation of minority groups in the trades (Bernstein, 1993). While numerous studies focused on the relationship between prevailing wage laws and the demographic structure of the construction labor market, none of these addressed the issue at the stage of training.

This chapter starts with background information on apprenticeship programs in the U.S. construction industry, and a description of the data and methodology. Next, the empirical analyses of relationship between prevailing wage laws and the recruitment rate of apprentices, completion and cancellation rates, and the share of minorities in apprenticeship are presented in three consecutive sections. The concluding section summarizes major findings.

Apprenticeship Programs in Construction Sector

The importance of apprenticeship in the construction industry derives from the particular structure of this sector (Mills, 1972; Bourdon and Levitt, 1980). Construction trades are craft based. Workers are required to be skilled and flexible enough to apply their trades to individual projects that differ from one job site to another. In comparison with manufacturing, construction work is less repetitive, requires more self-planning and self-supervision. Thus, provisioning of training in the fundamentals of the trade as well as specialized skills is critical. The bond between employer and employee in construction is also looser than what is observed in other industries. Work is intrinsically temporary. As old projects are completed and new ones start, workers move between job sites and possibly are hired by different contractors. Formal apprenticeship training is a process whereby basic and specialized skills are imparted to new generations of workers. It culminates in certification of the worker as a qualified journey worker, and sustains a relatively homogenously skilled labor force that reduces information and search costs in an industry characterized by constant flow of workers among employers and projects.

In the U.S., the Bureau of Apprenticeship and Training (BAT) or federally approved State Apprenticeship Councils (SACs) lay out the basic standards of apprenticeship programs and register programs whose sponsors agree to follow these guidelines. Apprentices enrolled in these programs are certified as journey-workers after the successful completion of a pre-determined number of hours of on-the-job training (OJT) and related theoretical in-class training (RTI).[2] During training, they receive apprenticeship wages, which start usually at 50 percent of the journey worker wage and rise gradually as the worker progresses. Thus, the cost of training is partially paid by workers by accepting low wages. The bulk of the cost is the responsibility of the sponsor. Apprenticeship programs are sponsored either unilaterally by employers (singly or as a group) in the open-shop sector of the construction industry, or jointly by unions and signatory contractors under the aegis of the collective bargaining agreement in the organized sector (henceforth, non-joint and joint programs, respectively). Within the general standards set by the BAT or SACs, sponsors determine the content of the apprenticeship program and entry requirements, select apprentices among applicants, and monitor their progress. In joint programs, joint apprenticeship committees, formed by equal numbers of representatives from trade unions and employers, administer the program. The program is financed by fees contractors pay per hour of labor hired. The level of the training fee is determined by the collective bargaining agreement. In non-joint multi-employer programs, an employer association usually administers training, and financing comes out of the pool of funds to which participating contractors contribute.

From the perspective of the individual contractor, access to a pool of reliable well-trained labor force is critical. The familiar debate in economics is whether markets by themselves are able to provide incentives for adequate provisioning of training. The problem faced by the employer is that the expected return to investment in training of a worker is very low, even negative, if competing firms can recruit the trained worker. Mobility of workers and the intrinsic transferability of skills in construction industry imply that individual contractors would not be highly motivated to establish apprenticeship programs. In this context, the motivation for the multiple-employer programs is, presumably, to set up an institutional framework that creates incentives for supplying training by transforming general skills into specific skills. While skills supplied are general from the perspective of a single contractor, they are specific to an occupation in the local labor market. In a multiple employer program, a firm does not invest in one specific worker, who could be stolen by a competitor, but in a pool of skilled workers to which it has ready access. Put differently, contractors supplying training as a group acquire some monopsonistic power and receive a share of the returns to training. This structure reduces the likelihood of market failure in training, although it is not watertight because the control over the local labor market is not absolute.

The tradition of multiple-employer training goes deep in U.S. labor history and is a hallmark of the union-management joint programs. While it is a relatively new phenomenon among the open-shop contractors, multiple employer programs account for more than two-thirds of all apprentices registered in non-joint programs as well. Single-employer programs in the non-union sector are either in very large programs, which apparently are organized either by large contractors, or by very small contractors often admitting no more than a single new apprentice once in several years. Presumably, both kinds exercise some monopsonistic power, the former through its larger size and internal promotion mechanisms, and the latter through an informal contract between the supplier of training and the employee.

Methodology and Data

This chapter analyzes the relationship between wage regulation and apprenticeship training by estimating the effects of the prevailing wage law on the level of registrations across states, the likelihood of completion and cancellation, and the probability that an apprentice belongs to a racial/ethnic minority group. The source of the apprenticeship data is the Apprenticeship Information Management Systems (AIMS) compiled by the

BAT, which keeps track of apprentices from the time they enter training through the date of exit, via either completion or cancellation of apprenticeship. Thus, the analysis is based on the 'flow' of new workers entering the apprenticeship programs, not the 'stock' of the total number apprentices enrolled. The available data only cover apprentices who started training between 1989 and 1995. Fourteen states and D.C., which do not fully participate in the BAT/AIMS, are excluded from the analysis.[3] While apprenticeship programs are established in over a hundred occupations in the construction sector, the overwhelming majority of enrollments are in a handful of trades. For this study, I selected five occupations: carpentry, electrical, pipe (plumber and pipefitter), painting, and structural steel trades, totaling 126,702 new apprentices. The choice of trades is based on two criteria. First, these are large occupations, jointly accounting for almost 70 percent of all recorded apprenticeship registrations in construction industry programs. Secondly, matching data on output levels for the corresponding specialty contractors are available for these trades.

Variations in the state regulations are measured in two alternative ways. First, I distinguish between the states with and without prevailing wage laws over the 1989-1995 period. The second method goes beyond this dichotomy and allows for variations in the strength of the prevailing wage law. Here, I adopt Thieblot's classification of weak, average and strong law states (Thieblot, 1995).[4]

The first column of Table 6.1 reports the distribution of apprentices across the prevailing wage law regimes. According to these figures, the majority of enrollments was in the states with prevailing wage laws (72 percent), and within the prevailing wage law states, in the strong law states (35 percent). The second column of Table 6.1 underscores the significance of union participation in apprenticeship. About two-thirds of the apprentices were enrolled in the joint programs. While joint programs apprentices constituted the majority in each state group, the share of joint programs varied with the regulatory regime. As prevailing wage laws strengthened, the share of joint program registrations rose.

Supply of Apprenticeship Training

This section investigates how the number of enrollments varies with the state prevailing wage law regimes. Controlling for other factors,

Table 6.1 Distribution of apprentices by the prevailing wage law regime

	All Apprentices (percent)	Apprentices in Joint Programs (percent)
No-PWL States	28.0	56.7
PLW States	72.0	74.0
Weak PWL States	16.0	67.2
Average PWL States	21.3	66.1
Strong PWL States	34.7	82.0
All States	100.0	69.1
N	126,702	87,579

Source: Bureau of Apprenticeship and Training, Apprenticeship Information Management Systems.

contractors in the prevailing wage law (or stronger prevailing wage law) states may have an incentive to hire apprentices because registered apprentices are paid at rates below the prevailing wage in government contracts. The indirect impact through the trade union activities, however, could be more powerful. The strength of the prevailing wage law is directly correlated with the rate of unionization.[5] If the repeal or weakening of the prevailing wage law weakens trade unions and curtails their activities, then apprenticeship training through joint programs is also expected to decline unless the open shop sector raises its own training via unilateral apprenticeship programs. In one of the few studies on the question, Philips (1998) compared the registration figures over the 1973-1979 and 1987-1990 periods for a group of states and argued that apprenticeship training, on average, declined in all states but the decline in states that either repealed the prevailing wage law or never had one was twice as high as that of the states with prevailing wage law.

While the first column of Table 6.1 also suggests that enrollments are higher in the prevailing wage law states, these figures are hardly informative because they do not control for the size of the state construction industry. The latter variable is of critical importance in the training literature, both theoretically and empirically. It is commonly accepted in this literature that the demand for apprenticeship is perfectly elastic and the number of trainees is determined on the supply side by the providers of training. The main point of contention has been whether supply is determined by current production or expected future production. The first approach treats apprentices and skilled workers as substitutes and emphasizes the current production needs as the primary motive for hiring apprentices. Accordingly, apprentice enrollment is estimated as a labor demand function with current production level among the explanatory variables in empirical application. The alternative model discounts the contribution of apprentices to current production and contends that training supply is primarily an investment decision: the firm hires and trains apprentices in order to meet its future production goals. In this case, some measure of expected future output (e.g. lagged output levels, capital investment) is more appropriate than the current output in estimation. Empirical applications of both models are time-series studies that use additional explanatory variables such as the relative cost of hiring apprentices, interest rate, availability of skilled labor, and idiosyncratic policy factors (Lindley, 1975; Merrilees, 1983; Stevens, 1994).

In investigating the relationship between the number of enrollments across states and prevailing wage laws, I will also assume that the volume of training is determined on the supply side. In contrast to the aforementioned studies, however, the focus here is the local labor market regulation, not the output level. In fact, due to the lack of adequate proxies for the expected output levels, it is not possible to inquire presently into the question of whether the current or future production is more relevant in the supply decision. Furthermore, despite the availability of annual apprentice registration information by state and occupation for seven years, a panel analysis is not feasible because the output data are available for only 1992. Consequently, the training supply can be estimated only for a cross section of five trades across 36 states, yielding a total of 180 observations. Output level values were not disclosed in two cases, however, and only 178 observations were used in the following analysis.

Estimation consists of an OLS regression of the volume of training over the prevailing wage law dummies, output level of the trade, prevailing wage law-output level interactions, state unemployment rate over the period (annual average), and occupation fixed effects. The production level of the occupation is measured alternatively as the total sales and the total number of employees of the respective special trade contractors as reported in the 1992 Census of Construction Industries. The dependent variable is measured by the total registrations over the 1989-1995 period, not only the 1992 registrations. This aggregation is preferred in order to reduce the randomness in the annual numbers of registrations. By construction, then, the output variable in the following estimations is essentially a measure of the scale of the trade across states, and its purpose is not to discriminate between the current production or investment hypotheses mentioned above.

Table 6.2 Estimates of apprenticeship supply equation

Dependent Variable: ln(Apprentices registered $_{state,trade}$)

	(1)[a]	(2)[b]	(3)[a]	(4)[b]
Law state	5.65**	7.91**		
	(5.87)	(5.23)		
Weak PWL state			5.41**	6.58**
			(4.38)	(3.17)
Average PWL State			5.45**	7.45**
			(4.31)	(3.97)
Strong PWL state			6.33**	10.16*
			(4.07)	(4.48)
ln(Output level)	1.93**	2.01**	1.94**	2.00**
	(11.51)	(11.68)	(10.96)	(11.13)
ln(Output level)× Law state	-0.92**	-0.89**		
	(4.99)	(4.57)		
ln(Output level)× Weak PWL			-0.89**	-0.73**
			(3.74)	(2.76)
ln(Output level)× Average PWL			-0.84**	-0.79**
			(3.39)	(3.22)
ln(Output level)× Strong PWL			-1.04**	-1.14**
			(3.97)	(4.19)
Unemployment Rate	0.12	0.15	0.10	0.11
	(0.98)	(1.28)	(0.68)	(0.76)
Constant	-5.06**	-11.24**	-5.00**	-10.96**
	(4.53)	(7.49)	(3.59)	(6.16)
Trade dummies		Included		
Region dummies		Included		
Adjusted R^2	0.63	0.64	0.62	0.64
N		178		

Source: Bureau of Apprenticeship and Training, Apprenticeship Information Management Systems.

Notes: t-values are in parentheses. * and ** indicate statistical significance at the 5 and 1 percent levels two-tailed tests.

[a] Output level is measured by the total sales of the specialty trade.

[b] Output level is measured by the total employees of the specialty trade.

The estimated impact of prevailing wage laws on the apprenticeship enrollment is reported in Table 6.2. The 'no-law' state category is the reference point in all regressions. As reported in columns one and two, the prevailing wage law has a strong impact on the registrations, both economically and statistically, even after controlling for the size of the trade. Point estimates under alternative proxies for production levels indicate that enrollments are six and eight percent higher in the prevailing wage law states than in no-PWL states. Regressions three and four distinguish among the prevailing wage law states in terms of the strength of the law. These findings indicate that enrollments increase as the law gets stronger. The estimates, however, are quite close to each other, especially in regression three, and the hypotheses that they are equal are not rejected at the conventional levels of statistical significance. Thus, the supply of training is definitely higher in the prevailing wage law states than in the no-PWL states, but within the prevailing wage law states the effect does not vary significantly with the strength of the law.

Since both enrollment and output are in logs, coefficients of the output variable are elasticities. These estimates indicate that the regulatory environment, again, matters. The estimated elasticity of enrollment with respect to either measure of output in the no-law states is equal to two and statistically highly significant. This suggests a strong response of apprentice recruitment to an increase in output level. This is not the case in the prevailing wage law states, however. Interaction dummies in regressions one and two indicate that this responsiveness declines sharply in the prevailing wage law states, and the elasticity becomes unitary. This result carries over in regressions three and four as well. The elasticity of recruitment with respect to output declines with the strength of the state, although, as before, differences among these states are not statistically significant. Interpretation of this finding hinges on the interpretation of the output level variable and raises the interesting question of whether the motivations for hiring apprentices differ between the prevailing wage law and no-PWL states. If, for instance, the output variable is essentially a measure of the current production level, then the higher sensitivity of enrollments in the no-PWL states may be taken to mean that the current (rather than future) production needs are more prominent in the training supply decision. Given the ambiguity of the variable used, such an interpretation is presently unwarranted. Nonetheless, whether the regulatory regime affects recruitment decision is a puzzle that deserves attention.

Attrition and Retention

A historical pattern noted by many observers of apprenticeship in the U.S. is that a large number of apprentices do not complete their training. The objective of this section is to investigate whether there is any relationship between the completion and cancellation rates of apprenticeships and the regulatory environment. The BAT data report the status of each apprentice as of the beginning of November 1995 as 'completed', 'cancelled', or 'still active'. In the section, I use duration analysis to estimate hazard rates of attrition and retention as functions of the prevailing wage law, controlling for program- and individual-specific variables. The dependent variable is the duration of apprenticeship, measured as the time that has elapsed between the entry into apprenticeship and the exit, conditional on the mode of exit.

      For this analysis, I selected a subset of apprentices. First, graduation requires completion of a pre-determined number of hours of OJT (in addition to RTI). I chose only programs with the modal OJT requirement, which is 8,000 hours. The overwhelming majority of these apprentices were in the carpentry, electrical, and pipe trades, and the few apprentices who were training for other occupations were excluded. Secondly, I limited the sample to the incoming class of 1989 in order to allow for a sufficiently long period for completion.

      Third, the asymmetry between the two exit types led to the loss of some observations. While an apprentice faces the 'risk' of cancellation starting with the first day, this is not the case for completion. Assuming continuous employment, an 8,000-hour program is expected to take four years to complete. Therefore, an apprentice should face the risk of completion only after the passage of this length of time. Apprentices can and do complete in periods shorter than four years, however. One reason for the shorter duration is the fact that apprentices with prior experience in the trade receive OJT-hour credits upon entry. Since OJT-credit information is available, it is straightforward to adjust the observed completion duration accordingly. In this study, I converted the hours of OJT credit to days at the rate of eight hours per day, and added this figure to the observed duration of completed apprenticeships. Even after this modification, however, a significant number of early completions remained. These may be explained by overtime work or advancement at a faster pace at the discretion of the program sponsor. The completion duration cannot be adjusted for these factors due to the lack of data. Nonetheless, the presence of these early completions makes it

Table 6.3 Status of the apprentices of the class of '89 by November 1995

	N	Percent Complete	Percent Cancel	Time* to Complete	Time* to Cancel
No-PWL States	3,529	28.1	40.1	49.8	21.6
PLW States	7,600	52.3	41.0	51.0	28.3
Weak PWL States	1,374	32.5	57.2	51.2	28.9
Average PWL States	2,147	53.8	40.5	49.7	26.9
Strong PWL States	4,079	58.2	35.7	51.6	30.1
All States	11,129	44.6	40.7	50.8	26.6

Source: Bureau of Apprenticeship and Training, Apprenticeship Information Management Systems.
Note: *Average duration measured in months.

inappropriate to use 1460 days (four years) as the starting point of the completion hazard. Consequently, I set the completion duration threshold at the compromise value of 730 days (two years). Consequently, completions with less than 730 days are dropped. This left 11,129 observations.

Table 6.3 reports the status of these apprentices and the mean durations of apprenticeship by the prevailing wage law. Of all apprentices, 45 percent completed training while 41 percent cancelled. Completion rates were substantially higher in the prevailing wage law states (52 percent vs. 28 percent) and increased with the strength of the prevailing wage law. Ranking in terms of the attrition rate did not yield as clear an outcome. Although the share of cancellation decreased with the strength of the law in the prevailing wage law states, the mean values were virtually identical in the prevailing wage law and no-PWL states. It is also noteworthy that a significant fraction of apprentices in no-PWL states was still in training by the end of the period (32 percent), while the corresponding figure in prevailing wage law states is much smaller (7 percent). Time to complete was approximately the same across the board, about two months longer than the four-year term. There was a wider difference in durations of cancelled apprenticeships. The average cancellation period was six months shorter in states without the prevailing wage law.

Apprentices registered in joint programs have higher completion rates (Bilginsoy, 2003), and as Table 6.1 suggests, these apprenticeships are more likely to be in the prevailing wage law states. Therefore, figures in Table 6.3 may simply be a reflection of the impact of the program type.

The multivariate analysis to follow, however, indicates that regulation also has an impact on the completion and cancellation rates that is independent of the program sponsor.

I use the Cox proportional hazard model to estimate the impact of a set of variables on the hazards of completion and cancellation. This flexible semi-parametric model allows estimation of the impact of explanatory variables on the hazard rate without imposing a 'baseline' hazard function (Hosmer and Lemeshow, 1999). The estimated coefficients measure the proportional effects of explanatory variables on the conditional probability of ending apprenticeship, and they are assumed to be independent of the duration. Since there are two alternative modes of exit, the model will be applied in a competing risks framework.

In addition to the prevailing wage law, explanatory variables in the analysis are the apprentice's age, gender, race/ethnicity, veteran status, program sponsor type, OJT credit received (in the cancellation regression), size of the program, annual state construction industry unemployment rate (a time-varying covariate), and state occupational licensing requirement. Regressions are stratified by occupation. Table 6.4 reports the estimated hazard ratios. An estimate that is greater than unity indicates that the associated variable results in a higher hazard, or a shorter period of apprenticeship. In regression one, for instance, the value of the estimated coefficient of the Joint Program variable is 1.64, indicating that apprentices in joint programs are more likely to complete and receive certification than those in non-joint programs. Symmetrically, the corresponding coefficient of 0.47 in regression three shows that they are less likely to cancel out of the program.

The variable of interest in Table 6.4 is the prevailing wage law. The estimated prevailing wage law coefficient in regression one is greater than unity, meaning that the completion hazard is higher, or the average completion duration is shorter, in the prevailing wage law states. Thus, apprentices in these states fulfill the OJT and RTI requirements at a faster pace than those in the no-PWL states, regardless of the program sponsor type or variations in the availability of jobs. Once the prevailing wage law states are differentiated by the strength of the law, it is observed that the hazard ratios are especially high in the average and strong-law states. The difference between hazard ratios of these states and that of the weak prevailing wage law state is statistically highly significant ($p<0.01$).

In regressions three and four, cancellation hazard ratios in prevailing wage law states are also higher than unity. In combination with the completion hazard ratio, this implies that the duration of

Table 6.4 Cox regression estimates of completion and cancellation hazards

	Completion		Cancellation	
	(1)	(2)	(3)	(4)
PWL state	2.45**		1.66**	
	(22.38)		(12.94)	
Weak PWL state		1.49**		1.87**
		(7.05)		(13.28)
Average PWL state		2.85**		1.55**
		(21.39)		(8.74)
Strong PWL state		2.87**		1.57**
		(24.36)		(10.00)
Joint program	1.64**	1.54**	0.47**	0.48**
	(13.07)	(11.09)	(21.89)	(21.12)
Ln (program size)	1.05**	1.04**	0.94**	0.94**
	(4.60)	(3.48)	(6.37)	(6.34)
Licensed occupation	0.82**	0.78**	1.16**	1.19**
	(5.04)	(6.07)	(3.88)	(4.24)
Age at entry	1.00	1.00	1.00	1.00
	(0.96)	(0.73)	(1.65)	(1.69)
Apprentice of color	0.59**	0.63**	1.07	1.05
	(12.03)	(10.45)	(1.62)	(1.08)
Woman apprentice	0.73**	0.72**	1.21*	1.22**
	(4.37)	(4.59)	(2.52)	(2.57)
Apprentice was	0.85**	0.88*	1.07	1.07
Veteran	(3.00)	(2.36)	(1.56)	(1.38)
OJT Credit			0.69**	0.70**
			(4.62)	(4.56)
Unemployment rate	0.93**	0.92**	0.94**	0.94**
	(15.47)	(17.69)	(14.43)	(12.82)
Log-likelihood	-36,770	-36,683	-33,060	-33,053
N (events)	4,964		4,529	
N (apprentices)		11,129		

Source: Bureau of Apprenticeship and Training, Apprenticeship Information Management Systems.
Notes: Stratified by occupation. Reported values are estimated odds ratios. z-values are in parentheses. * and ** indicate statistical significance at the 5 and 1 percent levels two-tailed tests.

apprenticeship, independent of the mode of exit, is longer in no-PWL states. This result is in line with Table 6.3 where, as noted earlier, a relatively larger number of apprentices neither completed nor cancelled in the no-PWL states by the end of the period.

While the higher completion hazard is clearly an indication of greater efficiency of apprenticeship in prevailing wage law states, interpretation of the cancellation hazard is not straightforward. The difficulty arises from the lack of information on why the apprenticeship was cancelled. In the absence of information on post-apprenticeship tenure of the workers it is also difficult to ascertain whether cancellations are symptomatic of a failure on behalf of the apprentices or the programs. A cancelled apprenticeship may be the result of dissatisfaction of the trainee with the occupation (e.g., if the trainee is not well matched with the occupation), or with the program (e.g., if the sponsor does not adequately deliver the promised skills). Alternatively, for an apprentice who has acquired sufficient skills, quitting could be the optimal decision once a better paying non-training job offer materializes. In this case the cancellation can hardly be viewed as a failure of the individual or the program. In order to determine the implications of cancelled apprenticeships and their variations across states with differing regulatory environments, it is necessary to obtain further information on the post-apprenticeship labor market experiences of workers regarding their wages, access to jobs, and attachment with the industry.

In addition to the lower completion hazard in the no-PWL states, the longer duration of apprenticeships may also be taken as an indication of the lesser efficiency of apprenticeship training in these states. Whether this is an outcome of a looser link between the sponsor and the apprentice, difficulty of locating training jobs, or inability of program sponsors to monitor and keep track of apprentices remains as a topic for future research. It is worth emphasizing that these findings are independent of program sponsorship. It appears that the regulatory environment affects performance of both joint and non-joint programs in the same direction

One final word of caution concerns the impact of regional factors on the estimated hazards. In the regression analysis, estimated coefficients of the prevailing wage law variables were robust under different specifications except in the case where the regression was stratified by geographic region. Once stratified by region, estimates of completion and cancellation hazards both turned out to be lower, although still significantly higher than unity. While the decline in the cancellation hazard was not statistically significant, the risk to complete was significantly lower. Thus, the estimated impact of prevailing wage law on the completion and cancellation may be picking the effect of regional factors as well.

Ethnic and Racial Minorities

In this section, I will discuss the relationship between prevailing wage laws and the participation of ethnic and racial minorities (Blacks, Hispanics, Asian Americans, Native Americans and Pacific Islanders) in apprenticeship training. Since racial discrimination is often alleged to be the underlying motivation for supporting prevailing wage laws, it is worth asking whether the participation of minorities is higher in states without, or weaker, prevailing wage laws. At first sight, this indeed appears to be the case. Among new apprentices registered in no-PWL states between 1989 and 1995, 21 percent were minorities, while the corresponding figure was 17 percent in the states with the prevailing wage law. Shares of minorities were especially lower in the average and strong prevailing wage law states. These figures, however, do not control for confounding factors such as the distribution of minorities in the labor force across the states. Another variable of interest is the trade union participation in apprenticeship training. Trade unions are frequently attacked for using their influence on the admissions process as a vehicle to exclude minorities from the skilled trades. If trade unions engage in discriminatory behavior, then minorities are more likely to be found in non-joint programs. Thus, the focus here is the likelihood that an observed apprentice belongs to a minority group across combinations of the prevailing wage law and sponsor type.

The appropriate methodology here is to estimate and compare the admission probabilities of whites and minorities to the program conditional on having applied to the apprenticeship program. Unfortunately, this avenue of investigation is blocked because data do not provide any information on the pool of applicants. The analysis is therefore limited to apprentices who entered training. In view of this constraint, I proceeded to the estimation of the likelihood of an apprentice is a minority controlling for the minority share in the state labor force. To the extent that the latter variable approximates the share of minorities among the applicants, this alternative may be satisfactory. Even then, it should be borne in mind that this approach is rather crude due to the lack of controls on the relative educational levels, basic skills and other individual level traits or whites and minorities.

Table 6.5 Estimated odds that an apprentice belongs to a minority group

PWL Program Type	Odds ratio	z-statistic
No PWL Non-joint	1.00	----
Regression 1		
No PWL Joint	1.11**	3.74
PWL Non-joint	1.05	1.55
PWL Joint	0.97	1.58
Regression 2		
No PWL Joint	1.11**	3.68
Weak PWL Non-joint	1.31**	7.45
Weak PWL Joint	0.90**	3.25
Average PWL Non-joint	0.87**	3.03
Average PWL Joint	0.92*	2.27
Strong PWL Non-joint	1.17**	2.89
Strong PWL Joint	1.26**	4.90

Notes: Estimated odds are calculated at the mean values of other explanatory variables (share of minorities in the state labor force, state unemployment rate, region, and trade). * and ** indicate statistical significance at the 5 and 1 percent levels two-tailed tests. $N=126,655$.

I estimated a logistic regression of the likelihood that an apprentice is a minority as a function of the prevailing wage law, program sponsor type, interactions of the program sponsor and the prevailing wage law (or the strength of the prevailing wage law), the minority share in the state labor force, the rate of unemployment in the year of entry into training, and occupation and region dummies. Table 6.5 reports the estimated odds of an apprentice being a minority for combinations of the prevailing wage law and program sponsor type from two specifications. In the first regression, the law is a dichotomous variable and the second regression distinguishes between the strength of the state law. In both cases, the base is non-joint program in no-PWL state.

Estimated odds do not reveal a clear pattern. The first panel of the Table 6.5 shows that the odds of being a minority are highest among no-PWL state joint-program apprentices (11 percent higher than the base). There are, however, no other statistically significant results, indicating that the odds that an apprentice is a minority are statistically identical among the three remaining combinations.

According to regression two, there are significant variations within the prevailing wage law states, but no distinct pattern emerges. In comparison with the no-law states, the odds of being an apprentice of color are significantly higher in the strong law states across program types, but lower in the average law states. In the case of weak-law states, odds are higher for the non-joint programs, but lower in the joint.

These results suggest that while there are statistically significant variations in the share of apprentices of color across states identified by the prevailing wage law laws, these do not lend themselves to any obvious interpretation. They do not support, however, the argument that minorities are worse off in states with prevailing wage laws.

Conclusion

This chapter presented a statistical study of the relationship between prevailing wage laws and the apprenticeship training. It focused specifically on the impact of the prevailing wage law on the recruitment of apprentices, completion and cancellation rates, and the minority share in apprenticeship programs. The most important finding is that, controlling for the size of the trade, the supply of apprenticeship is higher in the prevailing wage law states. It also rises with the strength of the prevailing wage law. Thus, regulation clearly raises the recruitment rate. Secondly, apprentices complete graduation requirements at a slower rate in states without prevailing wage laws, indicating a lower efficiency in producing certified skilled workers. This finding is not attributable to variations in program sponsorship, the unemployment rates, or other factors controlled for in the analysis. The relatively large number of apprentices in the no-PWL states who has not exited after the passage of at least six years is also indicative of lower efficiency of apprenticeship training in these states. The question of the source of this inefficiency remains an interesting subject for future study. The cancellation hazard is also higher in the prevailing wage law states. Since the reasons for cancellation are not known, however, it is not possible to identify whether the earlier cancellation indicates an inefficiency of the program or the ability of workers to find better jobs prior to completion of the program. Finally, there is no evidence that prevailing wage laws serve as a means to exclude minorities from training for the skilled trades.

Given the nature of the data, results reported in this chapter are preliminary findings. Four concerns stand out. First, the analysis of recruitment did not differentiate between the effects of the prevailing wage law and the program sponsor type. Therefore, the higher recruitment levels observed in the prevailing wage law states may be attributable to the pervasiveness of joint programs in these states. It would also be interesting to study whether the regulatory regime has an impact on recruitment that is independent of the sponsorship (similar to the observations made in the analysis of retention and attrition rates). This would require estimation of the recruitment regression separately for the joint and non-joint programs. Due to the lack of data on the relative sizes of the organized and open-shop sectors of the trades by state, this avenue of research is not yet feasible. Second, on the question of minority representation, information on the pool of applicants in addition to those actually admitted to the program is essential for definitive findings. Third, information on the post-apprenticeship tenure of workers is necessary in order to interpret the figures on cancelled apprenticeships. Fourth, the arbitrariness of the classification by the strength of prevailing wage law as weak, average, and strong-law states should be pointed out. The lines of demarcation between these categories lack precision. Other methods of aggregating distinct aspects of the state laws could give different rankings by the strength of the law. Defining the strength as a vector instead of a single score and measuring the impact of different dimensions of the prevailing wage law on apprenticeship would enhance the predictions concerning the outcomes of the wage regulation.

Notes

[1] I thank Jeffrey Petersen and Erin Godtland for comments on an earlier version of this chapter. This chapter was written while the author was visiting professor at the College of Administrative Sciences and Economics, Koç University, Istanbul.

[2] In construction trades, OJT is usually 6,000 or 8,000 hours and RTI is 432 or 576 hours.

[3] The list of participating states are in Table 6.6.

[4] Thieblot's classification is based on five factors: 1) The threshold contract amount above which the prevailing wage law is applied; 2) the level (county, municipal, state) of public work contracts; 3) the types of work or trades included or excluded; 4) The way the prevailing wage is identified; 5) other items (e.g., prevailing wage not applied in rural areas, lower rates for helpers, indexation of the rate to collective bargaining during the contract). Thieblot assigned points to each one of these factors and then added them up to reach the law severity index. Weak, average, and strong laws are defined on the basis of these points. It should be noted that both the method of aggregation and the choice of cut-off points concerning the strength of the law are somewhat arbitrary. An alternative approach that could at least partially avoid this problem

is to define the strength variable as a vector and estimate the impact of each factor Thieblot identified on the market outcomes separately.
[5] A regression of the unionization rate (in logs) on law variables indicates a direct relationship between the strength of the law and the rate of unionization in 1990:

$$\ln (union\ density) = 2.02 + 0.60\ WL + 0.99\ AL + 1.47\ SL, \quad R^2=0.50.$$

WL, *AL*, and *SL* are dummy variables for the weak-, average- and strong-law states, respectively (control: no-law states). All coefficients are statistically significant at least at the 5 percent level.

Table 6.6 Distribution of apprentices by the prevailing wage law

No Law States		Weak Law States		Average Law States		Strong Law States	
AL	2,248	KY	2,000	AK	959	IL	11,580
AZ	3,119	ME	514	AR	3,243	MA	1,297
CO	3,496	MT	840	IN	7,384	MI	5,856
FL	11,605	NE	846	NM	3,098	MN	3,132
GA	4,079	OK	1,504	NV	3,176	MO	6,529
IA	3,256	TN	3,877	PA	7,775	NJ	5,029
ID	1,534	TX	10,639	WV	1,127	OH	10,016
KS	818			WY	288	RI	564
MS	1,296						
ND	327						
SC	1,008						
SD	463						
UT	2,180						
	35,429		20,220		27,050		44,003

Source: Bureau of Apprenticeship and Training, Apprenticeship Information Management Systems.

References

Bernstein, David (1993), 'The Davis-Bacon Act: Let's Bring Jim Crow to an End', *Cato Briefing Paper No. 17,* Cato Institute, 1000 Massachusetts Avenue, N.W., Washington, D.C., 18 January.

Bilginsoy, Cihan (2003), 'The Hazards of Training: Attrition and Retention in Construction Industry Apprenticeship Programs', *Industrial and Labor Relations Review,* vol. 57(1), pp. 54-67.

Bourdon, Clinton C., and Levitt, Raymond E. (1980), *Union and Open-Shop Construction,* Lexington Books, Lexington, MA.

Hosmer, D.W., and Lemeshow, S. (1999), *Applied Survival Analysis,* John Wiley & Sons, New York, NY.

Lindley, R.M. (1975) 'The Demand for Apprentice Recruits by the Engineering Industry, 1975-71', *Scottish Journal of Political Economy,* vol. 22, pp. 1-24.

Merrilees, William J. (1983), "Alternative Models of Apprentice Recruitment: With Special Reference to the British Engineering Industry," *Applied Economics,* vol. 15, pp. 1-21.

Mills, Daniel Q. (1972), *Industrial Relations and Manpower in Construction,* The MIT Press, Cambridge, MA.

Philips, Peter (1998), 'Kansas and Prevailing Wage Legislation', Report prepared for Kansas Senate Labor Relations Committee.

Stevens, Margaret (1994), 'An Investment Model for the Supply of Training by Employers', *The Economic Journal,* vol. 104(424), pp. 556-570.

Thieblot, A. J. (1995), *State Prevailing Wage Laws: An Assessment at the Start of 1995,* Associated Builders and Contractors, Inc., Rosslyn, VA.

U.S. General Accounting Office (GAO) (1992), *Apprenticeship Training: Administration, Use, and Equal Opportunity,* GAO/HRD-92-43, Government Printing Office, Washington D.C.

Chapter 7

Prevailing Wage Laws and Injury Rates in Construction

Hamid Azari-Rad[1]

Introduction

Construction is one of the most dangerous industries in the United States. While the construction industry constitutes only 6 percent of the private sector workforce, it accounts for 23 percent of fatal, and 9.7 percent of non-fatal occupational injuries (Bureau of Labor Statistics, 2001a). This paper investigates the relationship between the presence of the prevailing wage laws and workers' safety in terms of non-fatal injury rates in the construction industry. Prevailing wage laws have mainly been enacted to keep the government, as a large purchaser of construction services with a considerable market power, from adversely affecting local labor markets. The regulatory environment of the prevailing wage laws, affect construction injury rates in several possible ways. The relationship between prevailing wage regulations and collective bargaining is a main factor that explains this connection, though indirectly. Earlier work by Philips *et al.* (1995) finds that experience is a major determinant of safety and productivity.

Employment in the construction industry is inherently unstable since the industry fluctuates cyclically and seasonally. Firms expand and contract their employment as they win or lose job bids. Construction, particularly industrial construction, requires a highly skilled workforce, yet the short-term nature of worker attachment to construction contractors discourage firms from investing in training workers. Skills acquired by a worker could benefit competitors, at no cost to the firm, once a project is completed and workers leave to work on other projects with different contractors. This creates a human capital free-rider problem for construction firms, and consequently discourages training by them.

Union halls provide a pool of highly trained workers from which all firms that are signatories to the collectively bargained agreement can recruit when they win bids. Construction unions provide a mechanism to address the human capital free-rider problem through investment in formal apprenticeship training programs by employers and journeymen.[2] Unions also encourage career attachment of trained journeymen by providing relatively high wages and benefits such as health and retirement insurance, which are attractive to workers as they age. By creating careers in a casual labor market, construction unions create the institutions needed to make human capital investment and its preservation, a rational market activity (Azari-Rad *et al.*, 1994). This in turn contributes to higher levels of experience and lower rates of injury.

The decline of the construction unionization rates in conjunction with the repeal of various state prevailing wage laws have resulted in a drop in apprenticeship training through union programs. Significant decline of more formal training provided in a unionized context leads to younger,[3] less experienced, and perhaps more accident-prone workers among non-union contractors (Philips *et al.*, 1995). Furthermore, construction unions have historically established more formal safety procedures, and provided workers with more formal avenues to address hazardous work conditions than the non-union sector. Occupational Safety and Health Administration (OSHA) safety standards are more diligently enforced in a unionized context leading to a safer workplace, and more accurate reporting of injuries (Elling, 1986; Berman, 1978; Weil, 1992). The institutional context provided by unions with formal rules, lower anxiety and stress among workers, which could otherwise result in higher rates of poor judgment and injuries (Freeman and Medoff, 1984; Levi *et al.*, 1982; Syme, 1988).

The relationship between prevailing wage laws and injuries was first examined in a study by Philips *et al.* (1995). However, their analysis was confined to the injury rates for plumber and pipe fitters employed by specialty contractors. This study extends Philips *et al.*'s study, by examining injury rates for the entire construction workforce over a longer period of time (1976-1999). It examines the effects of the presence of prevailing wage laws on injury rates in construction by their severity.

Injury Data

The major injury data employed in this study is the construction component of the *Survey of Occupational Injuries and Illnesses* published annually by the Bureau of Labor Statistics, for 1976-1999 time period. This survey is a

Federal/State program in which employer reports are collected from approximately 179,800 private industry establishments and processed by State agencies cooperating with the Bureau of Labor Statistics. The survey measures nonfatal injuries and illnesses only. The survey excludes the self-employed; farms with fewer than 11 employees; private households; Federal government agencies; and, for national estimates, employees in State and local government agencies. The annual survey provides estimates of the number and frequency (incidence rates) of workplace injuries and illnesses based on logs kept by private industry employers during the year. These records reflect not only the year's injury and illness experience, but also the employer's understanding of which cases are work related under current record-keeping guidelines of the U.S. Department of Labor (Bureau of Labor Statistics, 2002).

Our analysis focuses on workplace injuries to the exclusion of workplace related illnesses. Injuries are reported per 100 full-time equivalent workers. The broadest available measure of injury incidence is the *total* number of reported injuries (cases) per 100 full-time equivalent workers. This is decomposed into three measures based on the severity of injuries. The rate of injury cases *with days away from work* measure the incidence of injuries of greatest severity. The rate of injury cases *with lost-workdays* measure the incidence of injuries with less severity than the former measure, and does not require the worker to leave the workplace. Finally, the rate of injury cases *without lost-workdays* measure the least severe injuries.

The incidence rates represent the number of injuries and illnesses per 100 full-time workers and were calculated as:

$$\frac{N}{EH} \times 200,000 \qquad (7.1)$$

Where N is the number of injuries and illnesses; EH represents the total hours worked by all employees during the calendar year; and 200,000 is the base for 100 equivalent full-time workers (working 40 hours per week, 50 weeks per year). Lost workday cases are comprised of two case types, those requiring at least one day away from work, with or without restricted work activity, and those requiring restricted activity only. The latter type of case may involve shortened hours, a temporary job change, or temporary restrictions on certain duties (for example, no heavy lifting) of a worker's regular job.

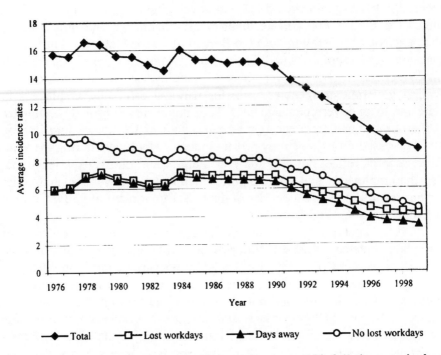

Figure 7.1   Construction non-fatal injury cases per 100 full-time equivalent workers, 1976-1999

For this study, a balanced panel of Bureau of Labor Statistics' occupational injury data for construction is created for 17 states, and an unbalanced panel for 50 states and the District of Columbia. Prevailing wage laws are present in 69.9 percent of states in the balanced, and 62.3 percent of the unbalanced panel. Data for state unemployment rates are from the Statistical Abstract of the United States (U.S. Census Bureau, 2002).

Injury Trends

Figure 7.1 shows that non-fatal construction injury rates, by all measures of severity, have been declining since 1976. This downward trend appears to be more pronounced in the 1990s, and is at different rates for each type of injury. Decline in various injury rates reflects in part the shifting over time of how a particular injury is treated. For instance, in the past, an injury of the exact same character may have resulted in a lost workday case where

Table 7.1 Workers' compensation rates for 1996

Plumbing	$7.89	Florida	$30.10
Plastering	$12.93	Minnesota	$26.25
Roofing	$30.90	New Jersey	$10.34
Structural Steel Erection	$37.65	Nebraska	$8.93

Source: Engineering News-Record.

the worker was absent from work for at least one day. In more recent times it may be that the worker with the exact same injury was assigned light duty work and never lost a workday due to absence from work. This may explain why the injury rate with lost workdays did not decline as quickly and shapely as, the more serious, lost workdays with days away from work.[4] It may be that contractors in construction were shifting the treatment of similar injuries away from sending the worker home to assigning the worker light duty work. The widening of the gap between the lines representing injury rate with lost workday and that representing the injury rate of lost workdays with days away from work indicates that either the nature of construction injuries have become less severe over time or the handling of injuries has shifted towards light duty work or both.

The fact that the rate for the least severe category of injury—injuries that did not result in lost workdays—fell first (see note 4) is also open to a dual interpretation. It may be that contractors found that in attempting to limit injuries, the least severe injuries were more easily controlled and/or it may be that less severe injuries were more likely to be reported in the past and simply go unreported today.

Along with feeling a moral obligation to provide a safe environment for their workers, contractors have a strong and increasing incentive to make the construction site safe. Worker compensation premiums are a significant labor cost in construction and during certain periods they have risen dramatically. Worker compensation premiums range as high as $50 for every $100 of payroll and average around $15 to $20 per $100 of payroll. Generally, workers' compensation premiums vary widely by occupation and state, as shown in Table 7.1. For the U.S. as a whole, the average premium for iron workers (structural steel) was almost five times higher than the average premium for plumbers. Florida's average premium, for all occupations, was more than three times higher than Nebraska's premiums. As shown in Table 7.2, the average U.S. workers' compensation premiums for three typical construction occupations rose between 87 and 116 percent in real terms, over the period 1983 to

Table 7.2 Workers' compensation insurance cost per $100 of payroll

Occupation	1983	2001	Percent Change
Masons	$7.01	$15.15	116%
General Carpenter	$9.65	$18.22	89%
Iron Workers	$20.27	$37.96	87%

Source: Engineering News-Record.

2001. Most of this increase occurred in the mid-to-late 1980s prior to or coincident with the decline in injury rates.

The surge in workers' compensation costs over the past decades cannot be tied to rising injury rates as these rates have been falling. Nor can it be tied to inflation because worker compensation rates are calculated as a percent of payroll which has more or less kept up with inflation. However, clearly a main driving force behind this upsurge has been the rising medical costs. Figure 7.2 shows the rate of inflation of the Medical Care component of the Consumer Price Index (CPI-Medical care) as a percentage of the general rate of inflation calculated using the Consumer Price Index for all urban consumers (CPI-U). When medical cost are rising in tandem with overall inflation, the line in Figure 7.2 would be at 100 percent, which is marked by a bold line. When medical costs are rising in any one year faster than overall inflation, the line is above 100 percent. With few exceptions, the line has been above 100 percent of overall inflation. This shows that price-inflation in the medical care sector has consistently been above the general rate of inflation since the early 1980s, reaching as high as 400 percent in 1986.

In addition to rising medical care costs, many state workers' compensation systems have been open to abuse through lax and sometimes arbitrary management of workers' claims. State laws that allow injured workers to bring independent civil lawsuits against employers in the state courts, that may not consider the findings of the state's workers' compensation enforcement agency's judgment,[5] leaves the door open for abuse through litigation. For example, in Texas these types of 'court proceedings are a key part of the problem because insurance companies often settle out of court to avoid jury trials ... it encourages a legion of "ambulance chasing" attorneys to swamp the system with questionable claims' (Setzer, 1989).

These alarmingly high premiums have prompted construction contractors, unions, and the government to take various measures to address on-the-job safety and injuries. State governments undertook major legislative reforms of workers' compensation laws in the 1980s to tighten

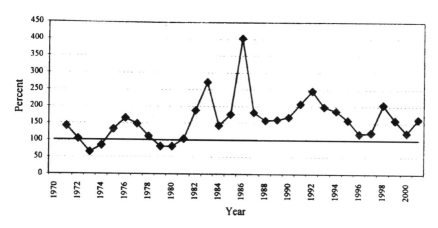

Figure 7.2 CPI-M as a percent of CPI-U inflation

Source: Economic Report of the President (2003).

compliance issues, address fraud, and reform payment schemes (Setzer, 1989, 1990; Powers and Korman 1991). OSHA, in its strategic plan, addresses workplace safety in construction through both educational programs and enforcement strategies. In the mid 1990s OSHA concentrated 'on rooting out the four principal causes of construction fatalities—falls, bodily injuries from equipment operation, falling objects and electrocution' (Rosenbaum, 1994). To this end, OSHA allocated its limited enforcement resources to worksite inspections.[6] The Utah Labor Commission, on the other hand, reports that for the last five years 'Utah's injury and illness incidence rate ... has been falling' as the result of OSHA's safety awareness programs (Ellertson, 1999). This saves on costs associated with on-the-job accidents, injuries, and fatalities, by way of improved experience rating and consequently reduced workers' compensation premiums.[7]

To address the rising cost of workers' compensation insurance, contractors formed self-insurance, individually or through a pool, since such plans allowed firms with better safety records to reduce their insurance costs. Also, self-insurance could save up to 30 percent on the overhead, profits, and residual market charges of conventional insurance companies (Mullen and Carr, 1986; Grogan, 1991). Presently, workers' compensation insurance is compulsory in all states but Texas, and about 47 states allow employers to self-insure workers' compensation costs either by individual employer or a group of employers. 'Not all contractors can be self-insured, however. To be eligible, they must be approved by the state they operate in and must be able to purchase catastrophic insurance to cover losses in excess of the amount they are approved to cover'[8] (Grogan, 1991). This would leave out smaller firms, putting further financial pressure on them as they cannot capitalize on savings of self-insurance.

Contactors increasingly make efforts to bring injured employees back to work as quickly as possible. 'Even when an injured employee may not be fully recovered, the employer may create a light-duty position or rearrange the employee's job duties to accommodate any physical limitations. By taking such steps, many employers have found that employees are able to return to work more quickly and, as a consequence, workers' compensation payments by employers are significantly reduced' (Mook 1995). This reduction in premiums results from reclassification of injury from more to less serious type that does not require days away from work. *Engineering New Record* (1990a, 1990b) confirms that the light-duty return to work program succeed, because many choose to get back on the payroll with light duty or alternate work than to sit at home collecting workers' compensation checks, even after severe injuries. 'Craft workers yearn to return to their trade, even at a reduced capacity, and get back to the comradeship of the workplace. Contractors can help workers feel better about themselves while shaving compensation costs' (*Engineering News-Record*, 1990a). This phenomenon may in part explain the widening of the gap, over time, between the injury rate with lost workday and the injury rate of lost workdays with days away from work.

A pronounced reaction by construction firms to high workers' compensation premiums has been to subcontract the injury risks. General contractors often subcontract more dangerous tasks to specialized contractors that are either better trained and equipped to handle these risks or, for other reasons, are willing to assume these risks. Figure 7.3 shows that, in the construction industry, as the average U.S. workers' compensation premiums increased in 1980s, the percentage of self-employed subsequently increased and remained high in the 1990s. While work is pushed away from the owner and general contractor, the control of materials are with the general contractor so that subcontracts are increasingly on a labor-only basis (International Labor Organization, 2001).[9] Aside from heavy and highway work, general contractors' share of the workforce fell from 35 percent in 1967 to 24 percent in 1997,[10] while the share of the labor force employed by specialty trade contractors rose from 48 percent to 63 percent during the same period (Philips, 2003).

Increased subcontracting points at potential underreporting of injuries as subcontractors with fewer workers may be more likely than larger contractors suppress injuries to keep costs under control. Changes in

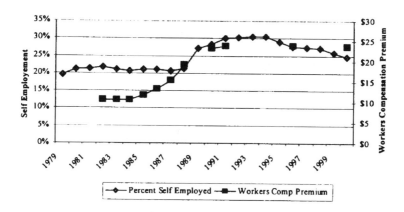

Figure 7.3 Workers' compensation premiums and percent self-employment in the construction industry

Sources: Current Population Survey and *Engineering News-Record.*

the racial and ethnic composition of construction workforce may be another source of unreported injuries. Hispanic employment has increased in both absolute and relative terms in the construction industry. Hispanics account for 10.9 percent of the total labor force while comprising 17.4 percent of the construction labor force (Current Population Survey, 2001a), thus, they are over-represented in the construction industry. The increased employment share of Hispanics in the construction industry in 1990s may have contributed to underreporting of injuries in construction as well.

Injuries by undocumented immigrants may not be reported since these immigrants may not know about their entitlement to workers' compensation or due to their undocumented status are afraid to seek out these benefits (Rodriguez, 2002). Thus, the official injury data may miss the undocumented day laborers who are picked up by trucks or walk casually onto job sites. This exacerbates the underreporting for Hispanics. Fields and Mena (2000) report that in California's open-shop sector

> [contractors] are augmenting a work force stretched taut by the boom with cheap, untrained workers, many of them Latino immigrants ... Injuries to these workers are rarely reported, but the men who gather near Home Depot stores each day looking for work carry the marks that attest to their reality.
>
> Raul Cevallos' hands have smooth shiny scars that make his skin look like a topographical map, the result of being burned by hot tar, he said.

And Oscar Diaz said his thumb hasn't worked right since a drywall he put in at a Laguna Beach catering business fell on him two months ago. He ignored the pain for the promise of $10 an hour and stuck his thumb in saltwater to ease the swelling, rather than seeing a doctor. 'I have no money, I have no papers and I needed to work', he said.

Trends and conditions begun in the Southwest are now a nationwide phenomenon. The *Atlanta Journal-Constitution* reports that:

> Many injured Hispanic workers, a large share of whom are in the country illegally, are either afraid to report injuries that may entitle them to workers' compensation, or assume they do not qualify because of their immigration status. Sokas says that fear is apparent in the statistics, which show Hispanics don't have higher injury rates than others, but a far higher death rate (Warren and Goldberg, 2001).

Thus, reported injury rates have fallen. The fall in the least serious injuries began in the 1970s while the fall in more serious injuries began in the late 1980s. The fall was prompted by increased workers compensation premiums. These increased premiums, in turn, were caused primarily by increased medical care costs. The fall in reported injury rates probably reflect safer working conditions in construction. But they also may reflect a change in how contractors treat injuries, shifting from sending workers home to putting them on light duty work. The decline in reported injuries may also reflect underreporting especially of less serious injuries. Underreporting may have become easier as the industry has increasingly hired undocumented workers who have less knowledge about or feel less comfortable claiming their workers compensation benefits.

In the following section we will address the question whether or not the presence or absence of prevailing wage regulations lead to more or fewer reported injuries. The connection between prevailing wage regulations and injury rates runs through the role prevailing wage regulations play in promoting construction training. Prevailing wage regulations promote training both directly when these regulations require contractors to contribute to apprenticeship programs, and indirectly when they encourage collective bargaining. Collective bargaining in construction promotes training by providing a vehicle whereby contractors can collectively contribute to an apprenticeship training without the problem of other contractors free-riding on this training by hiring graduated apprentices without having contributed to their education. The hypothesis to be tested is the proposition that training leads to fewer injuries and that by encouraging training, prevailing wage regulations lead to a safer construction workforce.

The question arises—do the problems of underreporting or changing management of injuries muddy the analysis of prevailing wage regulations and their effects on injuries? The answer lies in the role unions play in informing their members of their rights under workers compensation insurance. Union members, even undocumented immigrants who are union members, are more likely to be aware of their worker compensation rights and are more likely to seek benefits when injured. Union job protections as well as member education make union construction workers less likely to allow contractors to dismiss an injury or treat it with less attention than it deserves. So, all other things being equal, the presence of collective bargaining should lead to less underreporting of injuries. Thus, the problem of underreporting or mishandling of injuries in construction may confound an examination of the hypothesis that prevailing wage regulations lead to a lower injury rate.

Model

Four fixed effects models are employed to examine the effects of the presence of prevailing wage laws on the *total* number of injury cases, number of injury cases with *days away from work,* with *lost-workdays*, and *without lost-workdays* as the dependent variable. A dummy variable for each state and year are employed (but not reported in Table 7.3 for simplicity) to control for differences in injury rates across individual states and trends in injury rates over time. The log of unemployment rate is used in the model to control for variations in injury rates associated with the business cycle. During periods of high unemployment marginally experienced workers tend to exit from the industry first, leaving disproportionate numbers of experienced and less accident-prone workers. Also during these periods of slow construction activity there is less pressure on firms, hence, they become more careful as the rush jobs diminish and the workload becomes less hectic. Thus, an inverse relationship between unemployment rate and injury rates is hypothesized and controlled for.

Finally, the effects of the presence of state prevailing wage laws on injury rates are assessed through a dummy law variable which equals one if and when a state has a prevailing wage regulation in force. As of the beginning of 1979, prevailing wage laws were in effect in all states except Georgia, Iowa, Mississippi, North Carolina, North Dakota, South Carolina,

South Dakota, Vermont, and Virginia, which never enacted these laws. Starting in 1979 the following states repealed their prevailing wage laws: Florida (1979), Arizona (1979), Alabama (1980), Utah (1981), Colorado, Idaho and New Hampshire (1985), Kansas (1987), and Louisiana (1988). In 1995 Oklahoma Supreme Court judicially annulled their prevailing wage law. The Michigan law was judicially suspended for the 1995-1997 period. Kentucky exempted schools and municipalities from prevailing wage laws for the period 1982-1996. Ohio exempted schools from prevailing wage laws in July of 1997. Thus, we focus on the relationship between the existence or the absence of state prevailing wage laws and injury rates in construction controlling for other state differences in injury rates, time trends in injury rates and business cycle variation in injuries.

Results

Table 7.3 summarizes the regression results. The dependent variable in each model is an injury rate. Models 1 through 4 present the four separate construction injury rate measures arrayed from least to most severe injuries. Coefficients for two key independent variables are presented for each model while coefficients for each state dummy variable and each year dummy variable are not reported in Table 7.3 for simplicity of presentation. (The year coefficients are reported in note 4)

Along with state and year dummy variables the additional control variable in each model is the state unemployment rate as a measure of the local business cycle. As explained in note 4, the hypothesis is that the coefficient for this control variable would be negative. A negative coefficient implies that as the unemployment rate rises in a given year and state, all other things being equal, the injury rate would fall. This is because when the construction economy is down, less experience and younger workers are most likely to leave the industry first. Furthermore, construction work sites may be less stressed as both owners and contractors are in somewhat less of a hurry to get done. Thus, both workers and work sites may be safer in the slow times of a downturn. Conversely, in a construction boom, inexperienced and younger workers enter the industry. Work schedules are tightened and both work and workers become less safe.

This theorizing is consistent with the results reported in Table 7.3. In all four models, the unemployment rate is negative and statistically significant at the one percent level. Thus, we conclude that there is a business cycle pattern to injuries in the construction industry.

Table 7.3 Fixed effects regression estimates of prevailing wage laws on injury rates

	Model 1[*]	Model 2[*]	Model 3[*]	Model 4[*]
Dependent Variable: Injury Rates	No Lost Workdays	Total Injury Rate	Lost Workday	Days Away from Work
(Constant)	14.78	24.5	9.66	9.6
	(0.76)	(1.29)	(0.67)	(0.64)
Prevailing wage law in effect	-0.53**	-1.12**	-0.59**	-0.58**
	(0.23)	(0.39)	(0.20)	(0.19)
Unemployment Rate	-2.2**	-4.07**	-1.85**	-1.89**
	(0.31)	(0.52)	(0.27)	(0.26)
Adjusted R Square	0.75	0.78	0.77	0.81
Number of observations	408	408	408	408

Notes: * Fixed effects model, states and years are omitted for simplicity of presentation.
** Significant at the 1 percent level one tailed test. Standard errors are in parenthesis.

The focus variable in Table 7.3 is a dummy variable indicating whether or not in a given state and year that state has a prevailing wage regulation in effect. The hypothesis is that the coefficient for this independent variable would be negative. A negative coefficient implies that the presence of prevailing wage regulations lead to a lower injury rate. Prevailing wage regulations influence injury rates through training and promoting the retention of experienced workers. Prevailing wage regulations do this directly by often requiring that contractors on public works participate in and contribute to apprenticeship training programs. Prevailing wage laws indirectly promote training and worker retention by encouraging collective bargaining. Collective bargaining in turn establishes not only apprenticeship programs through contractually required contributions for training but also collective bargaining encourages the retention of older and more experienced workers through the establishment of health and welfare programs. This, in turn, preserves the human capital accumulated in the welfare programs provide the family medical insurance and pension programs that encourage older workers and married workers to remain in industry through apprenticeship training and on-the-job experience. More training and experience in turn lead to safer working practices and lower injury rates.

There is another probable connection between prevailing wage regulations and a safer work environment in construction. When contractors are accustomed to working within and complying with prevailing wage regulations, this helps set a climate legitimizing other construction labor market regulations. One key regulation is the providing of workers' compensation benefits. Contractors are required to participate in workers' compensation insurance. They also should provide injured workers with the means and information needed to receive workers' compensation benefits when injured. This, however, can raise the insurance premiums paid by contractors. Thus, absent a sense of duty, contractors may succumb to the temptation of avoiding worker comp costs by creating a work environment where worker injuries go unreported and possibly untreated. By helping create an environment of regulatory compliance and legitimacy, prevailing wage regulations can help internalize the cost of injuries through compliance with worker comp regulations. By internalizing the cost of injuries, worker comp costs create an incentive to make construction sites safer. Indirectly, prevailing wage regulations by encouraging collective bargaining and union representation, helps create structures of worker representation on construction sites that also discourage strategies of workers' compensation cost evasion. So again, injury costs are internalized to the firm creating incentives to make construction work safer.

The coefficients in Table 7.3 for the prevailing wage indicator are in each model negative and statistically significant at the one percent level. These results are consistent with the hypothesis that prevailing wage regulation lower injury rates through the encouragement of training and the retention of experienced workers. The magnitude of the prevailing wage regulation effect on injury rates may be calculated from the coefficients reported in Table 7.3 and the average injury rate for each type of injury. The coefficients estimate the decline in each type of injury rate associated with the existence of a prevailing wage law. Thus, for the least serious type of injury—injuries that do not result in lost workdays—the decline in that rate associated with prevailing wage laws is -0.53. The average over states and years for this type of injury rate is 7.43 injuries per 100 full-time equivalent construction workers. Thus, the percent decline in this injury rate evaluated at the mean is -0.53/7.43 which equals a 7.13 percent fall in the rate of least serious injuries. Table 7.4 calculates the percent decline in injuries for each type of injury rate and they range from a 7.13 percent decline in the least serious injuries associated with prevailing wage

Table 7.4 Percent decline in injury rates associated with the presence of prevailing wage laws, by severity of injuries

	Type of Injury			
	Less Serious	Total	More Serious	Most Serious
Estimated Coefficient	-0.53	-1.12	-0.59	-0.58
Average Injuries per 100 Full-Time Equivalent Workers in Construction	7.43	13.54	6.09	5.67
Percent Decline in Injury Rate Associated with Existence of Prevailing Wage Law	7.13%	8.25%	9.76%	10.19%

regulations to a 10.19 percent decline in the case of the rate for most serious injuries—injuries resulting in lost workdays with the worker absent from work.

Conclusion

Market competition that focuses on cheap labor strategies will also tend to encourage strategies that evade tax laws, insurance coverage, and safety regulations. Circumventing workers' compensation payments reduces incentive to create a safe worksite, and shift the full cost of injuries to the workers and the society as explained by Waddoups in chapter 9. On the other hand, regulated markets lead to compliance not only with wage regulations but also with safety and workers' compensation regulations. Evidence presented here suggests that the absence of prevailing wage regulations lead to higher injury rates in the construction industry and conversely, the presence of prevailing wage regulations leads to safer construction work particularly in the case of more severe injuries. The causal processes that create the connection between prevailing wage regulations and safer construction work include the role prevailing wages play in promoting training, encouraging the retention of experienced workers and creating an environment where other regulations are followed.

These include the payment of workers compensation benefits which in turn creates the economic incentives to avoid accidents.

Further research could also address the savings by the publicly supported hospitals, and the society in general, from presence of prevailing wage laws and reduction in injuries, especially the most serious and potentially more costly injuries.

Notes

[1] This paper was presented in a panel on prevailing wage laws at the annual conference of the Eastern Economic Association in New York City (2003), and benefited from comments of the referees and participants of this panel. I would like to thank Peter Philips and Mark J. Prus for their valuable comments. I am responsible for all remaining errors. I would also like to acknowledge the financial support of the State University of New York—New Paltz's Research Grant (2001-2002).

[2] Union apprenticeship programs have higher retention rates than their non-union counterparts, due in part to higher wages of union apprentices. This also induces the unions and employers to promote the passage of apprentices to journeymen in order to preserve their investment (Bilginsoy, 1996).

[3] The Current Population Survey data shows that the average age of construction workers in no-law states have consistently been lower than their counterparts in states with prevailing wage laws during 1977-2000 period. Philips *et al.* (1995) assert that the with declining wages and loss of health and pension benefits, industry level labor turnover has increased significantly, as even the older, more experienced workers leave the construction industry for other industries.

[4] These trends are clear in the following figure that reports the coefficients for the year dummy for each year in the data after 1976, of the fixed effects linear regression model employed in this study. The values of these coefficients may be interpreted as how much the injury rate has changed relative to 1976 controlling for the other factors in the model (prevailing wage effects and unemployment effects as well as a fixed effect for each state). When the coefficient (or year intercept) is less than zero, then all other things being equal, the injury rate is below that of the base year of 1976. The least serious injury rate—injuries with no lost workdays—is negative for all years after 1976 and is increasingly negative after 1982. This means that the rate of least serious injuries has been falling steadily for two decades controlling for the business cycle and changes in prevailing wage regulations. The decline in the rate of more serious injuries (controlling for the business cycle and prevailing wage regulations) came only in the late 1980s for the most serious days away from work cases and

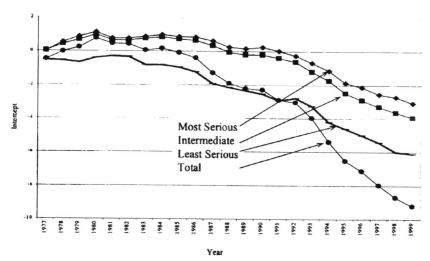

Year

early 1990s for all lost workday cases. In explaining their survey, the Bureau of Labor Statistics repots that 'Lost workday cases are comprised of two case types, those requiring at least one day away from work, with or without restricted work activity, and those requiring restricted activity only. The latter type of case may involve shortened hours, a temporary job change, or temporary restrictions on certain duties (for example, no heavy lifting) of a worker's regular job' (Bureau of Labor Statistics, 2002).

[5] Such as the state's Industrial Accident Board.

[6] Other examples of cooperation between private industry and federal government include signing of a partnership charter agreement between the Associated General Contractors of America (AGC) and the Occupational Safety and Health Administration (OSHA), in March 1998, to assist OSHA in achieving its strategic plan of reducing workplace accidents and injuries in the construction industry by 15 percent and reducing fatalities by 20 percent over the following five years (see http://www.agc.org)

[7] Ellertson (1999) reports that Utah's workers' compensation rates enjoyed a 16.3 percent reduction in 1999 as the result of safety awareness programs such as OSHA's Workplace Safety Training Course.

[8] Self-insurance also increases contractors' motivation to improve safety to protect their bottom line.

[9] The transformation of the individual worker to a self-employed subcontractor shifts the burden of payroll taxes and the risk of injury to the workers. Also, workers typically lose unemployment and retirement insurance.

[10] Of this workforce, one-third are not construction workers.

References

Azari-Rad, H., Yeagle A., and Philips P. (1994), 'The Effect of the Repeal of Utah's Prevailing Wage Law on the Labor Market in Construction', in Friedman, S., Hurd, R., Oswald, R.A., and Seeber R.L. (eds.), *Restoring the Promise of American Labor Law*, Cornell University ILR Press, Ithaca, New York, pp. 207-221.

Berman, D. (1978), *Death on the Job: Occupational Health and Safety Struggles in the United States*, Monthly Review, New York.

Bilginsoy, C. (1996), 'Regulation and Training: Prevailing Wage Laws and Apprenticeship in Construction', Paper Presented to the Center to Protect Workers' Rights Meeting. Washington, D.C.

Council of Economic Advisers (2003), *Economic Report of the President*, Government Printing Office, Washington, D.C.

Ellertson, R.L. (1999), 'Safety Awareness Program Essential To Preventing Accidents, Saving Money', *Intermountain Contractor*, vol. 61(12), May, p. 14.

Elling, R.H. (1986), *The Struggle for Workers' Health: A Study of Six Industrialized Countries*, Baywood Publishing Company, Farmingdale, NY.

Engineering News-Record (2000), 'Labor Campaign is a Sign of Bigger Battle to Come', vol. 244 (32), August 14, p. 12.

Engineering News-Record (1990a), 'Treat Workers Better and Save', vol. 225 (22), December 3, p. 70.

Engineering News-Record (1990b), 'Return-to-Work Plan Pays', vol. 225(22), December 3, p. 19.

Fields, R., and Mena J. (2000), 'State's Building Boom is Taking a Fatal Toll', *Los Angeles Times*, August 18, p. A1.

Freeman, Richard B., and Medoff, James L. (1984), *What Do Unions Do?*, Basic Books, New York.

Grogan, T. (1991), 'Alternatives to Workers' Comp', *Engineering News-Record*, vol. 227(25), December 23, p. 43.

International Labor Organization (2001), *The Construction Industry in the Twenty-First Century: Its Image, Employment Prospects and Skill Requirements*, International Labor Office, Geneva, Switzerland.

Korman, R. (1989), 'California Deepens Rate Split', *Engineering News-Record*, vol. 223(19), November 9, p. 24.

Levi L., Frankenhaeuser M., and Gardell B. (1982), 'Report on Work Stress Related to Social Structures and Processes', in Elliott G. R. and Eisdorfer C. (eds.) *Stress and Human Health*, Springer Publishing, New York.

Mook, Jonathan R. (1995), 'Employer Dilemma: Reducing Workers' Comp Costs May be Undercut by Conflicting Federal Laws', *American Bar Association Journal*, vol. 81, July, p. 52.

Mullen, T., and Carr, F.H. (1986), 'Workers' Comp on the Rise', *Engineering News-Record*, vol. 244(32), August 14, p. 11.

Philips, Peter, Mangum, Garth, Waitzman, Norman, and Yeagel, Anne (1995), *Losing Ground: Lessons from the Little Davis-Bacon Acts*, mimeo, Department of Economics, University of Utah, Salt Lake City, Utah.

Philips, Peter (2003), 'Dual Worlds: The Two Growth Paths in U.S. Construction', in Bosch, G., and Philips, P. (eds.), *Building Chaos: An International Comparison of the Effects of Deregulation on the Construction*, Routledge Press, London, pp. 161-187.

Powers, Mary B., and Korman, R. (1991), 'Two States Grapple Over Who is 'Disabled'', *Engineering News-Record*, vol. 226(20), May 20, p. 23.

Rodriguez, C. (2002), 'Union Alleges Exploitation, Plans Protest at Salem Site', *Boston Globe*, April 16, p. B1.

Rosenbaum, David B. (1994), 'AGC Firms Fairly Frustrated', *Engineering News-Record*, vol. 233(15), October 10, p. 15.

Setzer, Steven W. (1990), 'Florida Law Aimed at Abuses', *Engineering News-Record*, vol. 224(25), June 21, p. 12.

Setzer, Steven W. (1989), 'Steady Rise in Workers' Comp Rates Sparks Big Texas Reform Effort', *Engineering News-Record*, vol. 222(8), February 23, p. 10.

Smith R.S. (1979), 'Compensating Wage Differentials and Public Policy: A Review', *Industrial and Labor Relations Review*, vol. 32, pp. 339-352.

Syme S.L. (1988), 'Social Epedimiology and the Work Environment', *International Journal of Health Services*, vol. 18(4), pp. 635-645.

The Center to Protect Workers' Rights (1997), *The Construction Chart Book: The U.S. Construction Industry and Its Workers*, CPWR, Washington, D.C.

U.S. Census Bureau (2002), *Statistical Abstract of the United States*, Government Printing Office, Washington, D.C.

U.S. Department of Labor, Bureau of Labor Statistics (1976-1999), *Occupational Injuries and Illnesses: Industry Data*, Government Printing Office, Washington, D.C.

U.S. Department of Labor, Bureau of Labor Statistics (2001b), 'National Census of Fatal Occupational Injuries in 2000', *News*, 14 August, Government Printing Office, Washington, D.C.

U.S. Department of Labor, Bureau of Labor Statistics (1993-2001), *Census of Fatal Occupational Injuries*, Government Printing Office, Washington, D.C.

U.S. Department of Labor, Bureau of Labor Statistics (2002), 'Workplace Injuries and Illnesses in 2001', *News*, 19 December, Government Printing Office, Washington, D.C.

Warren, B., and Goldberg, D. (2001), 'Latino Work Deaths Climbing: A Third of Georgia's Job Fatalities Last Year were Hispanic', *Atlanta Journal-Constitution*, December 17, p. 1D.

Weil, David (1992), 'Building Safety: The Role of Construction Unions in the Enforcement of OSHA', *Journal of Labor Research*, vol. 13(1), pp. 121-132.

PART III
PUBLIC POLICY:
COMPENSATIONS

Chapter 8

Benefits vs. Wages: How Prevailing Wage Laws Affect the Mix and Magnitude of Compensation to Construction Workers

Jeffrey S. Petersen and Erin M. Godtland[1]

Introduction

This chapter examines the impact of the repeal of state-level prevailing wage laws on compensation to construction workers. Using data from the 1980s and 1990s, we compare compensation levels of construction workers in (1) states that never had prevailing wage laws, (2) states that repealed their prevailing wage laws, and (3) states that have retained their prevailing wage laws. Specifically, we examine the impact that prevailing wage laws, and their repeals, have on compensation to construction workers, in terms of both wages and benefits. We also examine the relationship between prevailing wage laws and the mix of compensation packages between wages and benefits. We find that compensation levels to construction workers are significantly higher under prevailing wage laws. When states repeal the prevailing wage law, compensation levels decline to the levels of states that never had prevailing wage laws. We also find that prevailing wage laws are positively related to the share of benefits in compensation packages. Given the economic incentives in the construction sector that discourage the provision of benefits, the latter result is of particular importance.

The chapter is organized as follows: the first section provides background information about previous research on the impact of prevailing wage laws for the compensation of construction workers. The next section describes the data sources and key variables used in our empirical analysis. The final sections present our empirical results and a discussion of these results.

Background

Public construction represents approximately one-quarter of total construction dollars spent in the United States (U.S. Census, 2002). Prevailing wage legislation sets pay floors for construction workers on the majority of these public construction projects. The Davis-Bacon Act, the federal prevailing wage law, establishes floors for all federally-funded construction, and 31 state prevailing wage laws set floors for state-funded construction. With such a large proportion of construction labor costs mandated by prevailing wage laws, it is imperative to understand the impact of prevailing wage laws—and their repeals—on compensation levels in the construction industry.

Researchers have only recently begun to address this question. Kessler and Katz (1999) use Current Population Survey (CPS) individual-level data from 1970-1993 to measure the impact of the repeal of state prevailing wage laws on construction wages. They use a difference-in-difference-in-difference approach, which compares the wages of construction workers with workers in other blue-collar occupations in both prevailing wage law and non-PWL states. They find that repeals have a significantly negative effect on the average wage in construction. They show that the burden of the repeal is borne most heavily by white workers and union workers.

Petersen (2000) uses state-level data from 1982-1992 to compare the compensation of construction workers (both wages and benefits) in different states. He finds that prevailing wage laws have significantly positive effects on wages and benefits, and that prevailing wage law repeals have significantly negative effects on compensation levels.

This chapter expands on Petersen's results by providing additional analysis and updated statistics. In particular, we use data up to 2000 to assess the long-run trends in compensation in states that repealed their prevailing wage laws. We also conduct regression analyses to test the impact of prevailing wage laws on the percentage of compensation that is received in wages (as opposed to benefits).

Data and Sample

In this analysis, we use data from four national datasets: the Form 5500 series, the Census of Construction Industries, the Current Employment Statistics, and the Current Population Survey. Information on employee benefits comes from the Form 5500 series—an annual report that is filed with the Internal Revenue Service by all employers that have employee benefit plans.[2] Data on construction spending levels by state come from the Census of Construction Industries (CCI). The CCI is conducted every five years as part of the Census Bureau's Economic Census program and covers all employers that are primarily engaged in construction.[3]

Information on employment and earnings is taken from the Current Employment Statistics (CES). These data are collected through surveys by state employment security agencies, and are compiled and made available by the Bureau of Employment Statistics. The CES data are used to compute total annual wages (as opposed to wage rates) in construction. Finally, information on unionization rates comes from the Current Population Survey (CPS). CPS is a monthly survey of about 50,000 households conducted by the Bureau of Census for the Bureau of Labor Statistics.

The 50 states can be divided into three categories: (1) states that currently have prevailing wage laws, (2) states that repealed their prevailing wage laws, and (3) states that never had prevailing wage laws. Nine states have repealed their prevailing wage laws: Colorado (repealed in 1995), Louisiana (1988), Kansas (1987), Idaho (1985), New Hampshire (1985), Arizona (1984), Utah (1981), Alabama (1980), and Florida (1979). Oklahoma's prevailing wage law was invalidated in a court decision in 1995. Nine states never had prevailing wages laws: North Dakota, South Dakota, Iowa, Virginia, North Carolina, South Carolina, Georgia, Missouri, and Vermont. The remaining 31 states currently have prevailing wages laws.

Not all 50 of the states, however, are included in the sample. We exclude from our analysis the three states that repealed their prevailing wage laws prior to 1982 because our data begins in 1982, and we want to examine the impact of the actual repeal. We also exclude Alaska, Kentucky, Montana, Wyoming, Iowa and the District of Columbia because the data was incomplete for these states. This leaves 42 states in the study: 27 that kept their law, 8 that never had a law, and 7 that repealed their laws.

Impacts of Prevailing Wage Laws

Our data indicate that construction workers in states with prevailing wage laws have significantly higher compensation levels than in states without prevailing wage laws. This can be seen in Table 8.1, which shows the changes in compensation levels from 1982 to 1999 in states that currently have prevailing wage laws, states that never had prevailing wage laws, and states that repealed their prevailing wage laws. All figures are expressed in 2001 dollars. Total compensation packages in states with prevailing wage laws in 1999 were 33 percent higher than in states without prevailing wage laws. Benefit packages were 6.6 times higher for workers in states with prevailing wage laws than in states without prevailing wage laws. Similarly, for each component of compensation—wages, pension benefits, and health benefits—workers in states with prevailing wage laws had higher levels than workers in states without prevailing wage laws. Workers in states with prevailing wage laws also received a higher percentage of their compensation package in the form of benefits: 7.6 percent, versus 1.4 percent in states without prevailing wage laws.

Table 8.1 also shows that repeals of prevailing wage laws are associated with declines in compensation levels, approaching the levels of states that never had prevailing wage laws. From 1982 to 1999, total average compensation does not change substantially in states that kept their prevailing wage laws and in states that never had prevailing wage laws. In contrast, compensation levels fall by 20 percent in states that repealed their prevailing wage laws, coming close to the level of states that never had prevailing wage laws. Looking at the components of compensation, total average wages decrease dramatically in states that repealed their prevailing wage laws, with wages adjusting to the level of wages in states that never had prevailing wage laws. Total benefits and health benefits, in particular, increase markedly in states that kept their prevailing wage laws, but decline in states that never had prevailing wage laws and in states that repealed their prevailing wage laws. Pension benefits increase in states that never had prevailing wage laws, but drop by 59 percent in states that repealed their prevailing wage laws. Again, the average pension benefit in states repeal their prevailing wage laws is converging towards that of states that never had prevailing wage laws. Finally, the percentage of compensation in the form of benefits falls by 61 percent in states that repealed their laws, leaving just 1.4 percent of total compensation going to benefits—the same level as states that never had prevailing wage laws.

Empirical Models

To ensure that the results of the cross tabulations in Table 8.1 hold when other factors are considered that may affect compensation to construction workers, we run two sets of regressions.

Table 8.1 Comparison of average compensation and wage/benefit mix in states with and without prevailing wage law

	State with PWLs			Percent Change 1982-2000	State Never Had PWLs			Percent Change 1982-2000	State Repealed PWLs			Percent Change 1982-2000
	1982-1983	1991-1992	1999-2000		1982-1983	1991-1992	1999-2000		1982-1983	1991-1992	1999-2000	
Average Total Compensation	42,040	42,217	42,358	1	32,902	36,370	31,886	-3	42,012	35,045	33,656	-20
Average Wages	39,545	38,807	38,888	-2	32,480	35,816	31,429	-3	40,511	34,346	33,182	-18
Average Benefits	2,494	3,302	3,470	39	422	556	457	8	1,500	698	474	-68
Average Pension Benefits	1,320	1,386	1,307	-1	249	208	315	27	803	268	330	-59
Average Health Care Benefits	1,281	1,914	2,162	69	173	345	143	-18	697	430	144	-79
Percent of Compensation in Benefits	5.90	7.80	7.60	29	1.30	1.50	1.40	8	3.60	2.00	1.40	-61

Note: All figures, except the percents, are expressed in 2001 dollars. We excluded Kansas from our sample of states that repealed their prevailing wage laws because its benefit levels were extreme outliers relative to the other repeal states.

The first set measures the impact of prevailing wage laws on compensation, while controlling for unionization, the size of the construction industry, and the percentage of construction spending that is public. We run six regressions. The dependent variables for the six regressions are: (1) average total compensation, (2) average annual wages, (3) average percentage of compensation that is paid in wages, (4) average total benefits, (5) average health benefits, and (6) average pension benefits.[4] The explanatory variables are the same for each regression; they are: a dummy variable for whether there was a prevailing wage law in that state during that year (the primary variable of interest), the percentage of constructions workers who are union members, the log of total construction spending, and the percentage of construction spending that is for public construction.[5]

The second set of regressions measures how long it takes for repeals of prevailing wage laws to influence compensation levels. The dependent variables are the same as in the first set of regressions. And the explanatory variables are also the same, except that we use dummy variables to capture the effects of years since the repeal.

Note in our regression analysis, we assume that prevailing wage law repeals are not correlated with unobserved time-varying economic conditions, such as changes in unemployment levels in the construction sector. We believe this assumption is well founded because Petersen (2000) found no correlation between changes in state unemployment rates and the time of prevailing wage law repeal. However, the driving force behind whether states repeal their prevailing wage laws might be related to observed state characteristics that do not vary over time, such as the political leaning of the state. To control for unobserved state characteristics that do not vary over the years of the sample, we include state-level dummy variables in both sets of regressions.[6]

In order to better estimate the effect of the repeal, we run both sets of models with two different comparison groups. The first group compares the states that kept their prevailing wage law with states that repealed. The second group compares states that never had a prevailing wage law with states that repealed.

Results

The results of the first set of regressions show that prevailing wage laws have a significant and positive impact on compensation levels. (See Table

Table 8.2a Estimation of the effect of prevailing wage legislation on total compensation, wages, and the percentage of compensation in wages

	Dependent Variable					
	Total compensation		Wages		Percent of compensation in wages	
Independent variables	Kept and Repeal States	Never Had and repeal States	Kept and Repeal States	Never Had and repeal States	Kept and Repeal States	Never Had and repeal States
Presence of a P-W law (dummy variable)	0.114*** [0.03] -3.76	0.137** [0.04] -3.05	0.101*** [0.03] -3.35	0.138** [0.04] -3.04	-0.01*** [0.00] (-3.58)	-0.003 [0.51] -0.51
Unionization rate in construction industry	0.413** [0.14] -2.92	1.126*** [0.32] -3.55	0.388** [0.14] -2.75	1.100*** [0.32] -3.44	-0.025 [0.15] (-1.43)	-0.024 [0.44] (-0.77)
Total construction spending	0.191** [0.07] -2.78	0.194 [0.12] -1.57	0.192 [0.07] -2.82	0.232 [0.13] -1.85	0 [0.57] -0.57	0.000*** [0.00] -4.86
Percentage of construction spending that is public	0.211 [0.33] -0.64	-0.082 [0.56] (-0.15)	0.166 [0.33] -0.5	0.051 [0.57] -0.09	-0.04 [0.12] (-1.57)	0.11** [0.01] -2.53
Adjusted R^2	0.72	0.52	0.66	0.51	0.15	0.03
F Value	21.78	7.22	16.58	6.83	7.25	3.32
Prob > F	0.0001	0.0001	0.0001	0.0001	0	0.0002
Observations	374	154	374	154	374	154

Notes: T-statistics are in brackets and the p-value for the t-test is in parentheses. Statistical significance is indicated by ****=.0001, ***=0.001, **=0.01, and *=0.05. The other variables that were included in the regression, but are not included in the table are dummy variables for the years 1982-1991 (excluding 1992 as the reference category) and dummy variables for each state in the analysis.

The Economics of Prevailing Wage Laws

Table 8.2b Estimation of the effect of prevailing wage legislation on total benefits, pension benefits, and health care benefits

	Dependent Variable					
	Total compensation		Wages		Percent of compensation in wages	
Independent variables	Kept and Repeal States	Never Had and repeal States	Kept and Repeal States	Never Had and repeal States	Kept and Repeal States	Never Had and repeal States
Presence of a P-W law (dummy variable)	0.114*** [0.03] -3.76	0.137** [0.04] -3.05	0.101*** [0.03] -3.35	0.138** [0.04] -3.04	-0.01*** [0.00] (-3.58)	-0.003 [0.51] -0.51
Unionization rate in construction industry	0.413** [0.14] -2.92	1.126*** [0.32] -3.55	0.388** [0.14] -2.75	1.100*** [0.32] -3.44	-0.025 [0.15] (-1.43)	-0.024 [0.44] (-0.77)
Total construction spending	0.191** [0.07] -2.78	0.194 [0.12] -1.57	0.192 [0.07] -2.82	0.232 [0.13] -1.85	0 [0.57] -0.57	0.000*** [0.00] -4.86
Percentage of construction spending that is public	0.211 [0.33] -0.64	-0.082 [0.56] (-0.15)	0.166 [0.33] -0.5	0.051 [0.57] -0.09	-0.04 [0.12] (-1.57)	0.11** [0.01] -2.53
Adjusted R^2	0.72	0.52	0.66	0.51	0.15	0.03
F Value	21.78	7.22	16.58	6.83	7.25	3.32
Prob > F	0.0001	0.0001	0.0001	0.0001	0	0.0002
Observations	374	154	374	154	374	154

Notes: T-statistics are in brackets and the p-value for the t-test is in parentheses. Statistical significance is indicated by ****=.0001, ***=0.001, **=0.01, and *=0.05. The other variables that were included in the regression, but are not included in the table are dummy variables for the years 1982-1991 (excluding 1992 as the reference category) and dummy variables for each state in the analysis.

Table 8.3a Estimation of the effect of prevailing wage legislation on total compensation, wages, and the percentage of compensation in wages over time

Dependent Variable

Independent variables	Total compensation		Wages		Percent of compensation in wages	
	Kept and Repeal States	Never Had and repeal States	Kept and Repeal States	Never Had and repeal States	Kept and Repeal States	Never Had and repeal States
One year since P-W law repeal	-0.104*	-0.104	-0.105*	-0.111	-0.001	-0.006
	[0.05]	[0.06]	[0.04]	[0.07]	[0.82]	[0.33]
	(-2.19)	(-1.61)	(-2.24)	(-1.69)	(-0.23)	(-0.98)
Two years since P-W law repeal	-0.05	-0.081	-0.049	-0.085	0.002	-0.004
	[0.05]	[0.07]	[0.05]	[0.06]	[0.75]	[0.54]
	(-1.06)	(-1.23)	(-1.03)	(-1.28)	-0.32	(-0.62)
Three years since P-W law repeal	-0.113*	-0.125	-0.100*	-0.123	0.013**	0.002
	[0.05]	[0.07]	[0.05]	[0.07]	[0.03]	[0.76]
	(-2.37)	(-1.87)	(-2.12)	(-1.82)	-2.24	-0.31
Four years since P-W law repeal	-0.122*	-1.135*	-0.105*	-0.13	0.017***	0.005
	[0.05]	[0.07]	[0.05]	[0.07]	[0.00]	[0.51]
	(-2.56)	(-1.99)	(-2.23)	(-1.90)	-2.86	-0.67
Five years since P-W law repeal	-0.201****	-0.261***	-0.185***	-0.256***	0.016**	0.005
	[0.05]	[0.07]	[0.05]	[0.08]	[0.01]	[0.50]
	(-3.85)	(-3.49)	(-3.37)	(-3.38)	-2.59	-0.68
Six years since P-W law repeal	-0.068	-0.14	-0.038	-0.126	0.030***	0.014
	[0.06]	[0.09]	[0.06]	[0.09]	[0.00]	[0.13]
	(-1.16)	(-1.63)	(-0.66)	(-1.46)	-4.2	-1.54
Seven years since P-W law repeal	-0.048	-0.125	-0.014	-0.109	0.035***	0.016*
	[0.06]	[0.08]	[0.06]	[0.08]	[0.00]	[0.07]
	(-0.83)	(-1.50)	(-0.24)	(-1.29)	-4.89	-1.82
Adjusted R^2	0.72	0.52	0.66	0.5	0.01	0.08
F value	19.51	6.02	14.92	5.65	6.92	1.82
Prob > F	0.0001	0.0001	0.0001	0.0001	0	0.026
F value (1-7)	3.04	2.04	2.73	1.92	6.15	1.09
Prob > F	0.0042	0.0557	0.0091	0.072	0	0.37
Observations	374	154	374	154	374	154

Notes: T-statistics are in brackets and the p-value for the t-test is in parentheses. Statistical significance is indicated by ****=.0001, ***=0.001, **=0.01, and *=0.05. The other variables that were included in the regression, but are not included in the table are dummy variables for the years 1982-1991 (excluding 1992 as the reference category) and dummy variables for each state in the analysis.

Table 8.3b Estimation of the effect of prevailing wage legislation on total benefits, pension benefits, and health care benefits over time

	Total compensation		Wages		Percent of compensation in wages	
Independent variables	Kept and Repeal States	Never Had and repeal States	Kept and Repeal States	Never Had and repeal States	Kept and Repeal States	Never Had and repeal States
One year since	-0.201	-0.065	-0.268	-0.141	0.16	0.078
P-W law repeal	[0.13]	[0.43]	[0.19]	[0.52]	[0.35]	[0.65]
	(-1.56)	(-0.15)	(-1.44)	(-0.27)	-0.45	-0.12
Two years	-0.348**	-0.316	-0.371	-0.46	0.074	0.112
since P-W law	[0.13]	[0.44]	[0.19]	[0.53]	[0.36]	[0.66]
repeal	(-2,67)	(-0.72)	(-1.97)	(-0.88)	-0.21	-0.17
Three years	-0.715****	-0.671	-1.064****	-0.9	-0.271	-0.536
since P-W law	[0.13]	[0.45]	[0.19]	[0.53]	[0.36]	[0.67]
repeal	(-5.52)	(-1.51)	(-5.67)	(-1.68)	(-0.76)	(-0.80)
Four years	-0.488***	-0.5	-0.615**	-0.518	0.461	0.098
since P-W law	[0.13]	[0.45]	[0.19]	[0.54]	[0.35]	[0.68]
repeal	(-3.77)	(-0.50)	(-3.27)	(-0.96)	-1.3	-0.14
Five years	-0.578****	-0.61	-0.564**	-0.48	-0.2	-0.637
since P-W law	[0.14]	[0.50]	[0.21]	[0.59]	[0.39]	[0.75]
repeal	(-4.07)	(-1.22)	(-2.74)	(-0.80)	(-0.52)	(-0.85)
Six years since	-0.618****	-0.877	-0.874***	-0.895	0.663	-0.04
P-W law repeal	[0.16]	[0.57]	[0.23]	[0.68]	[0.44]	[0.86]
	(-3.87)	(-1.54)	(-3.78)	(-1.31)	-1.51	(-0.05)
Seven years	-0.614****	-0.955	-0.788***	-0.991	0.614	-0.037
since P-W law	[0.16]	[0.56]	[0.23]	[0.67]	[0.44]	[0.94]
repeal	(-3.86)	(-1.71)	(-3.41)	(-1.48)	-1.4	(-0.04)
Adjusted R^2	0.94	0.67	0.88	0.55	0.81	0.66
F value	104.45	10.5	51.57	6.77	30.64	9.92
Prob > F	0.0001	0.0001	0.0001	0.0001	0.0001	0.0001
F value (1-7)	7.61	0.8	6.67	0.68	1.037	0.24
Prob > F	0.0001	0.5972	0.0001	0.6891	0.4048	0.9733
Observations	374	154	374	154	374	154

Notes: T-statistics are in brackets and the p-value for the t-test is in parentheses. Statistical significance is indicated by ****=.0001, ***=0.001, **=0.01, and *=0.05. The other variables that were included in the regression, but are not included in the table are dummy variables for the years 1982-1991 (excluding 1992 as the reference category) and dummy variables for each state in the analysis.

8.2a and 8.2b for the results.) The presence of a prevailing wage law is associated with highly significant increases in total compensation, wages, total benefits, and especially pension benefits. Prevailing wage laws also improve the percentage of compensation in benefits.

Specifically, when comparing states that repealed their prevailing wage laws with states that kept their prevailing wage laws, prevailing wage laws boost total compensation by 12 percent, wages by 11 percent, total benefits by 61 percent, and pension benefits by 105 percent.[7] For this comparison group, prevailing wage laws also significantly reduced the percentage of compensation devoted to wages. Unionization and total construction spending have a highly significant and positive impact on total compensation and wages.

When comparing states that repealed with states that never had laws, prevailing wage laws raised compensation. In particular, total compensation increased by 14 percent, wages by 15 percent, and pension benefits by 104 percent. For this comparison group, the presence of a prevailing wage law does not significantly impact the percentage of compensation devoted to wages. Again, unionization has a highly significant and positive impact on total compensation, wages, and pension benefits. Total construction spending, however, does not have a significant effect on compensation.

The results of the second set of regressions show that the effects of prevailing wage law repeals on compensation levels are not immediate. (See Table 8.3a and 8.3b for the results.) In fact, the most significant effects of prevailing wage law repeals on total compensation and wages occur five years after the repeal has taken place. When comparing states that kept their prevailing wage law with states that repealed, the results show that total benefits, especially pension benefits, begin to decline significantly after three years have passed. With this comparison group, the lag effects of the prevailing wage law also have a significantly positive effect on the percentage of compensation devoted to wages.

When comparing states that repealed with states that never had prevailing wage laws, the impacts of the prevailing wage law become significant at the five-year mark for total compensation and wages. However, no significant lag effect is evident for the percentage of compensation devoted to wages.

Discussion

Cost incentives might explain why prevailing wage laws have a stronger impact on benefit levels—particularly pension benefits—than on wage levels. Healthcare and pension contributions are tax-free, whereas wages have a payroll tax. Thus, once prevailing wage laws require employers to pay benefits, the employers have an incentive to establish benefit plans (as opposed to paying the benefits through wages) in order to reduce their labor costs. Given the two choices—health benefits or pension benefits—employers are likely to choose pension plans because they typically have lower start-up and administrative costs (Kruse, 1995).

Economic incentives arising from the structure of construction employment might explain why construction workers receive a greater proportion of their compensation in wages after prevailing wage laws are repealed. First, the cyclical and seasonal nature of construction employment provides an incentive not to lock money in health and retirement plans. Instead, to cope with intermittent bouts of unemployment, construction workers might prefer to receive their compensation in wages. This is especially true if compensation levels are reduced after a prevailing wage law repeal. On the employer side, high turnover among construction workers removes a primary incentive for employers to provide benefits – to induce loyalty to the firm. Additionally, construction firms typically employ a small number of workers. Consequently, the cost of providing benefits per worker is higher among construction firms than among larger firms that can achieve economies of scale in the provision of benefits.

There are several possible explanations for why the effect of a repeal might not be immediate. First, compensation will fall as workers' bargaining power erodes over time after the repeal (Kessler and Katz, 1999). Workers will lose bargaining power because non-union employers will underbid union employers, who are still constrained to union compensation levels. Over time, union employers will renegotiate compensation packages to lower levels. However, packages could take years to adjust if workers have multi-year contracts. The typical union contract lasts for three-years. Thus, it is not surprising that the repeal begins to have a highly significant impact on benefit levels at the three-year mark when the entire construction labor force has undergone at least one renegotiation since the repeal.

Conclusions

This chapter analyzes the effects of prevailing wage laws—and their repeals—over an eighteen-year period. The primary result is that after a repeal, compensation levels decline to the level of states that never had prevailing wage laws. This is true for compensation in both wages and benefits. In showing that the proportion of compensation devoted to wages also returns to the market level after a repeal, this chapter highlights an important and potentially negative side-effect of the repeal: construction workers, when left to their own (or their employers') devices, receive their compensation in the form of wages. This is an important consideration for policymakers in choosing whether or not to repeal a prevailing wage law. The prevailing wage law may, in fact, be operating in the long-run interest of the construction worker, while the construction worker and his employer operate in the short-run.

Notes

[1] Jeffrey Petersen is an Economist at Allman Economic Analysis and Erin Godtland is an Economist with the United States General Accounting Office. The opinions expressed in this article are the authors' and should not be attributed to Allman Economic Analysis or the General Accounting Office.

[2] The data are made available to the public through the Pension and Welfare Benefits Administration of the Department of Labor. The Form 5500 began in 1976 following the passage of the Employment Retirement Income Security Act (ERISA). The data only became available to the public in 1982. To calculate average health and pension benefits per construction worker at the state level using the Form 5500 data, employer contributions to benefit plans were summed up by state and divided by the total number of construction workers. To impute values for the years between the survey years, a 5-year moving average was applied.

[3] The CCS was conducted in 1977, 1982, 1987, 1992, and 1997. Data in the CCI is broken down by public (federal and state government) and private sector spending. CCI data was used to calculate the total level of construction spending per state and the percentage of construction spending that is publicly financed.

[4] Each of the continuous dependent variables is logged to normalize the distribution of the variable and deflated by the consumer price index.

[5] The regression equation is specified following Cutler and Gruber (1996).

[6] This is known as a fixed-effect technique.

[7] The coefficients are logged differentials, so the percentage changes are calculated with $(\exp\beta-1) \times 100$.

References

Cutler, David M., and Gruber, Jonathan (1996), 'The Effect of Medicaid Expansions on Public Insurance, Private Insurance, and Redistribution', *American Economic Review,* vol. 86(2), pp. 378-383.

Ghilarducci, T., Mangum, G, Petersen, J., and Philips P. (1995), *Portable Pensions for Causal Labor Markets: Lessons from the Operating Engineers Central Pension Fund,* Quorum Books, Westport , CT.

Kessler, Daniel P., and Katz, Lawrence (1999), 'Prevailing Wage Laws and Construction Labor Markets', *NBER Working Paper Series.* Working Paper 7454.

Petersen, Jeffrey S. (2000), 'Health Care and Pension Benefits for Construction Workers: The Role of Prevailing Wage Laws', *Industrial Relations,* vol. 39(2), pp. 246-264.

Thieblot, A.J. (1995), *State Prevailing Wage Law: An Assessment at the Start of 1995,* Associated Builders and Contractors, Rosslyn, VA.

U.S. Department of Commerce, Census Bureau (2002), *Current Construction Reports,* February, Government Printing Office, Washington, D.C.

Chapter 9

Health Care Subsidies in Construction: Does the Public Sector Subsidize Low Wage Contractors?

C. Jeffrey Waddoups

Introduction

Employer based health insurance (EBHI) is the primary method for financing health care among the non-poor and non-elderly in the U.S.[1] Workers in the construction industry, however, are left without access to EBHI at exceptionally high rates compared to their counterparts in other industries. The restricted access to health insurance is primarily a result of institutional rules in health insurance markets and the organization of work in the industry. Whether insured or not, workers and their dependents still require health care, and without health insurance their medical bills are less likely to be paid. To clarify the relationship between EBHI and uncompensated health care, especially as it is connected to workers in the construction industry, the present study explores 1) market failures that result in a low incidence of EBHI among construction workers; 2) the role collective bargaining plays in resolving such market failures; and 3) the relationship between EBHI and uncompensated care costs at safety-net hospitals and clinics.

To address the three issues, I use evidence on rates of EBHI and other health insurance programs in the March supplement of the Current Population Survey (CPS) combined with information on uncompensated care that is provided to employed guarantors by a major safety-net hospital and its clinics in southern Nevada.[2] Southern Nevada is a good venue for a study of such employment issues in the construction sector, because a relatively high percentage of the region's total employment is in the industry.

The Distribution of Uncompensated Health Care Costs

A preponderance of the evidence indicates that lack of health insurance imposes costs on the uninsured through poorer health status than they would otherwise experience (Hadley, 2002). The uninsured tend to delay care, are sicker when they receive treatment, and often obtain medical attention in hospital emergency rooms, which is a particularly inefficient method of delivering most health services. Inadequate access to health insurance may also impose costs associated with financial insecurity related to a lower probability of employment and insufficient asset protection (Stern, 1989).[3]

Besides costs imposed on the uninsured themselves, the community also bears costs resulting from the lack of EBHI. Poorer health outcomes among the uninsured impose negative externalities. For example, in the case of communicable diseases, others are put at greater risk when treatment is delayed or avoided.

Adverse health outcomes that affect households' economic well-being also impose external costs. Poor health status associated with lack of insurance has been related to lower incomes and rates of labor force participation, which increase the risk of impoverishment and reliance on publicly funded social welfare programs. In addition, when a patient receives uncompensated health care, the costs are shifted elsewhere. Such costs may be paid through higher local taxes to subsidize safety-net health care providers, and if the tax subsidies are not forthcoming, a decline in the quantity and quality of health care may be expected. Uncompensated care costs may also be reflected in higher prices for medical care to paying patients and higher insurance premiums.

To the extent that higher prices for health care are incorporated into insurance premiums, employers who offer health insurance face higher costs of doing business. Such costs are distributed among employers, workers, and consumers through a combination of lower profits, lower wages, and/or higher prices for goods and services. The incidence of the relative cost burden depends on the elasticities of supply and demand in the relevant labor and product markets.

The Construction Industry: Market Failure and a Low Incidence of EBHI

A number of institutional and economic problems reduce the probability that workers in the construction industry can gain meaningful access to

EBHI. Traditional EBHI programs are built on the assumption of relatively long-term employment relationships between workers and firms. In the construction industry, however, short-term employment relationships are often observed. Construction workers may work for several contractors over the course of any given year (Grob, 1994). Consequently, tenure of employment with a single employer may not last long enough to meet an EBHI program's eligibility requirements, which generally range from three to six months. Construction work is also highly sensitive to seasonal and cyclical factors, which increase the probability of unemployment spells and further decrease the probability of obtaining EBHI (Ghilarducci *et al.*, 1995).

Rules governing eligibility for health insurance coverage also exclude pre-existing conditions. Suppose a construction worker successfully obtains EBHI with a contractor. If a serious health condition arises during the current employment spell, the insurance plan of the next contractor generally would not cover the condition because it would have become pre-existing with the change of employers.

Another problem in the market for insurance is the small size of construction firms (The Center to Protect Workers Rights, 1998, p. 3). Small firms in general find EBHI relatively expensive, because economies of scale in administration cannot be realized and the small group over which the risk is spread. Administration costs for small firms average about 40 percent of total costs, while administrative costs for larger firms (over 10,000 employees) average only 5.5 percent (Helms, Gauthier, and Campion, 1992). In addition, small groups and groups with higher levels of turnover increase the risk for insurers, which leads them to charge higher premiums (Henderson,1999). Consequently, small employers in general, and small construction contractors in particular, are less likely to provide EBHI.

Collective Bargaining and the Resolution of Market Failures

Problems in the insurance market that restrict access to EBHI in construction apply mostly to the non-union sector. In the union sector, the problem caused by short-term work is solved by contractual arrangements between the union and employer that specify benefits payments to be paid into jointly managed health and welfare trusts. The trusts procure health insurance that covers workers in the same trades. Health insurance obtained in this manner is not employer specific, so that changing employers does not automatically result in a loss of health insurance or high COBRA payments. The size of the contractor is also no longer an issue because the risk pool includes workers employed by numerous small employers. Thus economies of scale in administration and lower underwriting charges based on a larger and more stable risk pool are realized. The problem with seasonal and cyclical work is addressed with the relatively modest amount of annual work hours required for eligibility.[4]

The Role of Prevailing Wage Laws

Along with collective bargaining in the construction industry, prevailing wage laws play a role in resolving market failure in the provision of EBHI. Union and non-union contractors who work on prevailing wage jobs—all federal government and many state and local government construction projects—must pay wages and benefits at a specified prevailing rate. For a non-union contractor that may not have a benefits program, any additional compensation may be paid as cash or by starting a benefits program. Fringe benefits, including EBHI, are tax advantaged over money wages, which makes them relatively more attractive than cash compensation to meet prevailing wage requirements. Prevailing wage laws also take compensation out of competition in the bidding process, thus protecting EBHI and other benefits offered in the union sector (Petersen, 2000).

In spite of the ability of collective bargaining and prevailing wage laws to resolve market failures, a minority of workers is covered under union contracts and only a small part of construction work is performed for prevailing wages. Hirsh and MacPherson (2002) estimate that approximately 20 percent of construction workers are covered under union contracts. A similar percentage of construction work was performed for prevailing wages (Petersen, 2000).

Predictions

A majority of construction work is performed without union coverage and outside prevailing wage laws, thus institutions that resolve market failures in the provision of EBHI do not generally operate in construction labor markets. Therefore, the following predictions appear plausible. (1) Of those reporting employment, workers in the construction industry (along with their dependents) are predicted to be among the least likely to have EBHI. (2) Because collective bargaining resolves problems with market failures that reduce access to EBHI, unionized workers in the construction sector are more likely to hold EBHI than their non-union counterparts. (3) Because market failures are particularly acute in construction, union coverage is predicted to be a more important predictor of EBHI coverage for workers in construction than for workers in other industries. (4) Restricted access to EBHI in construction is predicted to cause workers in the industry (and their dependents) to receive a disproportionate share of uncompensated health care.

The four predictions are addressed in the following case study of health insurance and uncompensated care provided by a large safety net hospital and associated clinics in southern Nevada. The area, which encompasses most of the Las Vegas standard metropolitan statistical area (SMSA), employs a larger proportion of its workers in the construction industry than average in the U.S. Between 1997 and 1999 approximately 10.1 percent of region's total employment was in the industry, compared to 6.6 percent nationally.[5] Data from the March supplement of the CPS are used to establish the incidence of health insurance coverage by various characteristics, including industry of employment and other dimensions of employment status. Data drawn from administrative records of a local safety-net hospital and associated clinics are used to obtain estimates of uncompensated care costs by various types of care (inpatient, emergency room, and outpatient). The data also contain information on the industry of guarantors' employment.

Incidence of EBHI: Estimates from the CPS

The CPS contains a number of questions pertaining to health insurance coverage. Although the sampling methodology used to gather CPS data guarantees representativeness at the state level, the number of observations available to estimate insurance coverage for a given state may be quite small. The State Health Access Data Assistance Center (2001) suggests that three years of CPS data at the state level should be aggregated to make the estimates more statistically reliable. Following the Center's suggestion, I use data in the March CPS from the years 1998-2000. The questions on health insurance coverage are retrospective and pertain to the previous year, thus all insurance and employment numbers in this study derived from the CPS pertain to the 1997-99 period.

Sub-samples of the CPS generally are not guaranteed to be representative of the population at the level of a single county or SMSA. The results reported in Table 9.1 through 9.4, therefore, are calculated using data on the state of Nevada.[6]

The figures on EBHI coverage for the U.S., Nevada, and Clark County are virtually identical, as demonstrated in Table 9.1 (0.622, 0.629, and 0.614). Insurance coverage from all sources is substantially higher in

The Economics of Prevailing Wage Laws

Table 9.1 Proportion with health insurance (1997-99)

| Source of Coverage | Location | | |
	United States	Nevada	Clark County*
Employment Based	0.622	0.629	0.614
Private (Including Employment Based)	0.708	0.712	0.690
Government (Medicare, Medicaid, Military)	0.244	0.215	0.210
Total Coverage	0.842	0.818	0.805

Source: Current Population Survey (CPS), March Supplement (1998-2000).
Note: *The CPS does not guarantee representative sampling below the state level.

the U.S., however, because of the relatively smaller proportion of Nevada's residents covered under government-sponsored programs such as Medicaid, Medicare, and military-related insurance. In particular, the Medicaid coverage rate in Nevada is quite low compared to the U.S. in general.[7]

Ethnicity, Race, Gender, National Origin, and Age

Focusing on workers in Nevada, health insurance coverage is especially sparse in the Hispanic population. Over 16 percentage points separate the white non-Hispanic and Hispanic populations. Respondents who report Hispanic ethnicity are less likely to be insured through both employment-based and government-sponsored programs. Non-citizens are also particularly likely to be uninsured. Although gender does not appear to be a predictor of insurance coverage, there is a clear trend toward increasing insurance coverage with age among adults.

Income

Respondents in families at or near the poverty level are less likely to be covered by health insurance. Members of households with incomes below the poverty cut-off are covered by EBHI at a rate of only 0.203 compared to a 0.795 rate for those with incomes over 300 percent of poverty. Impoverished families are more likely to be covered under a government-sponsored program than their higher income counterparts, but that still leaves them with lower rates of coverage. Nearly 91 percent of families above 300 percent of poverty are covered compared to approximately 62 percent for those below the poverty line (see Table 9.2).

Table 9.2 Proportion of Nevada's population with health insurance by demographic characteristics

Characteristics	Emp.-Based	Private Incl. Emp.-Based	Govt.	Total Cov.
White Non-Hispanic	0.636	0.718	0.208	0.816
Other Race	0.602	0.641	0.214	0.792
Hispanic	0.544	0.578	0.124	0.653
Foreign Born	0.573	0.698	0.256	0.826
Citizen	0.637	0.724	0.226	0.833
Non-citizen	0.534	0.559	0.079	0.624
Female	0.634	0.715	0.214	0.826
Male	0.625	0.708	0.216	0.809
Age less than 18	0.625	0.708	0.216	0.809
Age 18 to 24	0.486	0.582	0.118	0.659
Age 25 to 54	0.718	0.756	0.083	0.803
Age 55 to 64	0.678	0.779	0.190	0.855
Age over 65	0.298	0.608	0.958	0.997
Family Income Below Poverty	0.204	0.325	0.347	0.615
100 and 200 Percent of Poverty	0.446	0.534	0.285	0.712
200 and 300 Percent of Poverty	0.572	0.659	0.209	0.782
Over 300 Percent of Poverty	0.795	0.867	0.156	0.910

Source: Current Population Survey, March Supplement (1998-2000).

Industry, Employer Size, and Work Status

Results in Tables 9.3 support the discussion above on the problem with access to EBHI for construction workers. In fact the coverage rate is the lowest among all industries at 0.599. Although the EBHI coverage rate among workers in trade (0.617) is close to construction's rate, when total insurance coverage is accounted for the gap between construction and trade increases slightly from 0.686 to 0.736.[8] Workers in 'Government' and 'Hotel, Gaming, and Recreation' are the most likely to be covered by EBHI, with proportions of 0.873 and 0.804, respectively. Union density is high among workers in Las Vegas's Hotel Gaming and Recreation sector, which provides the industry's relatively unskilled workers with the economic power to bargain for health insurance. The union also sets a

Table 9.3 Proportion of Nevada's population with health insurance by work status

Characteristics	Emp.-Based	Private Incl. Emp.-Based	Govt.	Total Cov.
Construction	0.599	0.666	0.087	0.686
Trade	0.617	0.681	0.118	0.736
Hotel, Gaming, Recreation	0.804	0.816	0.090	0.852
Comm, Trans. Pub. Ut., Manufac.	0.787	0.821	0.103	0.836
Services	0.731	0.805	0.111	0.852
Government	0.873	0.887	0.191	0.927
Agriculture, Mining	0.625	0.672	0.040	0.712
No Work	0.386	0.583	0.532	0.842
Small Employer	0.536	0.659	0.128	0.716
Medium Sized Employer	0.731	0.765	0.093	0.783
Large Employer	0.807	0.835	0.106	0.878
Part Time	0.642	0.747	0.142	0.805
Full Time	0.760	0.795	0.073	0.820

Source: Current Population Survey, March Supplement (1998-2000).

compensation pattern that is generally met by non-union employers (Waddoups, 1999; Waddoups and Eade, 2002).

Another important determinant of EBHI is employer size. As Table 9.3 demonstrates, only about one-half of workers and their family members can rely on small employers for insurance coverage. The figure for large employers is over 80 percent. As mentioned previously, a disproportionate number of construction firms are small. In addition, part-timers are much less likely to have access to EBHI; however, when government-sponsored programs are considered the figures converge (0.805 for part-time workers and 0.820 for full-time workers).

Families and EBHI

Health insurance coverage is often a family matter that not only affects workers, but their spouses and dependent children as well. To capture this effect, I defined a 'Construction Families' category. A construction family is defined as two or more individuals living together who are related by

Table 9.4 Proportion of Nevada's population with health insurance coverage: working families,* Hispanic and non-Hispanic ethnicity (1997-1999)

Characteristic	Emp.-Based	Private Incl. Emp.-Based	Govt.	Total Cov.
Construction Family	0.586	0.643	0.094	0.681
Other Working Family	0.716	0.765	0.139	0.835
Hispanic Construction Family	0.426	0.443	0.063	0.506
Non-Hispanic Construction Family	0.677	0.756	0.112	0.779
Other Hispanic Working Family	0.641	0.659	0.082	0.698
Other Non-Hispanic Working Family	0.732	0.788	0.152	0.864

Source: Current Population Survey, March Supplement (1998-2000).
Note: *Families are defined as a group of 2+ people residing together related by birth, marriage or adoption.

marriage, birth, or adoption, and where one or more of the adults in the family are employed in the construction industry.

For comparison, I also defined an 'Other Working Families' category using similar criteria, but with the caveat that in a family with two working adults, one of which worked in construction, the family is considered a construction family. The results in Table 9.4 show that construction families hold EBHI at the rate of 0.586, compared to a rate of 0.716 for other working families The difference in total coverage between the two groups remains almost identical, but the rates increase to 0.681 and 0.835.

A striking difference among construction families emerges when the category is broken down according to Hispanic ethnicity. Well under one-half (0.426) of individuals in Hispanic construction families hold EBHI compare to a rate of 0.677 for non-Hispanic construction families. When other forms of health insurance are accounted for, a large gap in coverage remains (0.506 and 0.779). Although a similar pattern emerges between Hispanic families and non-Hispanic families working in other industries, the size of the gap is smaller with rates of 0.698 and 0.864.

Table 9.5 Probability of health insurance coverage by industry, union status, and insurance type[a]

Industry	Averages	Employment Based[b]		Difference Un-Nonun.
		Union	Nonunion	
Construction	0.691	0.889	0.612	0.277
Trade	0.718	0.817	0.711	0.106
Comm, Trans, Manuf., Util.	0.902	0.939	0.888	0.051
Services	0.779	0.876	0.769	0.106
Government	0.940	0.965	0.916	0.049
		Government[c]		
Construction	0.021	0.010	0.026	-0.016
Trade	0.064	0.042	0.065	-0.023
Comm, Trans, Manuf., Util.	0.028	0.023	0.030	-0.006
Services	0.054	0.045	0.055	-0.010
Government	0.061	0.046	0.074	-0.028

Source: Current Population Survey, March Supplement (1998-2000).

Notes: [a] probabilities calculated from logistic regression models, where the independent variables included controls for union coverage, employment size, managerial occupation, professional/technical occupation, part-time status, family income relative to the federally defined poverty cut-off, citizenship status, age, gender, race ethnicity, and national origin.

[b] Parameter estimate on union variable is statistically significant in all models.

[c] Parameter estimate on union variable is statistically significant in all models but Comm, Trans, Manuf., Util.

Union Coverage and EBHI

Numerous studies have documented the positive correlation between unions and fringe benefits (e.g., Freeman, 1981; Wiatrowski, 1994). The previous discussion, which described the difficulties non-union construction contractors face in providing EBHI without trade unions to resolve market failures, suggests that union coverage in the construction sector is more likely to be an important factor in predicting the incidence of EBHI than union coverage in other industries.

To test the prediction, I used March CPS data from 1998-2000 as before. However, region-specific or state-specific data would not provide reliable estimates on the union effect because of the dearth in observations. Instead, observations drawn from the entire March CPS data for the years

1998-2000 are used.[9] The probability of EBHI coverage was modeled as a function of a number of variables according to a logistic functional form. The variables included union coverage, along with other factors that might affect the probability of EBHI.[10] The model was estimated separately for five major industry categories as listed in Table 9.5. Numbers in the table are predicted probabilities evaluated at the sample means of all the independent variables except 'union coverage', which was evaluated separately at zero (non-union) and one (union). In addition, I set the values of the two dummy variables 'manager' and 'professional/ technical worker' to zero, which provides a more accurate simulation of the probability of EBHI among production workers.

The results show a striking gap between the probability of EBHI among union and non-union workers in the construction industry compared to the gap in other industries. The findings in Table 9.5 leave little doubt that unions play a vital role in correcting the market failures that lead to a disproportionately small number of construction workers with EBHI coverage. In fact, the union effect on increasing the probability of EBHI coverage for non-managerial, non-professional/technical construction workers is more than 2.5 times larger than the effect in the next closest industry.

The analysis thus far has indicated that workers in the construction industry are less likely to have access to EBHI than workers in other industries, and that union coverage plays a stronger role in providing EBHI to workers in construction than in other industries. In light of the current distribution of EBHI across industries, one would expect that construction workers would receive a disproportionately large share of uncompensated health care. In the next section, I will use administrative data from a local safety-net hospital and its associated clinics to address such an expectation.

Uncompensated Care and the Employed

There are three majors classifications of health care provided by the hospital and its complement of clinics: inpatient care, which occurs if a patient is admitted to the hospital; emergency room care, which is meant to provide care for particularly acute injuries and illnesses, and outpatient care, which consists of such functions as minor surgical procedures, pharmacy, radiology, primary care clinics, labs, among other types of care. The administrative data include patients who received uncompensated inpatient, emergency room, or outpatient care during fiscal years 1998-2000.

Table 9.6 Expected uncompensated care costs relative to actual uncompensated care costs by industry: inpatient care (FYs 1998–2000)

Industry	Percent Employ.	Percent Uncomp. Care	Expected (Exp.) Cost ($)	Actual (Act.) Cost ($)	Diff. ($)	Percent Act.>Exp.
Construction	10.1	19.1	1,882,371	3,553,790	-1,671,418	88.8
Wholesale, Retail Trade	20.3	24.8	3,778,823	4,618,868	-840,044	22.2
Hotel, Gaming, Recr.	17.1	17.7	3,181,991	3,286,167	-104,176	3.3
Comm, Transp., Manuf., Util.	8.8	7.1	1,630,295	1,315,560	314,735	-19.3
Services (excluding Hotel)	38.8	26.8	7,231,707	4,982,410	2,249,297	-31.1
Government	3.5	2.7	645,820	498,820	147,000	-22.8
Agriculture, Mining	1.4	1.9	267,430	362,823	-95,393	35.7
Total Acct. Balances	45,289,315		18,618,437	18,618,437		
Cost-to-Charge Ratio*	0.411					
Total Cost	18,618,437					

Sources: Current Population Survey, March Supplement (1998-2000) and hospital administrative data.
Note: *Industry specific cost figures are adjusted by the cost-to-charge ratio.

Particularly relevant for the present study is the proportion of the total costs that are attributable to guarantors who report employment. The administrative data contain the guarantors' employers, which I allocated into broad industry categories largely consistent with the industry codes used in the CPS.[11] The industrial categories were 'Construction', 'Wholesale and Retail Trade', 'Hotel, Gaming, and Recreation' 'Communication, Transportation, Manufacturing, and Public Utilities', 'Services (excluding Hotel)', and 'Agriculture and Mining'. If a reported employer could not be classified, the observation was excluded, which occurred in less than two percent of the cases. The same industrial categories were constructed using March CPS data. Casual inspection of Table 9.6 reveals that employment in 'Construction' and 'Hotel, Gaming, and Recreation' in the region are notably high compared to most locations, whereas employment in the 'Communication, Transportation, Manufacturing, and Public Utilities' category is quite low.

Table 9.7 Expected uncompensated care costs relative to actual uncompensated care costs by industry: emergency room care (FYs 1998-2000)

Industry	Percent Employ.	Percent Uncomp. Care	Expected (Exp.) Cost ($)	Actual (Act.) Cost ($)	Diff. ($)	Percent Act.>Exp.
Construction	10.1	14.1	1,184,672	1,654,862	-470,190	39.7
Wholesale, Retail Trade	20.3	29.2	2,378,205	3,419,596	-1,041,392	43.8
Hotel, Gaming, Recr.	17.1	19.1	2,002,588	2,233,710	-231,122	11.5
Comm, Transp., Manuf., Util.	8.8	6.7	1,026,027	786,972	239,055	-23.3
Services (excluding Hotel)	38.8	26.5	4,551,279	3,105,073	1,446,206	-31.8
Government	3.5	2.4	406,447	282,372	124,075	-30.5
Agriculture, Mining	1.4	2.0	168,307	234,940	-66,633	39.6
Total Acct. Balances	67,542,312		11,717,524	11,717,524		
Proportion Employed	0.422					
Cost-to-Charge Ratio*	0.411					
Total Cost	11,717,524					

Sources: Current Population Survey, March Supplement (1998-2000) and hospital administrative data.

Note: *Industry specific cost figures are adjusted by the cost-to-charge ratio.

The Distribution of Uncompensated Care by Industry

About one-third of uncompensated care goes to patients and/or guarantors who report employment.[12] A distribution of uncompensated care according to dollar costs by industry is compared to the distribution of employment by industry (as calculated using the March CPS data). If the uncompensated care is distributed among industries according to proportions of each industry's employment share, then approximately 10.1 percent of uncompensated care would be expected to go to workers in 'Construction' 20.3 percent to workers in 'Wholesale and Retail Trade', and so on. In contrast to the 10.1 percent employment share, the construction sector accounts for 19.1 percent of the uncompensated

Table 9.8 Expected uncompensated care costs relative to actual uncompensated care costs by industry: outpatient care (FYs 1998-2000)

Industry	Percent Employ.	Percent Uncomp. Care	Expected (Exp.) Cost. ($)	Actual (Act.) Cost ($)	Diff. ($)	Percent Act.>Exp.
Construction	10.1	16.1	693,091	1,105,715	-412,624	59.5
Wholesale, Retail Trade	20.3	21.0	1,391,366	1,440,377	-49,011	3.5
Hotel, Gaming, Recr.	17.1	22.2	1,171,612	1,521,889	-350,277	29.9
Comm, Transp., Manuf., Util.	8.8	6.1	600,276	419,250	181,026	-30.2
Services (excluding Hotel)	38.8	29.6	2,662,721	2,025,980	636,741	-23.9
Government	3.5	4.5	237,791	308,225	-70,433	29.6
Agriculture, Mining	1.4	0.5	98,468	33,891	64,577	-65.6
Total Acct. Balances	32,955,666			6,855,326	6,855,326	
Proportion Employed	0.506					
Cost-to-Charge Ratio*	0.411					
Total Cost	6,855,326					

Sources: Current Population Survey, March Supplement (1998-2000) and hospital administrative data.
Note: *Industry specific cost figures are adjusted by the cost-to-charge ratio.

inpatient care, which represents a substantial rate of over-representation relative to other industries. In the case of inpatient care, the construction industry is a source of disproportionately high uncompensated care costs, which are likely borne by the industry's workers, the hospitals, and the community. Over-representation in costs by 'Construction' is also evident in emergency room and outpatient care (see Tables 9.7 and 9.8). 'Wholesale and Retail Trades' and 'Hotel, Gaming, and Recreation' also show relative over-representation in uncompensated care costs.

At this point it is informative to assess the distribution of EBHI according to industry by reviewing Table 9.3 in order to make a connection between inter-industry differences in insurance coverage rates and the incidence of uncompensated care. Table 9.3 indicates that 'Construction and 'Wholesale and Retail Trade' are characterized by the lowest rates of both EBHI and total insurance coverage. Not coincidentally, Tables 9.6-9.8

Table 9.9 Expected (Exp.) uncompensated care costs relative to actual (Act.) costs: inpatient, emergency room, and outpatient (FYs 1998-2000)

Industry	Percent Employ.	(Exp.) Cost ($)	(Act.) Cost ($)	Diff. ($)	Percent Act.>Exp
Construction	10.1	3,760,134	6,314,366	-2,554,233	67.9
Wholesale, Retail Trade	20.3	7,548,394	9,478,841	-1,930,447	25.6
Hotel, Gaming, Recr.	17.1	6,356,190	7,041,765	-685,575	10.8
Comm, Transp., Manuf., Util.	8.8	3,256,598	2,521,782	734,816	-22.6
Services (excluding Hotel)	38.8	14,445,707	10,113,463	4,332,244	-30.0
Government	3.5	1,290,059	1,089,416	200,642	-15.6
Agriculture, Mining	1.4	534,205	631,653	-97,448	18.2
Total Costs		37,191,287	37,191,287		

Source: hospital administrative data and Current Population Survey, March Supplement (1998-2000).

Note: *Cost Figures are adjusted to reflect the cost-to-charge ratio.

also indicate that the two industries have the highest rates of uncompensated care relative to their employment shares.

In order to establish the dollar value of uncompensated care by industry, the account balances of employed guarantors are summed by industry. For comparison, the expected sums—given that uncompensated care was distributed proportionally across industries—are also reported. Finally, the percent by which *observed* sums exceed (or lag) *expected* sums is calculated for each industry. These results are also located in Tables 9.6-9.8. For inpatients, observed uncompensated care costs out-stripped expected costs by 88.8 percent for 'Construction'. Compare 88.8 percent for 'Construction' to 22.2 percent for 'Wholesale and Retail Trade' and 3.3 percent for 'Hotel, Gaming, and Recreation'. Workers (and their dependents) connected with the construction sector are especially over-represented among inpatients. Over the three year period the observed costs of uncompensated care amounted to nearly $3.6 million, which is nearly $1.7 million more than would have been expected if 'Construction' had the same rate of uncompensated care as its share of employment. Although the same pattern is evident for 'Wholesale and Retail Trade' and 'Agriculture and Mining', the differences in observed and expected sums are much smaller (22.2 percent and 35.7 percent).

Uncompensated emergency room and outpatient care costs connected to the construction sector do not stand out as noticeably as inpatient costs when compared to costs associated with workers in 'Wholesale and Retail Trade' and 'Hotel, Gaming, and Recreation'. In fact, uncompensated care in the emergency room is disproportionately attributable to recipients connected with 'Wholesale and Retail Trade;' however, 'Wholesale and Retail Trade' and 'Construction' both exhibit high rates of over-representation relative to other industries. For uncompensated outpatient care, as with inpatient care, the construction industry outpaces the others relative to their employment shares. Table 9.9 contains the aggregated findings from which to arrive at the total magnitude by which observed and expected industry specific uncompensated care figures deviate from each other. Observed uncompensated care figures attributed to construction are 67.9 percent higher than expected figures. The corresponding percentages for 'Wholesale and Retail Trade' and 'Hotel, Gaming, and Recreation' are 25.6 and 10.8 percent. The other industries remain under-represented in uncompensated care. In total, over a three-year period with no adjustment for inflation, the extra-normal costs of uncompensated care attributable to the patients connected to construction amounted to approximately $2.6 million. The analogous figure for 'Wholesale and Retail Trade' was somewhat lower at $1.9 million. All uncompensated care costs attributable to employed construction workers over the period amounted to $6.3 million, and the total costs of uncompensated care to the employed and their dependents was over $37 million for the years 1998-2000.

Conclusion

The connection between the lack of EBHI and disproportionate uncompensated care costs is clear when insurance coverage rates and uncompensated care distributions by industry are examined together. In particular the low incidence of EBHI among workers in the construction industry appears to result in a disproportionately high incidence of uncompensated care. The analysis also suggests that higher levels of EBHI among workers in construction, as is observed in the unionized segment, would likely reduce over-representation of construction workers in the uncompensated care category.

It is clear that a large share of uncompensated care is attributable to the construction industry relative to its size. Economic logic dictates that such costs must be subsidized from some other source. There is little doubt that construction workers and their families suffer from more precarious financial positions (not to mention poorer health) than would be the case with greater access to EBHI. And in all likelihood, local taxes supporting the hospital are higher than they would be otherwise. Furthermore, to the extent that cross-subsidies from paying patients cover uncompensated care costs, prices of health care and therefore insurance prices are higher than they would be without the high levels of uncompensated care.

If private sector employers that do offer insurance must pay higher prices to obtain it, then they must reduce money wages, be satisfied with lower earnings, and/or charge higher prices for their products or services. Public sector employers face similar choices in face of higher health insurance prices, wages must fall, or taxes must be increased to cover the costs of more expensive health insurance. If the public is not willing to pay higher taxes, fewer and/or lower quality publicly provided goods and services are to be expected.

On the other hand, suppose that lower compensation costs (lower because they do not include EBHI) are passed onto the consumers of construction services, then perhaps some consumers may enjoy lower quality adjusted prices and rents than they would if compensation reflected access to health insurance for construction workers. In effect some consumers may be trading, say, lower housing prices for higher taxes, lower money wages, and higher prices of other goods. However, if owners of construction projects (i.e. developers) have some degree of market power, they may be able to retain most of the benefits from the low rates of compensation, which suggests that lower costs originating from lack of EBHI in compensation packages will not be fully reflected in housing prices or in the prices of other construction products and services.

The above examples of how uncompensated care costs may be shifted from one economic entity to another certainly does not exhaust all possibilities for how cost shifting may occur, but it does suggest a complex system of economic interactions in which some parties shift costs to others. It appears that in this web of economic interactions uninsured workers and their dependents are among the disadvantaged, while developers and construction contractors are likely to be among the beneficiaries. Uninsured workers bear costs associated with restricted access to health insurance, including poorer health and more precarious financial circumstances.

The safety-net hospitals and clinics also appear to suffer substantial financial risk from costs of providing uncompensated care. The political climate in many locations makes raising taxes to cover costs associated with uncompensated care quite difficult. At the same time changing health care markets have reduced hospitals' ability to cross-subsidize non-paying patients by raising prices for those who pay. Thus the safety-net hospital and its clinics may not be able to pass uncompensated care costs along to taxpayers or paying patients.

Notes

[1] Employer based health insurance is defined broadly to encompass any group health insurance connected to employment, which includes insurance administered by joint union-management trusts.

[2] Guarantors are those responsible for payment. The patient may be either the guarantor or the guarantor's dependent.

[3] A report on asset development and protection issued by the Corporation for Enterprise Development (2002) suggests that health insurance is one of the key factors in protecting a household's assets.

[4] Petersen (2000) discusses in greater detail how construction trades unions solve market failure problems.

[5] The percentages are calculated from data in the March Supplement of the 1998-2000 CPS. Only those that reported employment were included in the sub-sample used to arrive at these numbers. Respondents in the sub-sample reported on the industry of their longest held job in the previous year.

[6] Clark County encompasses Las Vegas and all the major population centers in southern Nevada from Arizona on the east to California on the South. Because approximately two-thirds of the state's population resides in Clark County, similar figures are generally observed at the state and county levels. Results from Clark County are available up request from the author.

[7] Based on the author's analysis of March CPS data.

[8] The coverage rate for workers in the Agriculture/Mining sector is also quite low, however, the aggregation of agricultural workers and mining workers is somewhat suspect, given that mine workers are substantially more likely to hold insurance than agricultural workers. For purposes of uniformity, the aggregation scheme of the state has been adopted in this instance.

[9] Only respondents in the out-going rotation group (ORG) during March answer questions on union membership or coverage, thus other observations were excluded.

[10] I estimated another model with the dependent variable defined as the probability of government coverage as a function of the same vector of independent variables, the results of which are also displayed in Table 9.5.

[11] In some cases the industries were aggregated or disaggregated according to local employment patterns (i.e., 'Hotel, Gaming, and Recreation,' 'Agriculture and Mining,' 'Services (excluding hotel)').

[12] Based on the author's analysis of the hospital administrative data. Uncompensated care among the employed is attributable to 'self-pay' patients (i.e. patients without health insurance) whose bills were left unpaid. In some cases partial payments were made, and balances were adjusted downward by the hospital, but balances still remained. In others, partial payments were made and the remaining charges were forgiven. Such accounts did not, however, enter into the uncompensated care calculations. In no instances among these accounts were partial payments made through insurance that resulted in an unpaid balance. Such occurrences were recorded in the 'compensated care' accounts, but they accounted for only 2.3 percent of total charges to paying inpatients who reported employment during the 1998-2000 period.

References

Corporation for Enterprise Development (2002), 'State Asset Development Report Card', http://sadrc.cfed.org/index.php, 17 October.

Freeman, R.B. (1981), 'The Effect of Unionism of Fringe Benefits', *Industrial and Labor Relations Review*, vol. 34, pp. 489-509.

Freeman, R.B., and Medoff J. (1984), *What Do Unions Do?* Basic Books, New York, NY.

Ghilarducci, T., Mangum, G., Petersen, J., and Philips, P. (1995), *Portable Pensions for Casual Labor Markets: Lessons from the Operating Engineers Central Pension Fund*, Quorum Books, Westport , CT.

Grob, H. (1994), 'Developments in Collective Bargaining in Construction in the 1980s and 1990s', in P. Voos (ed.) *Contemporary Collective Bargaining in the Private Sector*, Industrial Relations Research Association, Madison, WI, pp. 411-445.

Hadley, J. (2002), *Sicker and Poorer: The Consequences of Being Uninsured*, report prepared for the Kaiser Commission on Medicaid and the Uninsured, Urban Institute, Washington, D.C.

Helms, D.W., Gauthier, A.K., and Campion, D.M. (1992), 'Mending the Flaws in the Small-Group Market', *Health Affairs*, vol. 11, pp. 7-27.

Henderson, J.W. (1999), *Health Economics and Policy*, Southwestern College Publishing, Cincinatti, OH.

Hirsch, B., and MacPherson, D.A. (2002), 'Unionstats.com: Union Coverage and Membership Database', www.trinity.edu/bhirsch, 16 October.

Petersen, J. (2000), 'Health Care and Pension Benefits for Construction Workers: The Role of Prevailing Wage Laws', *Industrial Relations*, vol. 39, pp. 246-264.

State Health Access Data Assistance Center (2001), 'The Current Population Survey and State Health Insurance Estimates', *Issue Briefs*, March, Issue 1.

Stern. S. (1989), 'Measuring the Effect of Disability on Labor Force Participation', *Journal of Human Resources*, vol. 24, pp. 361-393.

The Center to Protect Workers' Rights (1998), *The Construction Chart Book: The U.S. Construction Industry and its Workers*, The Center to Protect Workers Rights, Washington, D.C.

Waddoups, C.J. (1999), 'Union Wage Effects in Nevada's Hotel and Casino Industries', *Industrial Relations*, vol. 38, pp. 577-583.

Waddoups, C.J., and Eade, V.H. (2002), 'Hotels and Casinos: Collective Bargaining During a Decade of Expansion', In Clark, P.F., Delaney, J.T., and Frost, A.C. (eds.), *Collective Bargaining in the Private Sector*, Industrial Relations Research Association, Champaign, IL, pp. 137-177.

Chapter 10

Pension and Health Insurance Coverage in Construction Labor Markets

Mark A. Price

Introduction

Compared to most workers, those within construction are less likely to have important fringe benefits—like a pension plan and health insurance coverage—because even when employers want to offer benefits they face barriers, which limit their ability to offer coverage. For example, the typical construction contractor has fewer than 25 employees; these small employers must bear higher costs in the provision of benefits than their larger counterparts, because the pool of employees over which to spread administrative costs is smaller. Higher costs translate into lower rates of coverage for workers in small firms. Furthermore, employment within construction is highly sensitive to changes in the business cycle as well as the seasons, and thus construction workers are more likely to be unemployed and move between multiple employers during the year. This frequent movement between employers limits eligibility for health insurance and pensions within construction. Finally, the construction industry has always been a gateway to opportunity for immigrants both because of the prevalence of backbreaking manual labor and the basic need for shelter which imparts building trades skills that are portable the world over. Since the 1980s the pace of immigration from Mexico and South America has made Hispanics the fastest growing minority in the U.S. overall and within construction. A key feature of that immigration is the prevalence of documented and undocumented non-citizens. Generally non-citizens are unlikely to have a pension and health insurance whether through limited bargaining power or the greater priority placed on wages, which can be remitted to relatives back home. The greater prevalence of non-citizen-Hispanics within construction has thus meant that overall construction workers are less likely to have benefits coverage.

The barrier to benefits coverage presented by firm size, high turnover, and the absence of citizenship is overcome for construction workers when they are covered by a collectively bargained contract. Union benefit programs are multi-employer programs and thus, as unionized construction workers change employers their pension and health insurance plans follow them from employer to employer. These multi-employer programs also allow small employers to spread administrative costs over a larger pool of workers thus achieving cost reductions typically only available to very large employers. Finally, although labor law limits the protections available to non-citizens, those that achieve union membership are much more likely to have a pension and health insurance coverage. Collective bargaining thus overcomes the barriers to pension and health insurance coverage within construction and it does so with the support of state and federal prevailing wage laws.

Prevailing wage laws prevent bidders on public construction from using low wages to gain a competitive advantage in the public bidding process and thus encourage contractors to sign collective bargaining agreements, which while offering higher wages also provide high quality and highly skilled labor. The majority of state prevailing wage laws also mandate the provision of pensions and health insurance coverage. So while supporting collective bargaining, state prevailing wage laws also require contractors in the open shop to offer their workers pension and health insurance coverage in order to bid on publicly financed construction. Beginning in 1979 the repeal and or annulment of state prevailing wage laws has exacerbated the absence of pension and health insurance coverage within construction.

While it's difficult to determine whether the repeal of state prevailing wage laws leads to an erosion of union density (the percent of workers who are union members) or if repeal is merely a symptom of union weakness, it is clear that repeal leads to declining rates of pension and health insurance coverage for construction workers. There is also evidence that repeal is associated with larger reductions in benefits coverage for those workers facing barriers to coverage like high turnover.

Unlike the chapter by Petersen and Godtland, which analyzes wages and benefits at the firm level, this chapter will analyze trends in pension and health insurance coverage rates using individual data from the Current Population Survey (Unicon, 2003). Our use of the Current Population Survey will allow us to examine trends in coverage by individual characteristics such as turnover, race, ethnicity and citizenship. Our focus on health insurance coverage rates will also put into perspective the chapter by Waddoups, which explores the consequences of the

Table 10.1 Unemployment rate

Year	Overall	Construction	Ratio: construction / overall
1994	6.1	11.8	1.9
1999	4.2	7	1.7

Source: Bureau of Labor Statistics. http://www.bls.gov/iag/iag.construction.htm

absence of health insurance coverage for taxpayers and other consumers of medical services. These disparate themes are linked together through a focus upon the influence of prevailing wage laws and collective bargaining on the trends in pension and health insurance coverage within construction labor markets.

Barriers to Benefits Coverage in Construction

Turbulence

> From a window in a crowded van full of men in work boots, Julio Alexander has seen more of the United States in six years than most Americans see in a lifetime. He can't remember all the cities, but he remembers the daylong treks between construction sites—from Kansas to Tennessee to the Carolinas to New Jersey. Now he's in Salem, Mass.

> With a tool belt strapped to his waist, the 22-year immigrant from El Salvador leads one of the dozens of crews building a luxury apartment complex on Bridge Street. Nearly all of them are Latino immigrants who, like Alexander, are brought by subcontracting firms from one work site to the next, sleeping three or four to a room in apartments and motels. They are an employer's dream: young, strong, and willing to work for far less money than union carpenters (Rodriguez, 2002).

Perhaps there is not such thing as a typical construction worker. Still, in many ways, Julio Alexander is typical. He moves from town to town in search of work. As one job site wraps up, he must find a new job site. Unlike many construction workers who go from contractor to contractor, Julio stays with one, nonunion contractor.

The turbulence in construction employment associated with high seasonal and cyclical volatility of construction demand leads to relatively high unemployment and high labor turnover for construction workers.

Table 10.2 Share of total employment by turnover

Number of employers	Non-construction	Construction	Ratio: construction / non-construction
One	82.7	73.1	0.9
Two	12.5	16.1	1.3
Three or more	4.8	10.8	2.3

Source: Current Population Survey, March (1980-2002).
Notes: Sample includes blue-collar non-agricultural wage and salary workers, aged 16-64, who reported employment during at least one week last year. Observations weighted using Current Population Survey sample weights.

Table 10.1 shows that typically the unemployment rate of construction workers is close to twice the national average.

In 1994, when the national unemployment rate was 6.1 percent, the construction unemployment rate was 11.8 percent. As the economic boom of the 1990s peaked in 1999, national unemployment fell to 4.2 percent while construction unemployment fell to 7 percent. Despite the underlying changes in the business cycle, in both years construction unemployment remained almost twice that of the national average.

Unemployment usually means changing employers in construction. Table 10.2 shows that compared to national averages, construction workers are more likely to work for multiple employers during the year. The share of workers in construction that have three or more employers during the year is more than twice the national average.

It is hard for many contractors to pay health insurance. When labor turnover is high, insurers are reluctant to enroll new workers. The administrative costs and risks associated with new enrollees bringing with them pre-existing conditions make insuring transient workers difficult. With these workers gone soon, the whole process of insurance becomes difficult and expensive. Julio's employer may face less labor turnover because he moves his workers from town to town and state to state while continuing to employ them. But health insurance typically is tied to local providers. So it is difficult to provide health insurance.

For those construction workers who do change employers Table 10.3 identifies a decline in pension coverage from 29.6 percent to 23.4 percent and a decline in health insurance coverage from 47 percent to 41.3 percent for workers with two employers during the year.[1]

Table 10.3 Turnover and benefits coverage

Percent of workers with benefits at work

Number of employers	Pension Plan		Health Insurance Plan	
	Non-construction	Construction	Non-construction	Construction
One	37.9	29.6	54.8	47.0
Two	18.2	23.4	37.1	41.3
Three or more	12.7	30.9	29.1	42.9

Source: Current Population Survey, March (1980-2002).
Notes: Sample includes blue-collar non-agricultural wage and salary workers, aged 16-64, who reported employment during at least one week last year. Observations weighted using Current Population Survey sample weights.

There is only a small a difference in pension coverage between construction workers with only one employer and those reporting three or more employers. However, with only 42.9 percent of those with three or more employers reporting health insurance coverage these workers are less likely than those with only one employer during the year to have health insurance. Compared to workers in other industries, construction workers with multiple employers during the year are better off in terms of benefits coverage. As we shall see this is because there are institutions within the construction labor market, which have adapted to the industry's high degree of employment volatility by making benefits portable across employers. However, for those construction workers outside of these institutions, high turnover still remains a barrier to benefits coverage.

Small Firms

Due to the scale economies associated with pension plan administration, small employers have difficulty offering their workers pension plans (Ghilarducci and Terry, 1999; Mitchell and Andrews, 1981; Caswell, 1976). As shown in Table 10.4, as firm size gets smaller pension and health insurance coverage rates decline both outside and within construction.

However construction workers are more likely to be covered by a pension and health insurance than those outside of construction in similar sized firms. Despite this apparent advantage, only 27.7 percent of construction workers were covered by a pension plan between 1988 and 2001, compared to just under a third of all other workers. Similarly only

Table 10.4 Firm size and benefits coverage

Percent of workers with benefits at work

Number of employees	Pension Plan		Health Insurance Plan	
	Non-construction	Construction	Non-construction	Construction
Overall	32.9	27.7	48.2	42.5
<25	9.0	13.9	22.8	28.1
25-99	23.0	36.1	43.5	53.1
100-499	38.0	45.7	57.5	62.1
500-999	45.0	52.1	62.3	64.3
1000+	50.6	55.7	62.1	66.7

Source: Current Population Survey, March (1989-2002).
Notes: Sample includes blue-collar non-agricultural wage and salary workers, aged 16-64, who reported employment during at least one week last year. Observations weighted using Current Population Survey sample weights.

42.5 percent of construction workers were covered by a health plan compared to 48.2 percent of all other workers. Pension and health insurance coverage rates are lower within construction in part because, as illustrated in Table 10.5, over half of all construction workers are employed in firms with fewer than twenty-five employees compared to just one quarter of all workers. The larger number of small employers translates into lower rates of benefits coverage within construction.

Citizenship

An anonymous complainant had called to report an injury accident at a construction site. An adult male had slipped off a scaffolding board when a suspension line snapped. He fell 30 feet. When I [a police officer] arrived at the future site of the six-building apartment complex, an ambulance with two EMTs in the front seat was parked in the dirt with its engine running. The injured person was not on board. I stopped and talked to the driver. 'Where's the victim?' I asked. 'I don't know. He was gone when we got here', he explained. 'Somebody must have driven him to a hospital. But I can't confirm that because most of these workers don't speak English. I also have a hunch a lot of them are illegals and they're scared to get involved'. 'Did you talk to the foreman?' I said. 'Yeah we did', he grunted. 'The big guy with a heart the size of a pea told us everything had been taken care of. He canceled the call and then walked off. You know I drive by here all the time. These places are going up

Table 10.5 Share of employment by firm size

Number of employees	Non-construction	Construction
<25	25.5	52.8
25-99	16.6	22.6
100-499	16.8	13.6
500-999	6.0	3.0
1000 +	35.0	7.9

Source: Current Population Survey, March (1989-2002).
Notes: Sample includes blue-collar non-agricultural wage and salary workers, aged 16-64, who reported employment during at least one week last year. Observations weighted using Current Population Survey sample weights.

> faster than a shantytown. I think the company is pushing deadline instead of safety (Flemming, 2003).

Construction work is dangerous and is often made more so by the prevalence of workers who are vulnerable to abuse because of their fear of detection by immigration authorities. When workers get hurt on-the-job workers compensation is supposed to pay for their health care. Law requires workers compensation premiums paid by the contractor. But workers compensation premiums can cost anywhere from $7 to $36 per $100 of payroll depending on the occupation and the location of the work. So contractors sometimes have an incentive to avoid workers' compensation premiums and this illegal tactic is often easier when the workers themselves are illegal. In a previous chapter, Waddoups's case study of uncompensated care at a Nevada hospital illustrated the consequences for taxpayers of this cost shifting strategy. In this chapter, we will measure the impact that citizenship status has upon benefits coverage rates among construction workers.

Since 1994 the Current Population Survey (CPS) has collected information on a workers citizenship status. While it is unknown the degree to which the non-citizens identified by the CPS are undocumented, it is clear from Table 10.6 that the share of construction employment represented by Hispanic-non-citizens is almost one-and-half times the share of employment outside of the industry.

Blacks (non-Hispanic) are significantly under represented in construction employment relative to their share of employment outside the industry. The share of construction employment of both Whites (non-Hispanic) and Hispanic-citizens within construction is comparable to both

Table 10.6 Share of employment by race, ethnicity and citizenship

Race, ethnicity and citizenship	Non-construction	Construction	Ratio: construction / non-construction
White Non-Hispanic	65.8	71.3	1.1
Black Non-Hispanic	14.6	8.5	0.6
Hispanic citizen	7.6	7.1	0.9
Hispanic non-citizen	7.8	10.8	1.4

Source: Current Population Survey, March (1994-2002).
Notes: Sample includes blue-collar non-agricultural wage and salary workers, aged 16-64, who reported employment during at least one week last year. Observations weighted using Current Population Survey sample weights.

groups' respective shares of employment outside of the industry. As we will see in the next section union density within construction is comparable for all of these groups except Hispanic-non-citizens.

As reported in Table 10.7 the greater share of Hispanic-non-citizens within construction also translates into lower rates of pension and health insurance coverage in the industry. Within construction fewer than one in ten Hispanic-non-citizens has a pension, which is less than half the rate of pension coverage for Hispanic-citizens. With respect to health insurance one-fifth of Hispanic-non-citizens has coverage compared to over a third of Hispanic-citizens.

The transitory nature of the employment relationship, the prevalence of small firms, the presence of non-citizens (documented and undocumented), all operate as substantial barriers to the provision of health and pension benefits for construction workers.

Collective Bargaining Transcends the Barriers to Benefits Coverage

In the face of all these factors—transience, smallness and citizenship status—collective bargaining in construction encourages the payment of benefits by establishing multi-employer, union-management, jointly-trusted health and pension insurance funds. These funds are financed through employer-provided, hourly contributions called for by the collectively bargained agreement. Because the funds are multi-employer, union workers can move from signatory contractor to signatory contractor according to the dictates of fluctuating labor demand and their health and pension coverage

Table 10.7 Benefits by race, ethnicity and citizenship

Percent of workers with benefits at work.

	Pension Plan		Health Insurance Plan	
	Non-construction	Construction	Non-construction	Construction
White Non-Hispanic	37.1	32.7	51.2	47.4
Black Non-Hispanic	31.6	22.3	46.9	36.5
Hispanic citizen	26.8	23.1	43.0	38.1
Hispanic non-citizen	13.5	8.9	29.7	20.5

Source: Current Population Survey, March (1994-2002).
Notes: Sample includes blue-collar non-agricultural wage and salary workers, aged 16-64, who reported employment during at least one week last year. Observations weighted using Current Population Survey sample weights.

will follow. Thus, collective bargaining promotes portable benefits in a turbulent construction labor market.

In the open shop sector of construction, benefit payments tend not to be portable. In most cases, when a worker leaves one contractor to work for another, that worker's employer-provided health and pension benefits do not follow. Nonunion contractors have difficulty establishing multi-employer insurance because open shop contractors have no institutional mechanism to set standard employer contributions into a joint fund. Furthermore, open shop contractors are reluctant to reveal the wages and benefits they pay their workers to competing contractors or even to their own workers. Secrecy strategies further impede multi-employer funds in the open shop. Consequently, open shop contractors typically bifurcate their labor force between key workers they intend to retain through the ups and downs of business activity and non-key workers who are hired and laid-off based on work requirements. Key workers in the open shop tend to receive employer benefit contributions to single-employer plans while marginal workers are less likely to receive benefits.

Table 10.8 reveals that over two-thirds of construction workers working under collectively bargained contracts were covered by a pension compared to less than a fifth of those in the open shop. In the open shop, more than one-third of construction workers were covered by health insurance compared to over four-fifths of unionized construction workers.

Table 10.8 Benefits by union status 1993-2001

Percent of construction workers with benefits at work

	Pension Plan		Health Insurance Plan	
	Union	Non-Union	Union	Non-Union
Overall Coverage Rate	72.2	19.6	81.4	37.6
Number of Employers Last Year				
One	72.3	21.2	81.9	39.6
Two	78.5	13.0	85.1	31.5
Three +	<u>63.7</u>	<u>14.6</u>	<u>72.4</u>	<u>27.4</u>
Firm Size				
<25	<u>61.5</u>	<u>10.5</u>	<u>71.4</u>	<u>26.2</u>
25-99	74.5	29.7	84.2	49.3
100-499	75.5	31.3	87.7	60.3
500-999	77.8	45.0	84.7	62.1
1000 +	86.0	43.7	88.5	57.9
Race & Ethnicity				
White Non-Hispanic	74.3	22.2	82.4	39.6
Black Non-Hispanic	54.7	13.3	76.1	38.7
Hispanic	62.2	8.7	73.8	24.2
Hispanic citizen	63.4	17.4	81.9	32.3
Hispanic non-citizen	<u>60.3</u>	<u>4.2</u>	<u>60.4</u>	<u>20.1</u>
Asian and Other	69.5	15.4	80.5	41.7

Source: Current Population Survey, March (1994-2002).
Notes: Sample includes blue-collar non-agricultural wage and salary workers, aged 16-64, who reported employment during at least one week last year. Observations weighted using Current Population Survey sample weights.

Turbulence and Collective Bargaining

Table 10.8 shows that when union workers move from contractor to contractor, their health insurance and pensions move with them. On average, 72.3 percent of construction union members with one employer during any given year had pensions and 81.9 percent had health insurance. On average, 78.5 percent of union construction workers with two employers had pensions and 85.1 percent had health insurance. So basically health and pension coverage followed when these union construction workers switched from one employer to a second. For those going between three or more contractors in a year, 63.7 percent had pension coverage from their employer and 72.4 percent had employer provided health insurance. So there was a slight drop-off for those workers bouncing between three or more contractors per year.

In contrast, nonunion construction workers were less likely to have any pension or health coverage, and when these workers moved from one employer to the next, their already low rate of benefits coverage fell markedly. Only 21.2 percent of nonunion construction workers had pensions and 39.6 percent had health coverage if they stayed with one contractor throughout the year. But if they moved to a second contractor, pension coverage fell by more than a third to 13 percent and health insurance coverage fell by a fifth to 31.5 percent. Go between three or more nonunion contractors and both pension and health coverage fell by about a third to 14.6 percent and 27.4 percent respectively. Thus, nonunion contractors tended to pay pension and health insurance only for key workers and if workers moved between contractors, they typically lost their coverage.

Firm Size and Collective Bargaining

For union members working in firms with fewer than 25 employees between 1993 and 2001, 61.5 percent had a pension and 71.4 percent a health plan. As union members reported employment at larger firms their benefit coverage rates increased until roughly 86 percent reported having a pension and 88.5 percent a health plan. Although there is some improvement in coverage for union workers as they work in larger firms, those gains are modest compared workers in the open shop.

Among non-union workers in firms with fewer than 25 employees, 10.5 percent reported having a pension plan at work while 26.2 percent reported having a health plan. In the open shop, firm size has a dramatic effect on the both pension and health insurance coverage. Among workers employed at the largest contractors in the open shop, well over a third had a pension and over half had health insurance. Benefits coverage rates increase much faster as firm size gets larger in the open shop compared to the union sector because as open shop contractors grow, their benefits programs can spread administrative costs over a larger pool of workers, thus reducing the cost of offering these benefits. As explained earlier, union benefit programs are multi-employer programs, which allow small union contractors to provide their workers access to pension and health insurance at a cost that only the largest of open shop contractors enjoy. This explains why the gap in coverage between small and large contractors in the union sector is smaller than in the open shop.

Supporting the descriptive statistics reported in Table 10.8, even after controlling for differences in time, region and human capital characteristics, there is statistical evidence showing that collective bargaining facilitates the payment of benefits to construction workers in small firms and/or highly mobile workers. For construction workers reporting multiple employers over the year, union membership raises the odds of pension coverage by 40 percent and raises the odds of health insurance coverage by 9 percent. Among construction workers employed in firms with fewer than twenty-five employees, union membership raises the odds of pension coverage by 130 percent while increasing the odds of health insurance coverage by just 22 percent.

Citizenship Status and Collective Bargaining

Fewer than two-thirds of union members who were also Hispanic-non-citizens had a pension plan between 1993 and 2001. That is compared to 74.3 percent of Whites (non-Hispanic), 54.7 percent of Blacks (non-Hispanic) and 63.4 percent of Hispanic-citizens. In the open shop only 4.2 percent of Hispanic-non-citizens were covered by a pension compared to 22.2 percent of Whites, 13.3 percent of Blacks and 17.4 percent of Hispanic-citizens. Not only are the pension coverage rates for all workers in the open shop substantially lower than the coverage rates prevailing in the union sector the gap in coverage between Hispanic-non-citizens and all other groups is also substantially larger in the open shop.

For Hispanic-non-citizens working under a collectively bargained contract the rate of health insurance coverage was 60.4 percent compared to 82.4 percent for Whites, 76.1 percent for Blacks and 81.9 percent for Hispanic-citizens. Although the gap in health insurance coverage between the union and non-union sector is smaller than was the case for pension coverage it remains true that gap in coverage between Hispanic-non-citizens and other groups in the open shop is larger than in the union sector. Only a fifth of Hispanic-non-citizens had health insurance in the open shop compared to 39.6 percent of Whites, 28.7 percent of Blacks, and 32.3 percent of Hispanic-citizens. That's barely over half the rate of health insurance coverage for both Blacks and Whites and just under two-thirds the rate for Hispanic-citizens in the open shop. As was true of other groups of vulnerable workers the failure to provide benefits coverage in the open shop is most pronounced among non-citizen-Hispanics.

Engineering News Record, the standard industry publication for construction, in a recent editorial bemoaned the debilitating effects on the industry of the growing nonunion sector's inability to pay benefits.

> Today, the open shop [i.e., nonunion contractors] is dominant, and that segment of the industry appears even less capable of attracting and training talent, much less holding onto it through the most productive working years. Some big construction firms have resorted to 'bounty hunters' to bring in warm bodies possessing the skills needed for a particular project. Others in a crunch send people to hang around the gates of other nearby projects to offer workers a couple of dollars more an hour to lure them away ... But what about benefits and retirement packages for workers? After a career in the industry, many nonunion construction workers can expect only kind words from their employer for a job well done. That doesn't buy the groceries or pay the rent in retirement ... (*Engineering News-Record*, 1997).

What we have seen, thus far, is that collective bargaining promotes the payment of benefits in the face of high turnover, small firm size, and the absence of citizenship. The nonunion sector in general has a chronic inability to pay benefits, and this inability becomes more pronounced as workers move from employer to employer, work for small firms or lack citizenship. However, in the history of the construction industry up to the era of the civil rights movement, many construction unions practiced racial segregation policies. So the question arises, today, does the legacy of these policies of racial exclusion have the effect of currently depriving minorities of the benefits made possible by collective bargaining?

A Closer Look at Collective Bargaining, Race, Ethnicity and Citizenship Status

In 1960, according to one estimate, less than one percent of the building trades union membership was Black (Quadango, 1994). At the time, 5.3 percent of all construction workers were Black (U.S. Census Bureau, 1960). Thus, Blacks were significantly under-represented among construction union members. Blacks were also significantly under-represented among construction workers in general—a trend that remains true today.[2] Blacks accounted for 8.6 percent of all non-farm employment in the 1960s, meaning that with 5.3 percent of construction work, Blacks were under-represented in this industry. But among union construction

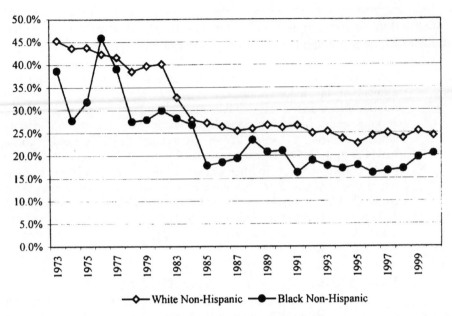

--◇-- White Non-Hispanic   --●-- Black Non-Hispanic

Figure 10.1 Union density within construction 1973-2000

workers, the under-representation was greater than the construction industry as a whole.

With the abolition of legal forms of discrimination in the first half of the 1960s, the attention of the civil rights movement shifted to the pressing need for employment and job training in the Black community. The inner cities were becoming disproportionately Black. The high visibility of urban construction projects situated in largely Black neighborhoods but utilizing an overwhelmingly White workforce were attractive targets for protest and legal action. As we have discussed, unions created multi-employer institutions to cope with the prevalence of small firms and volatile product demand. As a result, construction unions—typically institutions larger than any one contractor—provided the largest legal and political target for anti-discrimination initiatives. So while the activities of the unions were highly visible and thus prone to legal challenges, this high visibility should not be mistaken as evidence of a greater degree of discrimination than prevalent in the entire construction industry. However it is true that these large union multi-employer institutions did make possible the rapid reform of the employment practices of union contractors.

Community groups staged protests shutting down construction sites in major northern cities such as Philadelphia and Chicago. What emerged from these protests were a mixture of government imposed and voluntary programs designed to increase minority employment in the unionized construction industry and participation in primarily union apprenticeship programs (Marshall *et al.*, 1978). Change came dramatically, and in comparison to school or housing desegregation, change came fairly immediately.

Black apprentices in 1960 accounted for 2.2 percent of all apprentices (Marshall and Briggs, 1967, 28). By the mid-1970s, minority apprentices (primarily Blacks) represented 20 percent of all construction apprentices (primarily in joint labor-management programs).[3] Between 1973 and 1979 the percentage of all Blacks in construction that were union members rose to an average 34 percent (compared to 42 percent for Whites). Thus, while Black and White unionization rates were not equalized in the 1970s, convergence in these unionization rates took place rapidly in the late 1960s. These changes were driven by community protests, progressive union members, legal actions brought by individuals and the government, and ultimately, affirmative action.

Since the early 1970s, the relative unionization rate of Blacks compared to Whites has remained fairly constant with Black unionization rates just below that of Whites. On the other, hand this has occurred in an era of declining union strength, as illustrated in Figure 10.1, union density[4] for both Blacks and Whites in construction has declined from over a third to less than a fourth in the last 30 years.

Particularly in urban areas, the building trades have continued to struggle to increase the proportion of Blacks in their ranks. The problems they face are many. The high concentration of Blacks in urban areas remains a source of conflict between the building trades and many urban activists seeking employment opportunities for Black urban residents. While the racial composition of many building trades locals reflect that of their entire jurisdiction, the concentration of Blacks in urban areas has meant that Blacks are often underrepresented relative to their proportion of a city's population on urban construction projects. The entrance exams required by the building trades apprenticeship programs operate as a barrier for young urban Blacks coming from under funded and failing schools. Nepotism in the building trades leads naturally to a lack of diversity as sons and nephews obtain preferential treatment in obtaining work and access to information about apprenticeship programs. There is evidence that, despite these problems affirmative action coupled with community activism and pressure is an effective means of further diversifying the building trades (Glover, 1989; Schutt, 1987; Price, 2002).

Changing demographics has meant that issues of race no longer break only along Black-White lines. Table 10.9 reports union density by

Table 10.9 Union density within construction 1973-2000

Year	White Non-Hispanic	Black Non-Hispanic	Asian and Other	Hispanic	Hispanic Citizen	Hispanic Non-Citizen
1973	45.3	38.6	62.4	45.1		
1974	43.7	27.8	81.0	46.2		
1975	43.8	31.9	60.0	40.5		
1976	42.3	45.9	54.7	26.7		
1977	41.6	39.1	51.6	36.1		
1978	38.5	27.5	63.8	27.2		
1979	39.7	27.9	48.9	31.2		
1981	40.1	30.0	41.5	36.1		
1983	32.8	28.3	44.1	24.2		
1984	27.8	26.8	36.3	22.2		
1985	27.2	17.8	29.5	20.8		
1986	26.4	18.6	40.3	19.1		
1987	25.5	19.4	35.3	19.8		
1988	26.0	23.5	29.3	18.2		
1989	26.7	20.9	29.2	16.2		
1990	26.2	21.1	34.6	14.3		
1991	26.6	16.3	33.6	16.0		
1992	24.9	18.9	37.0	15.1		
1993	25.3	17.8	32.4	14.3		
1994	23.7	17.2	30.3	13.6	18.6	10.3
1995	22.6	17.9	31.1	11.1	17.7	6.3
1996	24.3	16.2	22.5	12.4	14.6	10.8
1997	24.9	16.6	19.0	11.3	18.5	6.2
1998	23.8	17.1	19.1	11.8	16.2	8.0
1999	25.4	19.6	25.3	13.0	18.8	8.8
2000	24.4	20.4	19.5	12.5	19.2	8.8

Source: Current Population Survey, May (1973-1979 and 1981). Monthly Outgoing Rotations Current Population Survey (1983-2000).
Note: Observations weighted using Current Population Survey sample weights.

race, ethnicity and citizenship status between 1973 and 2000. Union density, or the percent of construction workers who are union members, when examined by race reveals that the percent of Whites (non-Hispanic), Blacks[5] (non-Hispanic) and Asians who are union members has converged.

Or, to put it another way, the racial composition of the union and open shop sectors has become roughly comparable by 2000. The one exception is the disproportionate decline in union density among Hispanics.

While the anti-discrimination efforts of the 1960s focused on Black employment in construction, the biggest demographic change in the construction industry in recent decades has been the increased relative importance of Hispanic construction workers. Foreshadowing larger demographic trends, Hispanics became the largest minority employed in the construction industry in the mid 1980s, surpassing non-Hispanic Blacks. The share of Hispanics among construction workers has steadily increased from less than 5 percent in 1975 to just under a quarter in 2002.[6] The Hispanic workforce, in turn, has shifted from a primarily documented and legal workforce, to one with a significant component of undocumented workers. Between 1994 and 2002, the period in which we have data on citizenship status, the Hispanic share of construction employment rose from 14.1 percent in 1994 to 24.5 percent. Over the same period the share of Hispanics working in construction that were non-citizens rose from 56.2 percent to 63.6 percent. Undocumented non-citizens, because of their immigration status, have limited ability to organize, redress grievances or join unions.

> Latino construction workers picketing at Salt Lake City's Gateway commercial and residential development have endured more than months of unemployment and countless hours on asphalt so hot it burns through the soles of their shoes ... On April 30 [2001], they walked off their jobs of spraying toxic fire retardant on Gateway's steel skeletons after months of grumbling to bosses that their paychecks were mysteriously shrinking. They also said bosses were denying overtime pay, and some claim the company health insurance for which they paid about $300 a month was a sham. USC [Utah Structural Coatings] owner Chris Utley denies cheating workers out of pay and says they could have brought problems about health insurance straight to him ... But workers say when they did complain about getting shortchanged, bosses threatened to turn them into the Immigration and Naturalization Service. When, prodded by union organizers, the USC workers walked off the job for a one-hour protest, they were fired (Egan and Lopez, 2001).

This passage highlights the leverage unscrupulous employers have over undocumented workers seeking redress of workplace problems. Table 10.9 shows that union density among Hispanic construction workers tracked closely with that of Blacks up until the late 80s and early 90s. Hispanic unionization rates have fallen rapidly since about 1987 due the

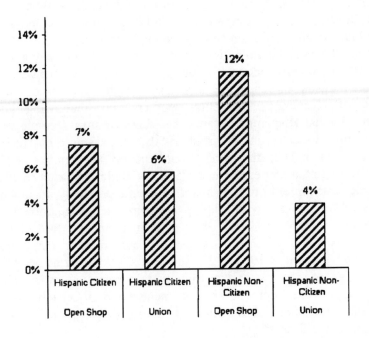

Figure 10.2   Share of employment across the union and open shop sectors: by citizenship status and Spanish ethnicity: 1994-2000

growing share of non-citizens among the Hispanic population. In 1987, 35.3 percent of all Asians, 25.5 percent of all Whites (non-Hispanic), 19.4 percent of all Blacks (non-Hispanic) and 19.8 percent of all Hispanics were union members in construction. By the year 2000, 24.4 percent of all Whites, 19.5 percent of all Asians, 20.4 percent of all Black, and 19.2 percent of all citizen-Hispanics were unionized. But only 8.8 percent of all non-citizen-Hispanics were unionized. Because of their often-illegal status, it is more difficult to unionize non-citizen construction workers.

> A Utah contractor acted illegally when it fired a group of Latino workers who walked off the job in April, the National Labor Relations Board (NLRB) has alleged in a complaint and hearing notice filed Friday. The complaint also alleges managers at Utah Structural Coatings Inc., a Draper company that fireproofs construction material, broke the law by threatening to turn in striking undocumented workers to the Immigration and Naturalization Service if they did not return to the job ... He [the

contractor] contends the company did not know workers were undocumented when they initially were hired. To rehire them now would put the contractor in the position of violating the law, Zoll [the contractor's attorney] said (Sahm, 2001).

As the quote illustrates when non-citizen-Hispanics seek out the protection offered by unionization employers who knowingly hired undocumented workers in the first place use these workers legal status as an excuse not to hire them back once the employer has been found guilty of labor law violations. It is not surprising that nonunion contractors have hired a disproportionate number of non-citizen-Hispanics. Figure 10.2 shows that union and open shop (nonunion) sectors are composed of roughly equal proportions of Hispanic-citizens where 7 percent of the open shop workforce is Hispanic-citizens compared to 6 percent of union sector.

Thus, union and open shop contractors hire essentially the same proportion of citizen-Hispanics. But Hispanic-non-citizens constitute 12 percent of the workers employed in the open shop and just 4 percent in the union sector. Nonunion contractors hire a significantly greater percentage of non-citizen-Hispanics (some of whom are documented and some not), than union contractors.

Recognizing that undocumented workers are often at the mercy of their employers, in recent years, unions have sought to empower these workers by legalizing their work status.

> The AFL-CIO also is putting its considerable political clout behind legislation to grant legal status to more than 5 million immigrants who are here illegally. For many years the labor federation adamantly opposed illegal immigrants, arguing that they took jobs away from U.S. workers and enabled employers to cut back the workers' pay, benefits and working conditions. It supported the current law calling for sanctions against employers who hire undocumented workers. But the AFL-CIO came to realize that undocumented immigrants are here to stay and that the rarely enforced sanctions simply allow employers to threaten to disclose to immigration authorities the illegal status of workers demanding better treatment. The AFL-CIO knows that if the undocumented workers are not unionized, they will continue undercutting other workers, but that unionizing them will be very difficult unless they are granted the legal rights and protections granted others—above all, the right to unionize (Meister, 2001).

Legal workers are more easily unionized. Undocumented workers are vulnerable. As we have seen, among the effects of their vulnerability in the construction industry is that they tend not to receive health insurance nor pension coverage from their employers. But as with other groups of vulnerable workers collective bargaining is a way to obtain coverage. We now turn our attention to the link between collective bargaining and state prevailing wage laws.

State Prevailing Wage and Collective Bargaining

Prevailing wage regulations in construction are the primary governmental policy promoting collective bargaining in this sector. Due to rapid labor turnover in construction, the process of construction subcontracting and the ephemeral nature of specific construction sites, National Labor Relations Board elections are uncommon in this industry. Furthermore, the Taft-Hartley Act provides an exception in construction permitting contractors to sign collective bargaining agreements without a prior representation election. In the absence of NLRB elections, "top-down" organizing— namely unions convincing contractors to become signatories to local collectively bargained agreements—is the primary mode by which union coverage in this industry is created and extended. Prevailing wage regulations encourage contractors to sign collective bargaining agreements and promote collective bargaining to the extent that proclaimed prevailing wages and benefits are similar to local collectively bargained wages and benefits. Under these circumstances, contractors feel they can sign collective agreements and still effectively compete for public work, which often accounts for about 20 percent of construction demand.

Starting in 1979 and ending in 1988, nine states repealed their state prevailing wage laws. In addition, in 1995, Oklahoma's prevailing wage law was judicially annulled. Table 10.10 shows that union density—a measure of the presence of absence of collective bargaining in construction—has fallen since 1979. Here union density is compared before and after repeal in the following three categories: Law states (Law) are those that would maintain a state prevailing wage law between 1979 and 2000[7], repeal states (Repeal) are those states that repealed their prevailing wage law at anytime between 1979 and 2000[8], and finally states that did not have a prevailing wage law during the period of analysis (Never). In states with prevailing wage laws, unionization has been and remains the highest and the practice of collective bargaining has fallen the least. In states that never had prevailing wage laws, union density is and has been the lowest and has fallen by 53.8 percent. Similarly, in states that had prevailing wage laws in 1979 but repealed or annulled them by the 1990s, the prevalence of collective bargaining fell by 54.6 percent (similar

Table 10.10 Union density within construction before (1979) and after (1993-2000) repeal of state prevailing wage laws

	Law	Repeal	Never
Before Repeal (1979)	45.3	30.2	14.4
After Repeal (1993-2000)	27.7	13.7	6.7
Percent Change	-38.9	-54.6	-53.8

Source: Current Population Survey, May (1979), Monthly Outgoing Rotations (1993-2000).

to states that never had this type of regulation). In short, prevailing wage regulations support collective bargaining and their absence discourages collective bargaining. How does the presence and absence of prevailing wage laws affect pension and health insurance coverage?

State Prevailing Wage Laws and Benefits Coverage

By mandating benefits for construction workers on publicly financed construction projects, state prevailing wage laws increase the numbers those in construction with benefits coverage. Where these laws are absent benefits coverage will be lower overall with those workers facing barriers to coverage suffering the lowest rates of coverage. Table 10.11 reports pension and health insurance coverage rates for construction workers before and after repeal or annulment of ten state prevailing wage laws.

Here workers are categorized according to whether their state of residence had a prevailing wage law covering state and locally funded construction projects.[9] Allocating workers into law and no law states before and after repeal means that in 1979 all of the workers from the 10 states that would eventually repeal their law are in the Law column. In the period after most of the repeals had occurred (1993-2001) all of the workers from these 10 repeal states were included in the No Law column. We find that over a third of construction workers in law states were covered by a pension compared to just under a quarter those in states without a law in 1979. Health insurance coverage was greater for all construction workers in 1979, with over half of those in law states covered, compared to well over a third of those in states without the law. By 1993, 9 of the 10 states had repealed or annulled their prevailing wage law with Oklahoma's repeal taking effect after 1996 (Michigan briefly suspended its law between 1995 and 1997). In the period after repeal, pension and health

Table 10.11 Benefits coverage in law and no law states before (1979) and after (1993-2001) repeal

Percent of construction workers with benefits at work

	Pension Plan		Health Insurance Plan	
	Law	No Law	Law	No Law
Before Repeal (1979)	37.5	23.9	56.7	42.7
After Repeal (1993-2001)	32.4	19.7	45.6	36.1
Percent Change	-13.7	-17.6	-19.6	-15.3

Source: Current Population Survey, March (1980, 1994-2002).
Notes: Sample includes blue-collar non-agricultural wage and salary workers, aged 16-64, who reported employment during at least one week last year. Michigan suspended its prevailing wage law in 1995 and reinstated it in 1998. Michigan is treated as a law state with observations collected during suspension (1995-1997) omitted from the analysis. Oklahoma's repeal became effective in 1996. Oklahoma is treated as a no law state with observations prior to repeal (1994-1995) omitted from the analysis. Observations weighted using Current Population Survey sample weights.

insurance coverage rates were lower across all states. Slightly less than a third of construction workers in law states were covered by a pension compared to one-fifth of those in states without a law with pension coverage falling faster in states without a state prevailing wage law. Just under half of all construction workers in law states had health insurance coverage, compared to just over one third of those in states without a law, unlike pension coverage, health insurance coverage actually declined faster in states with a prevailing wage law than it did in states without the law. The classification used here obscures the effect of repeal on benefits coverage so in the final section of this chapter we will examine trends in coverage in repeal states, states that kept their prevailing wage law and states that did not have a law over the entire period of our analysis.

Turbulence and State Prevailing Wage Laws

As we have shown, workers that report having multiple employers over the year are less likely have a pension and health insurance. Table 10.12 reports benefit coverage rates for this vulnerable group of workers before and after repeal in law and no law states. What emerges from these data is that workers living in states without a prevailing wage law and reporting multiple employers over the year experienced disproportionately larger declines in pension and health insurance coverage than their counterparts

Table 10.12 Turnover and Benefits Coverage in law and no law states before (1979) and after (1993-2001) repeal

Percent of construction workers with benefits at work

Number of employers	Pension Plan		Health Insurance Plan	
	Law	No Law	Law	No Law
	Before Repeal (1979)			
One	41.7	24.4	59.3	43.7
Two	30.5	17.7	51.7	39.6
Three or more	43.8	24.4	62.8	41.6
	After Repeal (1993-2000)			
One	33.2	20.6	46.2	37.7
Two	26.1	15.2	42.5	32.0
Three or more	35.2	18.1	44.6	28.0
	Percent Change			
One	-20.4	-15.5	-22.0	-13.9
Two	-14.6	-14.4	-17.8	-19.2
Three or more	-19.6	-25.7	-29.0	-32.6

Source: Current Population Survey, March (1980, and 1994-2002).
Notes: Sample includes blue-collar non-agricultural wage and salary workers, aged 16-64, who reported employment during at least one week last year. Michigan suspended its prevailing wage law in 1995 and reinstated it in 1998. Michigan is treated as a law state with observations collected during suspension (1995-1997) omitted from the analysis. Oklahoma's repeal became effective in 1996. Oklahoma is treated as a no law state with observations prior to repeal (1994-1995) omitted from the analysis. Observations weighted using Current Population Survey sample weights.

reporting only one employer during the year. The one exception to this trend was among workers reporting two or more employers; this group experienced a slightly smaller decline in pension coverage (14.4 percent) compared to the 15.5 percent decline in pension coverage experienced by workers reporting only one employer during the year. But for workers reporting three or more employers during the year pension coverage declined by 25.7 percent between 1979 and 1993-2001. The declines in health insurance coverage reported for workers in states without a prevailing wage law grew larger as those workers reported multiple employers. Health insurance coverage for workers with only one employer declined by 13.9 percent, declined by 19.2 for workers with two employers, and declined by 32.6 percent for workers with three or more employers.

This contrasts with the experience of construction workers in states with a prevailing wage law who, for the most part, experienced

Table 10.13 Benefits coverage by firm size in law and no law states

Percent of construction workers with benefits at work
After Repeal (1993-2000)

Number of employees	Pension Plan		Health Insurance Plan	
	Law	No Law	Law	No Law
<25	16.5	9.8	30.5	23.6
25-99	43.8	25.0	57.0	47.1
100-499	52.3	33.9	66.3	53.0
500-999	56.5	37.4	66.9	51.8
1000+	61.3	46.5	69.4	62.2

Source: Current Population Survey, March (1980, and 1994-2002).
Notes: Sample includes blue-collar non-agricultural wage and salary workers, aged 16-64, who reported employment during at least one week last year. Michigan suspended its prevailing wage law in 1995 and reinstated it in 1998. Michigan is treated as a law state with observations collected during suspension (1995-1997) omitted from the analysis. Oklahoma's repeal became effective in 1996. Oklahoma is treated as a no law state with observations prior to repeal (1994-1995) omitted from the analysis. Observations weighted using Current Population Survey sample weights.

proportionate declines in pension and health insurance coverage whether they reported one or multiple employers during the year. As in states without a law, the one exception to this trend occurred among workers reporting two employers; these workers registered a 14.6 percent decline in pension coverage. That is compared to a 20.4 decline for those reporting only one employer and a 19.6 percent decline for those with three or more employers. Over the same period in law states, health insurance coverage fell 22 percent for workers with only one employer while declining 17.8 percent for those with two or more employers. With health insurance coverage declining by 29 percent for workers with three or more employers these workers were worse off than their counterparts with fewer employers during the year. In sum, prevailing wage laws facilitate the payment of benefits to construction workers who frequently change jobs in response to fluctuating demand.

Firm Size and State Prevailing Wage Laws

As with turnover, firm size is a barrier to pension and health insurance coverage for construction workers. Unfortunately, firm size is not available in the March CPS until 1989 and thus unlike the previous tables, Table

Table 10.14 Benefits coverage by race, ethnicity and citizenship in law and no law states before (1979) and after (1993-2001) repeal

Race, ethnicity and citizenship	Percent of construction workers with benefits at work			
	Pension Plan		Health Insurance Plan	
	Law	No Law	Law	No Law
	Before Repeal (1979)			
White Non-Hispanic	39.4	25.2	57.8	44.5
Black Non-Hispanic	28.3	18.7	47.3	35.7
Hispanic	29.2	40.1	54.6	45.6
	After Repeal (1993-2000)			
White Non-Hispanic	37.5	22.1	51.0	39.1
Black Non-Hispanic	28.1	17.1	40.9	32.1
Hispanic citizen	25.3	15.6	38.7	36.6
Hispanic non-citizen	9.5	7.2	20.9	19.3
	Percent Change			
White Non-Hispanic	-4.9	-12.2	-11.8	-12.1
Black Non-Hispanic	-0.6	-8.7	-13.5	-10.0

Source: Current Population Survey, March (1980, and 1994-2002).
Notes: Sample includes blue-collar non-agricultural wage and salary workers, aged 16-64, who reported employment during at least one week last year. Michigan suspended its prevailing wage law in 1995 and reinstated it in 1998. Michigan is treated as a law state with observations collected during suspension (1995-1997) omitted from the analysis. Oklahoma's repeal became effective in 1996. Oklahoma is treated as a no law state with observations prior to repeal (1994-1995) omitted from the analysis. Observations weighted using Current Population Survey sample weights.

10.13 only reports benefits coverage by firm size between 1993 and 2001, the period after repeal.

Regardless of firm size, benefits coverage rates are greater in states with a prevailing wage law than in states without the law with the gap in coverage being smaller for health insurance than for pensions. The gap in benefits coverage between law and no law states shrinks as firm size increases. While it is not possible to identify the effects of repeal on benefits coverage for workers in the smallest firms, which also employ the majority of construction workers, it is clear from Table 10.13 that these workers are much better off working in states with a state prevailing wage law.

Citizenship and State Prevailing Wage Laws

Finally in Table 10.14, we examine benefits coverage rates by race, ethnicity and citizenship. Reflecting their relative share of employment the pattern of benefits coverage for White non-Hispanics follows the overall patterns described in Table 10.11. For Black non-Hispanic construction workers living in law states there has been no change in pension coverage since 1979, with over a quarter reporting having a pension plan at work. In states with no prevailing wage law there has been a slight reduction in pension coverage since 1979, with less than one-fifth of Black non-Hispanic construction workers reporting pension coverage over the entire period. The gap in pension coverage between Blacks and Whites *across* law and no law states has decreased as the White non-Hispanic pension coverage rate has declined.

In 1979, just under half of Black construction workers in law states had health insurance coverage compared to just over a third of those in no law states. In the period after 1993, over a third of Black construction workers in law states had health insurance compared to less than a third of those in no law states. As was the case with pension coverage, the gap between White and Black health insurance coverage has declined as coverage among Whites has fallen in both law and no law states. Although the gap in coverage between Blacks and Whites was greater in law states, a greater percentage of Black construction workers have access to both a pension and health insurance in prevailing wage law states.

Deciphering the trends among Hispanic construction workers is made more difficult by the demographic shift both within the U.S. population and construction employment, which culminated in Hispanics becoming the largest minority in the U.S. in 2003 (Associated Press, 2003). In 1979 less than one-third of Hispanic construction workers in law states were covered by a pension compared to over a third in no law states. In the same year more than half of Hispanic construction workers in law states had health insurance compared to less than half in no law states. In the period after repeal, benefits coverage rates for Hispanics are divided by citizenship status. One quarter of Hispanic-citizens were covered by a pension in law states while less than a fifth were covered by a pension in no law states. Over a third of Hispanic-citizens were covered by health insurance in both law and no law states. Barely a tenth of Hispanic-non-citizens were covered by a pension in law and no law states. Less than a quarter of Hispanic-non-citizen construction workers were covered by health insurance in both law and no law states. The experience of Hispanic-

Table 10.15 Benefits coverage in law, repeal, and never law states before (1979) and after repeal (1993-2001)

Percent of construction workers with benefits at work

	Pension Plan			Health Insurance Plan		
	Law	Repeal	Never	Law	Repeal	Never
Before Repeal (1979)	39.7	29.7	23.9	58.2	51.1	42.7
After Repeal (1993-2001)	32.4	19.1	20.4	45.6	34.5	38.3
Percent Change	-18.6	-35.6	-14.5	-21.8	-32.4	-10.4

Source: Current Population Survey, March (1980, and 1994-2002).
Notes: Sample includes blue-collar non-agricultural wage and salary workers, aged 16-64, who reported employment during at least one week last year. Observations weighted using Current Population Survey sample weights.

citizens in the construction industry tracks closely with that of Blacks while non-citizen-Hispanics receive substantially less benefits than any other group. Still non-citizen-Hispanics receive greater benefits coverage in states with prevailing wage laws compared to states without these regulations.

The Effect of the Repeal of State Prevailing Wage Laws on Benefits Coverage

Kessler and Katz (2001) examined the impact of state prevailing wage law repeal on wage rates by race and union status. They found repeal-induced wage rate declines were borne almost entirely by union construction workers (both on and off public construction). Kessler and Katz also found that there is a differential impact of repeal by race, with White construction workers experiencing wage reductions while Black construction workers were not harmed by repeal. These findings are puzzling because the percent of all Blacks in construction that are unionized is similar to the percent of all White workers in construction who are union members. Thus, if repeals cut the wage rates of union members, the effect on Blacks and Whites should be similar. However, they found no support for the hypothesis that Blacks benefited relative to Whites from repeal due to the reduction in the union wage premium, thus leaving the precise mechanism underlying their differential race effect unexplained.

Petersen (2000), examining total compensation, found that construction workers in repeal states experienced a 15 percent reduction in

Table 10.16 Benefits coverage by number of employers in law, repeal, and never law states before (1979) and after repeal (1993-2001)

Percent of construction workers with benefits at work

Number of Employers Last Year	Pension Plan			Health Insurance Plan		
	Law	Repeal	Never	Law	Repeal	Never
Before Repeal (1979)						
One	41.7	31.1	25.1	59.3	52.5	43.4
Two	30.5	20.5	18.3	51.7	44.8	41.8
Three +	43.8	36.0	27.0	62.8	54.1	41.1
After Repeal (1993-2001)						
One	33.2	20.2	21.1	46.2	36.3	39.4
Two	26.1	15.1	15.3	42.5	29.8	35.1
Three +	35.2	15.5	22.8	44.6	26.5	30.7
Percent change from 1979 to 1993-2001						
One	-20.4	-35.0	-16.2	-22.0	-30.9	-9.3
Two	-14.6	-26.2	-16.6	-17.8	-33.5	-16.1
Three +	-19.6	-56.9	-15.7	-29.0	-50.9	-25.2

Source: Current Population Survey, March (1980, and 1994-2002).
Notes: Sample includes blue-collar non-agricultural wage and salary workers, aged 16-64, who reported employment during at least one week last year. Observations weighted using Current Population Survey sample weights.

wages but a 53 percent decline in benefit levels. In addition Peterson found that repeals reduced total compensation in construction to levels comparable to those in states that never had a law, and those levels were significantly lower than total compensation in states that kept their law.

As previously noted in Table 10.10, the largest declines in union density since 1979 occurred in states that repealed or never had a prevailing wage law. While it is not clear whether state prevailing wage law repeal directly weakens unionization or if repeal operates merely as an accelerant of the inertia of union decline, there is agreement that state prevailing wage laws tend to support collective bargaining and by extension benefits coverage for all construction workers. Although a portion of the decline in pension and health insurance coverage for construction workers mirrors broader trends affecting all workers, Table 10.15 reveals the role that state prevailing wage laws and unionization in particular, have played in changing benefits coverage for construction workers.

Most state prevailing wage laws require contractors bidding for state financed projects to offer pension and health insurance coverage even if those contractors are not signatories to a collectively bargained contract. Thus, while the rate of decline in unionization observed in Table 10.10 was similar across repeal and never law states, the rate of decline in pension and health insurance coverage reported in Table 10.15 for repeal states was greater than a third compared to a decline of less than a fifth in states that never had a law and that kept their law. If declining unionization was the sole factor contributing to the decline of pension and health insurance coverage in repeal states, we would expect to see similar rates of decline in benefits coverage in never law states. Instead we see that despite roughly equivalent declines in union density across repeal and never law states, the decline in benefits coverage is two and in the case of health insurance, three times greater in repeal states compared to never law states. This is because as state prevailing wage laws are repealed, contractors in the open shop, which once offered pensions and health insurance as a condition of eligibility to bid for work on publicly financed projects, reduced or eliminated pension and health insurance coverage to gain a cost advantage in the bidding process.

Paralleling these overall findings, Table 10.16 shows the percent change in benefits coverage across three legal regimes by number of employers last year. In 1979, over one-third of construction workers in both law and repeal states that reported having three or more employers during the year had pension coverage. After repeal more than a third of these workers in law states had a pension compared to less than one-fifth in repeal states. For the most part, the declines in pension coverage experienced in both law and never law states did not differ between workers reporting one or more employers during the year. In repeal states the magnitude of the reductions in pension coverage was larger than experienced in law and never law states and was the greatest among workers reporting three or more employers during the year.

In 1979 slightly less than two-thirds of construction workers in law states had health insurance, compared to just over half of those in repeal states and well over a third of those in never law states. Currently less than a third of construction workers in repeal and never law states have health insurance compared to a little less than half of those in law states. For the most part, across all three legal environments (not just in repeal states as was the case with pension coverage), the declines in health insurance coverage get larger as workers report having additional employers during the year. However, consistent with the trends in pension coverage, the largest declines in health insurance coverage were experienced by construction workers reporting more than one employer during the year while living in a repeal state.

Conclusion

The lack of health care and pension coverage is a personal problem, a family problem, an industry problem and a societal problem. At the personal and family level, the lack of health insurance today means current health problems often go unmet. The lack of pension coverage means downstream problems for the elderly and increased pressure on their adult children to care for them. At the industry level, the inability of the open shop sector of construction to pay family-friendly benefits means that the workforce becomes younger and is less likely to stay in construction as family formation takes place. This means a loss of experience and training as middle-age workers migrate to other industries. At a societal level, the failure of the industry to pay benefits shifts the costs of health and old age in part to the taxpayer. It puts greater pressure on local health care providers and strains Social Security.[10]

Prevailing wage regulations support the payment of benefits by supporting multi-employer collective bargaining. The contracts that emerge from this bargaining do two good things at once. First, it forces contractors to embed in their bids the long-term costs of maintaining a healthy and experienced labor force. So these contracts short-circuit cost shifting and ultimately force the direct consumers of building services to pay the full cost of the buildings and roads they purchase. Second, collectively bargained contracts make pensions and health insurance portable across the shifting terrain of jobs generated by the turbulence of construction demand. This, in turn, not only means that workers remained insured, it also means that the construction labor force can be insured and retain the flexibility needed to respond to shifting and unpredictable demand. Collectively bargained contracts preserve flexibility in the construction labor force that would be lost if workers had to stay with one employer in order to stay insured. So prevailing wage regulations, by promoting collective bargaining—viewed by their critics as a source of inflexibility—are in fact a source of flexibility within construction labor markets.

Prevailing wage laws also encourage the payment of benefits independent of collective bargaining by requiring that on public works all contractors pay benefits. This induces some nonunion contractors to set up benefit programs that they otherwise would not have in order to qualify for public construction bidding. The fact that with the repeal of prevailing wage regulations, the payment of benefits falls more than the fall in collective bargaining is a measure of the independent contribution prevailing wage regulations have in encouraging the payment of benefits in construction.

While the repeal of prevailing wage regulations has contributed to the loss of pensions and benefits both indirectly by undercutting collective bargaining and directly by eliminating the requirement that open shop contractors pay benefits on public works, the loss of pensions has not affected all construction workers equally. Currently, in states with prevailing wage laws, all demographic groups—Anglos, Hispanic-citizens, Blacks and Asians—are more often covered by pensions and insurance compared to these same groups in states without prevailing wage regulations. However, since the repeal of prevailing wage laws in the 1980s, the fall-off in coverage has been much more sharp among Hispanics. This is due to the increased importance of non-citizen, often undocumented, Hispanics both among all Hispanics and within the general construction labor force. This group of workers is least able to be protected either by prevailing wage laws or collective bargaining. Unscrupulous contractors can exploit illegal workers holding out the threat that any redress sought either through appeal to regulators or to unions can be trumped by calling in the Immigration authorities. Furthermore, the Supreme Court has raised questions as to whether illegal workers can even receive the protection of labor laws.[11]

Thus, while the repeal of prevailing wage laws have reduced the pension and health coverage of construction workers, the proliferation of construction workers who fall outside the protection of unions and labor laws has exacerbated this problem.

Notes:

[1] All of the data presented on Pension and Health Insurance Coverage is based upon the authors analysis of the March Current Population Survey (CPS) 1980-2002. Please note that benefits coverage questions in the March CPS ask about coverage at work last year. Although the data analyzed was collected during the period between 1980 and 2002 the coverage rates are for the period between 1979 and 2001.

[2] See Table 10.6.

[3] Based on authors analysis of data from the United States Bureau of Apprenticeship Training.

[4] All of the data presented on union density is based on the author's analysis of the May Current Population Survey 1973-1981 and the Outgoing Rotations of the Current Population Survey 1983-2000.

[5] Although union density for Blacks is comparable to that of Whites, as illustrated in Table 10.6 Blacks remain underrepresented in construction employment overall.

[6] Based on author's analysis of data from the 1975 May Current Population Survey and 2002 March Current Population Survey.

[7] Michigan suspended its Prevailing Wage Law between 1995 and 1997 and thus is treated as a Law State with observations collected during repeal omitted from the analysis.

[8] Oklahoma was the last state to repeal its law in 1996; it is treated in this analysis as a repeal state. Observations collected for Oklahoma between 1994 and 1995 and therefore prior to repeal were omitted from the analysis.

[9] Michigan is treated as a law state with observations collected during suspension (1995-1997) omitted from the analysis. Oklahoma is treated as a no law state with observations prior to repeal (1994-1995) omitted from the analysis.

[10] In chapter 9, Waddoups's case study of public hospital costs in Southern Nevada shows that uninsured construction workers account for a disproportionate share of all employed patients whose medical bills are covered by the public.

[11] In Hoffman Plastic Compounds, Inc. v. NLRB, No. 00-1595 (S. Ct.), the Supreme Court ruled that the National Labor Relations Board (NLRB) did not have the authority to order back pay to an undocumented worker who was fired because of union activities.

References

Associated Press (2003), 'Hispanics Outnumber Blacks in U.S. Minority Population', 21 January.

Caswell, Jerry W. (1976), 'Economic Efficiency in Pension Plan Administration: Analysis of the construction Industry', *Journal of Risk and Insurance*, vol. 42, pp. 257-273.

Egan, Dan, and Lopez, Jesus Jr. (2001), ' "Little" Strike, Large Issues', *Salt Lake Tribune*, 8 July, p. A1.

Engineering News Record (1997), 'End of Puny Wage Hikes Had Better Be Here Soon', vol. 239(13), 29 September, p. 134.

Ghilarducci, Teresa, and Terry, Kevin (1999), 'Scale Economies in Union Pension Plan Administration: 1981-1993', *Industrial Relations*, vol. 38, pp. 11-17.

Flemming, Paul (2003), 'Construction Crew Put Up Walls to Hinder Probe, But OSHA Nailed Them', *Salt Lake Tribune*, 27 January, p. B2.

Glover, Robert (1989), 'Apprenticeship: A Route to the High-Paying Skilled Trades for Women?', in Harlan, Sharon L., and Steinberg, Ronnie J. (eds), *Job Training for Women*, Temple University Press, Philadelphia, PA, pp. 269-289.

Kessler, Daniel P., and Katz, Lawrence F. (2001), 'Prevailing Wage Laws and Construction Labor Markets' *Industrial and Labor Relations Review*, vol. 54(2), pp. 259-274.

Marshall, Ray F., and Briggs, Vernon M. Jr. (1967), *The Negro and Apprenticeship*, Johns Hopkins University Press, Baltimore, MD.

Marshall, Ray F., Knapp, Charles B., Ligget, Malcolm H., and Glover, Robert W. (1978), *Employment Discrimination: The Impact of Legal and Administrative Remedies*, Praeger Publishers, New York, NY.

Meister, Dick (2001), 'Influx Of Immigrants Offers U.S. Unions A Great Opportunity', *Buffalo News*, 2 September, p. H1.

Mitchell, Olivia, and Andrews, Emily (1981), 'Scale Economies in Private Multi-Employer Pension Systems', *Industrial and Labor Relations Review*, vol. 34(4), pp. 522-530.

Petersen, Jeffrey S. (2000), 'Health Care and Pension Benefits for Construction Workers: The Role of Prevailing Wage Laws', *Industrial Relations*, vol. 39(2), pp. 246-264.

Price, Vivian (2002), 'Race, Affirmative Action, and Women's Employment in US Highway Construction', *Feminist Economics*, vol. 8(2), pp. 63-86.

Rodriguez, C. (2002), 'Union Alleges Exploitation, Plans Protest at Salem Site', *Boston Globe*, 16 April, p. B1.

Sahm, Phil (2001), 'Contractor Fired Illegally, Says National Labor Relations Board', *Salt Lake Tribune*, 3 July, p. B4.

Schutt, Russel K. (1987), 'Craft Unions and Minorities: Determinants of Change in Admission Practices', *Social Problems*, vol. 34(4), pp. 388-402.

Unicon Research Corporation (2003), Santa Monica, CA: [producer and distributor of CPS Utilities], March (1980-2001), May (1973-1981), Outgoing Rotations (1983-2000) *Current Population Survey* (CPS), Conducted by the Bureau of the Census for the Bureau of Labor Statistics. Washington: Bureau of the Census [producer and distributor]. Unicon Research Corporation [producer and distributor of CPS Utilities], 2003.

U.S. Department of Commerce, Census Bureau (1960), *Census of Population*, Government Printing Office, Washington, D.C.

Quadagno, Jill (1994), *The Color of Welfare: How Racism Undermined the War on Poverty*, Oxford University Press, New York, NY.

Index